Dy

L

LUCKY LUPIN

CHARLIE MORTIMER

LUCKY LUPIN

Constable • London

CONSTABLE

First published in Great Britain in 2016 by Constable

1 3 5 7 9 10 8 6 4 2

A CIP catalogue record for this book
is available from the British Library.

ISBN: 978-1-47211-729-8 (hardback)

Typeset in Sabon by SX Composing DTP, Rayleigh, Essex
Printed and bound in Great Britain by Clays Ltd, St Ives Plc

Papers used by Constable are from well-managed forests
and other responsible sources.

MIX
Paper from
responsible sources
FSC
www.fsc.org   FSC® C104740

Constable
An imprint of
Little, Brown Book Group
Carmelite House
50 Victoria Embankment
London EC4Y 0DZ

An Hachette UK Company
www.hachette.co.uk

www.littlebrown.co.uk

To Tim and the NHS,
my life-support systems

Contents

Contents

Pre-med

When I was sixteen years old, my despairing dad wrote to my older sister: 'Charlie is the only person I know who got nothing, bar one or two criminal friends, out of Eton. He would have been just as happy, or perhaps equally indifferent, at a Yateley comprehensive. He is, of course, virtually illiterate. I don't think he finds that a handicap and everyone likes him.'

Almost a half a century later Charles Moore, former editor of the *Daily Telegraph* and Maggie Thatcher's biographer, reviewed *Dear Lupin*, a book based on the letters written to me by my father over some twenty-five years: 'Charlie Mortimer is apt with his hands and good, in that enviable way of the utterly feckless, at getting on with people. He is however spectacularly unfit for all the normal occupations of the upper middle classes.' So not much change there then. As my dad might have said, 'A good horse will always run true to form'.

In the summer of 2013, when *Dear Lupin* had clearly been far more successful than anyone had expected, I had a eureka, or rather a second-bottle-of-cut-price-Merlot, moment. It suddenly came to me that this was probably the only time in my entire life that a publisher was ever going to take me seriously, so I may as well take advantage of the situation. This was despite the fact that over ninety per cent of *Dear Lupin* consisted of my long, dear-departed father's letters; my only contribution being the disorderly conduct which had inspired the correspondence in the first place and the odd paragraph in between the letters, and even that, according to Charles Moore, had been pretty inadequate: 'Charlie edits the book in a shockingly slapdash and uninformative manner, but then reading his father's strictures, one would expect nothing else . . .'

Despite the sad fact that I hadn't actually managed to read a book for ten years, the publishers took a punt and gave me an amber light. Not unreasonably, before committing themselves they wanted some sort of written proposal from me outlining what I intended to write about. In the event I just about managed a sheet of A4. To my surprise they liked the idea and a deal was struck.

The original title we had agreed for *Lucky Lupin* was *My Virus and Me*. Some months into the project I was informed that 'Lupin' needed to be incorporated into the title somehow. Fortunately, I still had the same delightful editor Andreas, nothing if not the diplomat: 'The thing is Charlie,' he said putting on his most earnest expression, 'of course I understand that for you the big challenge is actually to write a book, but you must also understand that from our point of view the big challenge is to sell it. With the best will in the world your original title just isn't going to fly off the shelves, well is it?' Whatever the title the content remains much the same: a black comedy based around Aids, epilepsy, mental illness and depression. It's autobiographical and is loosely based around the board game 'Snakes and Ladders' – otherwise known as life.

In short, when I'm not suffering from some potentially terminal illness and being told by doctors to prepare for the inevitable, or feeling so off-the-wall and depressed that I'm seriously considering sticking my head in a gas oven, I'm cracking on as best I can. The life I lead maybe somewhat narrower than I might have chosen, but rather than resent the one I can't have, I tend to live to the full the one that I can.

There is, however, an altogether different way of looking at this book. Imagine that I'm extremely inebriated and by chance you get stuck in a lift with me for several hours. Should you find yourself enjoying the experience then there's a sporting chance you just might derive some pleasure from the next three hundred or so pages. If after the first minute you're clawing at the lift doors to get out, then clearly you won't – so I suggest you put the book back on the shelf, pronto.

1

Now Here's a Tip . . .

Now here's a tip.

You've made an appointment with your doctor to get your test results.

When you arrive he asks the practice nurse (Rosie in this case) to sit in on the consultation and quite suddenly she starts to cry.

You can, at this point, be pretty much guaranteed that the news he is about to deliver is likely to be on the bleak side of seriously distressing.

It's January 1986. About three months earlier I had taken an Aids test at my local hospital under the rather obscure pseudonym of Carlos Georgios. (I was going through a Greek period at the time.) Mind you I hadn't banked on being stuck with the name through thick and thin for the next nineteen years, and to be regularly greeted at the Kobler Clinic with 'Georgios? That's a Greek name isn't it? You don't look very Greek.'

'Ah well, the thing is it was just my dad who was Greek, and I inherited my mother's blonde . . . '

In fact it was only when I almost died from pneumonia in 2003 that I finally copped to my real name. I had a dreadful vision of being wheeled out from the mortuary fridge with a tag tied to my big toe that read Carlos Georgios and my poor grief-stricken and distraught mother, wig skew-whiff, shouting, 'I'm telling you that's not my bloody son!'

I never did collect the result from the hospital because I didn't have the balls, but equally, I guess, because I didn't want to have to confront or curtail the hedonistic riot I was then having in the saunas and other places that at the time constituted my lifestyle. It was only fairly recently at the age of thirty-two that I had finally come to some sort of acceptance with the fact that I was clearly gay. Having for years, as my dad might have put it in horse-racing parlance, ridden under both sets of rules, I decided one day to ask a pragmatic doctor in the local STD clinic (rather too pragmatic as it turned out) what he thought.

'Is this just a stage that, as a late developer, as all my family are, I am going to grow out of doctor?'

The response was both short and sharp and unexpected: 'When you close your eyes what do you think about when you're wanking, Charlie?'

'Well thanks for that doc, I had no idea you could be so subtle.'

That said, he actually did me a huge favour and from that defining moment I never looked back, although getting it across to friends and family was another matter altogether.

———•———

It was during a lecture at Broadway Lodge, a no-nonsense alcohol and drug treatment centre in which I'd unsurprisingly ended up in May 1984, I first heard about 'Acquired Immune Deficiency Syndrome'. I remember thinking, 'Well, I've managed to have every other bloody illness known to mankind that's associated with having fun so I'm sure to have this one.'

The accompanying slide-show, which largely portrayed young men, looking like they had just been liberated from Belsen, made compulsive and painful viewing, so much so that it was easier to go into a state of terminal shut-down about it all and move on. In the clichéd terminology of therapy, they call this denial. It's like sticking all your unpaid bills in a drawer in the insane hope that somehow matters will simply resolve themselves, whereas in reality you'd probably be better off writing a wish list to Father Christmas and sending it up the chimney mid-April.

Broadway Lodge was my last-chance saloon and, despite throwing my brandy glass through the open sunroof as a concerned friend drove me through the front gates, I had (unlike any of my other attempts at confronting addiction) no secret supply of narcotics stashed away. That said I had arrived fairly well tanked up and still have very little if any recollection of the first forty-eight hours.

Given its uncompromising stance and exceptional success rate, Broadway Lodge was very popular with the seriously affluent as well as local authorities. Thus the inmates consisted of a similar cross-section of society that makes horse racing so colourful. You were just as likely to be paired up with the offspring of a Greek ship owner as you were a 'Scouser' on probation for robbery with violence. I was very fortunate because ten years previously my poor, long-suffering and deeply concerned father had put me on a health insurance programme which despite forking out already for a number of 'cures' in cushier establishments in the Home Counties had rather generously agreed to fund my 'treatment' at Broadway Lodge. However, they made it clear, as had several other people, that if I screwed up this opportunity I was on my own.

In truth, there had been a fair number of 'final straws'. On one occasion, I sat down with a litre of 'Three Barrels' brandy and drank the entire bottle within an hour, only to find that I felt more or less exactly the same as before I'd started. I was of course also taking quite large quantities of prescribed speed in the form of Dexedrine together with an interesting variety of prescribed and street drugs. An old friend, Robin Grant-Sturgis (hardly a teetotaller himself), described my bedroom in undisguised shock as 'Hell's Kitchen'. He kindly suggested that I sort myself out at his farm in the country where he and his charming wife would look after me. There was only one house rule: no alcohol before noon. That, of course, was completely out of the question. Around that time another close friend, the late John Hobbs (society antiques dealer), used to tell people in his own inimitable East End style, 'Charlie fucking Mortimer came in the shop the other day and said he'd found the meaning to fucking life. At that my ears pricked up as I waited to hear his secret. Charlie explained, with a completely straight face, that it was four fucking cans of ice-cold Red Stripe lager before breakfast. It's fucking unbelievable.'

Needless to say I had had a little 'previous' on the general abuse front. In 1976, at the age of twenty-four, I had ended up in Basingstoke General Hospital with a survival prognosis of 50 per cent. I believe I hold the dubious honour of being the first patient in that hospital to have a liver biopsy. My dear mother, crucified with concern, and never one to get her facts straight at the best of times, rang a cousin who was a doctor: 'I'm most awfully worried about Charles. They've just done an autopsy on him.'

At the time heroin was all the rage across the social spectrum, in particular with trust-fund kids. It turned out that I had contracted a very chronic form of Hepatitis B from sharing needles while injecting heroin, among other stuff. I hadn't, rather astonishingly in retrospect, realised that this constituted risky behaviour. But even if I had, the overwhelming craving at that precise moment for the hit would have overridden any health concerns even if a clean syringe was available at a chemist less than five minutes away.

Injecting was a whole different ball game to smoking drugs or taking pills. For years afterwards I found having a blood test minor torture because as the doctor's needle went into my vein, there was always the anticipation for a wave of euphoria that never came. Bizarrely, to this day I still get a similar feeling if I catch the distinctively sweet smell of sulphur from a burning match and am subconsciously transported back to heating up heroin on a spoon when I often managed to use an entire box of Bryant and May matches in the process.

Although I survived Hepatitis B, there was a price: minor brain damage brought about by toxic fluids from the liver flooding the brain. At the time, I hadn't taken on board the potential consequences, and it was only a couple of years later when a whole load of strange and quite frightening stuff started happening. One night at a party given by a band, who had the misfortune to have me as their manager, I smoked, as I often did, a joint. I expected to simply become light-headed and silly. 'Grass' usually had the effect of making me laugh like some demented delinquent, but on the night in question something very different happened. If you could have conjured up a moment that was diametrically opposed to the comfort and euphoric warmth from jacking up heroin, this was it. It was like being injected with a shot of pure terror, like looking at life and people down the wrong end of a telescope. Everything familiar had in a nanosecond become alien, and normal consciousness felt strangely unreal, as if in a dream. I knew at that moment that nothing was ever going to be quite the same again. As the Australians so succinctly put it: 'the kangaroos had broken out of the upper paddock.'

That night I just lay on the floor upstairs, periodically getting up to splash my face with cold water and opening and closing my eyes in the vain hope that whatever it was would wear off. In the morning it was just as bad, if not worse, and I was convinced that I had gone mad. I also had a compulsion to tell people about it in some detail. I remember the writer Ian La Frenais kindly asking me how I was. Twenty minutes on, he swore he would never ask anyone that question again unless he genuinely wanted to know the answer.

For a long time, I was convinced that either the joint or the drink had been spiked with acid. And, for the first time in my life, I developed acute paranoia and was convinced that everyone had doctored any drink I was offered with some mind-bending drug. For years afterwards, I only ever asked for water in other people's homes and would insist on cleaning the glass first and then filling it from the tap myself. My close friend, wild man Charlie Shearer, used to call paranoia being 'a friend of Barry's (i. e. Barry-noia), and I had certainly become a friend of Barry's big-time.

This rather unsatisfactory state of affairs may just have had a touch of karma. John Hobbs used to claim, perhaps with good reason, that he was suffering from what he described as 'nut pressure', by which he meant chronic anxiety, rather than chronically tight Y-fronts. He was already taking Valium when I met him in 1973 (he was twenty-six and I was twenty-one). On a particularly bad day just after he'd swallowed a couple of 'mother's little helpers', I told him that I'd hidden some LSD in his pill bottle. In the blink of an eye, he turned ashen white and adopted the pained expression of a man who'd been told that half his family had just been murdered. Absolutely side-splitting for me at the time, but appallingly unkind in retrospect. I always remember my dad telling me that as a child he adored watching a silent Charlie Chaplin film in which a large gentleman gets his heavily bandaged foot caught in the revolving door of a grand hotel. My father found this hysterical until some sixty years later, suffering from painful gout, he also had a heavily bandaged foot . . . after which he considered the Chaplin film to be in 'exceedingly poor taste'.

The first and almost last time I took LSD turned out to be a fairly memorable experience for all concerned. It was the summer of 1971 and I was renting a room in a rather splendid stately home near Exeter that belonged to Robin Grant-Sturgis.

His father had recently fallen from the roof in unusual circumstances and sadly died leaving the entire estate to his oldest son. The house itself, although set in wonderful parkland, had seen better days and was now the epitome of decaying grandeur. Shotguns were regularly let off in the dining room, mushrooms the size of watermelons grew on some of the walls and alcoves designed for statuettes were stacked high with Weber carburettors and tractor parts. A famous Belgian architect staying locally, eager to see the interior, called by one afternoon. He took one look inside, put his hand to his head and exclaimed 'Mon Dieu!' before swooning in horror.

I had just left the Coldstream Guards after a rather short and unsatisfactory military career and was eager to escape from my very displeased family. I had moved down to Devon to be initially (and very briefly) employed as a salesman for an experimental stainless steel paint company. The other occupants of Hillersdon House were mainly students from Exeter University. I was most definitely the odd one out, if only for the fact that I still had a military number-one cut and the rest looked as if they were auditioning for the part of Jesus and his disciples in a provincial theatrical production.

One Saturday night a few of them dropped some LSD and politely asked if I would like some. Given the fact that I looked so straight, they thought it might be both an interesting and entertaining experience all round. My immediate reaction was, 'You must be having a laugh!' though a mere five minutes later I was on board.

The drug was called a 'micro dot' and resembled a tiny bit of blotting paper. After twenty minutes I decided I clearly hadn't enough as nothing was happening and took some more. Ten minutes later something did start happening. Unfortunately, for some reason that I cannot put my finger on, I thought it would liven things up a bit if I got out my beloved sixteen-bore shotgun 'Crippen'. Now suitably armed, I made all the students march up and down the hall, Brigade of Guards style, saluting the house-keeper's cat, which I had renamed General Fielding. As the sun finally came up I had them fighting off the Japanese across the cornfields. In many ways the joke had rather backfired on them but credit where credit is due and, surprisingly, they all took what was probably rather an alarming experience with good humour: that said they never did offer me LSD or indeed any other mind-bending drug again.

Five years on and now stuck with some obscure and permanent form of brain damage I realised just how debilitating and terrifying any form of mental illness can be and just how difficult it is to press the reset button. At home we had a remote control for the TV on which you could alter colour, contrast etc., though it also had a single button labelled 'Normal'. This meant that once you'd completely screwed up the settings all you needed to do was press the 'normal' button and, hey presto, everything was back in its proper place. If only brains had the same facility. Inevitably, I ended up being referred to a psychiatrist at the excellent Maudsley Hospital in south-east London. Despite the fact he was called Gaius, Welsh and a devout Christian, after a tricky start we got on rather well. From the outset, he suspected that I had Temporal Lobe Epilepsy (TLE), an unusual form of epilepsy that could be caused by severe liver disease. (This was later confirmed.) I used to go and see Gaius in his consulting rooms at Wimpole

Street fairly regularly but my most abiding memory of that period was of bumping into Frankie Howerd in the waiting room. If everything that represented the hideous pain and depth of depression could have been etched on to one face, at that moment it was Frankie's. It is engraved on my memory as clearly as Munch's *The Scream*.

———•———

Back to that day of reckoning in January 1986. As expensive lawyers tend to say, when they've run out of options and are just about to submit an eye-watering invoice, 'we are where we are' and we were at this precise moment awaiting my medical verdict with a certain amount of frisson.

There I am with my younger sister, who had sportingly insisted on accompanying me, in Doctor Michael's surgery along with Rosie, the nurse, who was in tears. Michael was an extremely charming man but even he could not put much gloss on the news he was duty bound to deliver.

Michael: Now, Charlie. [clears throat while shuffling papers] Well, the thing is, Charlie, it's not good news. In fact it's rather bad news.

Me: When you say bad news, Michael, in what way is it bad, exactly? Just quite bad, seriously bad or utterly catastrophic?

Michael: Well, the thing is, Charlie, I'm afraid that your results show that you've tested positive for

HTLV-III. In other words, you have been exposed to the virus which causes Aids and consequently, Charlie, you have contracted ARC, or Aids-related complex, which, since there is currently no treatment, will ultimately lead on to full Aids. Unfortunately things are liable to deteriorate from here.

Me: Sorry, Michael, but just homing in on that word there – 'deteriorate'. Just how quickly am I liable to deteriorate exactly? Are we talking days, weeks, months or years?

Michael: Unless you are very unlucky it will be years, Charlie. At least two maybe even three years.

Me: Oh well, that's all right then!

To be absolutely honest all the anticipation prior to this moment of truth had been such that, had the test results been fine, it would have been somewhat of an anticlimax, not to say disappointment. There was a feeling of fear (actually abject terror) but also of liberation to be told that I might, if I was lucky, have a mere two or three years left to live without a hint of a cure in sight. Certainly on the plus side, getting an overdue career going and a mortgage was off the cards.

My first stop was the local video store to arrange an annual platinum membership for unlimited access to its extensive film library. I was going to be taking this lying down. I settled into my sofa with copious quantities of Solpadeine and Valium for the comparatively short haul towards what I had been assured would be an early and rather unsatisfactory demise. On top of all this, I found out in the same week that virtually my entire savings had been wiped out. Unwisely, three months earlier I had made a loan to a friend of a friend who, it now transpired, had gone completely crackers and done a runner. Paradoxically, I also remember this as one of the happiest periods in my life.

Years earlier 'Chick', a childhood friend of John Hobbs, had told me that when he was driving home in the early hours, he had lost control of his car on a corner. He had desperately twisted the steering wheel this way and that until, and I quote, 'I thought bollocks to all this, folded my arms across my chest, gave up any attempt at keeping the car on the road, and waited for the inevitable. Do you know what, Chas?' he continued. 'It was one of the most serene moments of my entire fucking life.'

I guess I was just doing a different version of the same thing.

2

With the Best Will
in the World . . .

With the best will in the world in 1985 having any association at all with Aids was social suicide. It was like Ebola but with a raft of really unsavoury moral and other implications attached. The word 'pariah' comes to mind. The fact is you don't get Aids from watching telly.

I'd decided from day one to be open about my diagnosis, apart from to my parents whom I felt had suffered enough from my antics. Reactions varied. On the whole they were, for want of a better pun, positive. My then brother-in-law, 'Hot Hand Henry', who could have been Nigel Farage's twin, made a point, when I visited, of telling me to kiss his children goodnight, a gesture of extreme good faith. On the other hand, some old friends with whom I regularly spent Christmas never invited me again. As with most things, I tended to use gallows humour to fend off the more disturbing and depressing elements of this personal catastrophe that at times seemed utterly overwhelming.

Once, over coffee my then partner in a property company, Robin Grant-Sturgis, said to me, 'Christ, I think I've drunk out of your mug. I might have caught Aids.'

'Look mate,' I responded, 'that's all very well, but I'm far more frightened that I've drunk out of your mug and caught some of your pomposity, you cunt . . .'

At Rafatteer, a company I co-owned that manufactured boxer shorts in Asia (slogan: *Are the boxer shorts in your life as exciting as the life in your boxer shorts?*), my drinking receptacle had 'AIDS MUG' written on it. Without doubt sick humour. The more morbid and tasteless the better was my way of dealing with it. It stopped me zipping myself up into a bag of self-pity.

Aids seemed such a sleazy and dishonourable thing to have. My dad had been a real war hero, an honourable man in the old-fashioned sense. Five years stuck in various German POW camps had not been exactly a barrel of laughs, seeing as for many of those years it seemed likely that the Germans might win the war. He had been very brave, whereas I found myself sitting around confronting a terminal disease that I'd acquired either from jacking up drugs or having too much sex, which didn't seem a very honourable position to be in. But the fact is, I still had to confront it and live with it, so I had to stop giving myself an impossibly hard time.

It was not until 1987 that Princess Diana 'willingly and knowingly' hugged an Aids victim, which promptly earned her the title 'The Princess of Sodomy' from one national newspaper. Reaction was pretty unpredictable and, although on some fronts I was happy to take a risk, others less so. For example, I was fairly sure that had Parsons Green launderette heard about it they wouldn't have washed my sheets but burnt them. A close friend wouldn't even speak to me on the telephone as he thought he might get Aids down the phone line.

This was hardly surprising given the near hysteria in the tabloid press. One Sunday paper had published a poll in which about 90 per cent plus of its readers felt that any infected individual should be forcibly rounded up and sent to a quarantine camp on the Isle of Man. On the strength of that story I, quite legally at the time, bought a Berretta pump action shotgun with collapsible stock in matt black and rubber; my thinking being, 'If these fuckers are coming to get me I'm not going down without a fight.' The idea of being holed up on the Isle of Man in inclement weather with only Nigel Mansell as a neighbour . . . well, that would be a fate worse than death.

It crossed my mind from time to time what I would do if I got really ill. When I felt well, I hadn't a care in the world but when I felt ill, the old negative thinking kicked in and I could think of little else. I remember confiding to a friend of mine, 'It's a toss-up – either I'll accept it and go through the unmitigated hell of it all or I'll take the emergency exit route and blow my head off'. It wasn't so much that I couldn't face the prospect of terminal disintegration in slow motion: I just didn't want my family (my mother, in particular) and friends to be dragged through all that crap with me. Had I consulted them, I'd rather hope that they would go for the 'we'll nurse you through' option rather than 'go on take the shotgun one'.

If what was going on in my own head and the tabloid press wasn't bad enough, the government launched a number of hard-hitting health awareness campaigns both on TV and via pamphlets delivered to every household in the country. One consisted of a volcano erupting under a thunderous sky. Dramatic shots of cascading rocks preceded images of a tombstone being chiselled. The actor, John Hurt, delivered the voice-over with suitable gravitas: 'There is now a danger that has become a threat to us all. It is a deadly disease and there is no known cure.' The main message was revealed etched onto the granite gravestone at the end: 'AIDS. Don't die of ignorance.' This was all fine unless you were, as I was, apparently, already dying of ignorance.

Feeling a tad on the rough side, as I went downstairs to get the post, could take a serious turn for the worse if confronted by a 'tombstone' leaflet. A further decline could be generated by an interview on Radio 4 with then Chief Constable of Greater Manchester Police, James Anderton. He referred to Aids victims as 'swirling around in a human cesspit of their own making'.

One of the few amusing anecdotes at the time was the story of the current health secretary Norman Fowler persuading Maggie Thatcher that the word 'anal' had to appear in the list of unwise behaviour.

I bought a medical book on Aids, which was so depressing that I binned it after three pages and to cheer myself up, in an obscurely dark way, set about learning the entire James II funeral service off by heart. 'Man that it is born of a woman hath but a short time to live and is full of misery. He groweth up and is cut down like a flower, he fleeth like as shadow and never continueth in one stay. In the midst of life we are in death . . .' and so on. At the time the big challenge was to get the whole thing off pat before I was carted off in a body bag.

Although many people felt at the time that Aids victims had brought the whole thing on themselves, I personally felt no particular sense of shame or regret – only a sort of excitement at the madness of it all.

I was attending Narcotics Anonymous (NA) meetings fairly regularly and, despite there being a strict code of anonymity ('what is said here stays here'), my predicament was much too good a story not to get out. The only thing I'm really grateful for is that at exactly the same time another guy in NA, called John, had also been diagnosed, and from then on was always known, not without affection, as 'Aids John'. By the grace of God, I escaped being 'Aids Charlie'. Sadly, John died decades ago now.

At the Kobler Clinic, which I went to regularly, many of the other patients looked so emaciated and, in some cases, deranged that I sometimes wondered if they would make it through to the next day. It was especially depressing when I caught sight of a passing acquaintance from a year or so back who was now virtually unrecognisable from the fit and healthy person that they had been. In those early days, once the illness had taken hold there was no way back and it really was only a matter of time. For a while, I pitched up to a weekly NA meeting specifically for people with HIV/Aids. There was a lot of bonhomie and black humour but the death rate was such that I thought it was not unlike being in the trenches in the Great War. However, there was absolutely no point in feeling sorry for myself and dwelling on what I was assured by my various doctors was going to be a fairly brief and bleak future. So I just got on with other stuff.

My life in London was very separate from that of my

parents in Berkshire, and I was determined, one way or another, to spare them this little disaster; more so as my dad was pushing on in years and had enough problems with his own health.

On top of all the physical problems there were the mental difficulties. I once explained to a rather long-suffering GP that a remote ancestor of mine, the dastardly Roger de Mortimer, had murdered Edward II in Berkeley Castle with a red-hot poker 'per rectum' (as they say in medical speak). Not surprisingly (as poppers hadn't been invented then) the screams were heard, according to the history books, for miles around. My point was that the king had been murdered in this particularly gruesome fashion because he was gay and thus it followed that it was God's punishment that I, the last surviving de Mortimer of Wigmore (or so I liked to think), should not only be born gay but contract Aids and be condemned to an early and fairly hideous death. Try capping that for logic. The doctor clearly lacked the appetite to engage with me on this one and reached for his prescription pad. Around that time, I was introduced to a member of the Royal family and, desperate to make amends and put an end to the curse on the Mortimer family, my opening line was: 'I'm most frightfully sorry about the poker incident, ma'am.'

Several years later, in 1988, I bought an almost new BMW M5 from Sytner's of Nottingham. A month after purchase, I returned the car to the garage for a free service. This gave me several hours to while away, so I decided to visit Nottingham Castle. To my utter astonishment the very first thing I saw on arrival was a prominent sign pointing to 'Guided tours of Mortimer's Hole'. Intrigued by this faintly vulgar-sounding offer, I followed the various signs until I arrived at a rendezvous point where there was a larger sign stating that there were two tours a day of 'Mortimer's Hole', one at 11 a.m. and the other at 3 p.m. Pleased to find that I was just in time for the morning tour I waited more with curiosity than anticipation.

I was rather disappointed when a 'jobsworth' in a cloth cap appeared at the prescribed time and announced loudly to no one in particular that due to lack of numbers the morning tour had now been cancelled. 'Minimum number eight; next tour three o'clock this afternoon providing there's 'nuff people.' Before he had time to scuttle off I tapped him on the shoulder.

'If I told you that I was in fact the last surviving male Mortimer of Wigmore, would you be prepared to make an exception in my case regarding minimum numbers?'

Without showing the slightest interest he simply replied, 'No, it wouldn't,' and walked off.

Unfortunately, as it turned out, this was not the end of the matter. About ten minutes later, as I was meandering around the battlements, a very pleasant, scholarly individual caught up with me.

'I am told,' he said somewhat breathlessly, 'that you are the last surviving male Mortimer of Wigmore.'

I confirmed that indeed I was.

'Do you have any evidence to that effect?'

(In the absence of anything more substantial, a Barclaycard sufficed.)

It transpired that he was a senior curator at the castle and he offered, there and then, to take me on a personal tour of the famous hole. Well, all I can say is more bloody fool me for agreeing so enthusiastically. For the first thirty minutes of the tour I felt rather important. Some three and a half hours later, I felt somewhat less so, now bitterly regretting I had ever mentioned being a wretched Mortimer in the first place. For those not up to speed with the historical significance of 'Mortimer's Hole' it is really just a cave through which Edward III and his troops stole their way into the castle to arrest and subsequently hang my poor old ancestor, Roger de Mortimer, who was holed up (for want of a better pun) with Queen Isabella of France. As I confided to a friend, 'It's a sad old day when the only place mentioning my family's name can get me is in is some exceptionally uninteresting old hole.'

It is now some thirty years since the original diagnosis. I am not the sort of person who keeps a diary and, to be honest, at the time I didn't tend to dwell too much on my predicament beyond feeling somewhat 'grubby' in that by having sex with someone I could be passing on a death sentence. I had considered sex a fairly healthy activity, with minor inconveniences such as herpes or gonorrhoea being the worst outcome. One unexpected positive that came out of this was that I became somewhat cleanliness obsessed and acquired my first ever vacuum cleaner. My thinking was that if people were prepared to take the risk of visiting me, the very least I could do was to present myself shaved and washed in a home that didn't look like there was a virus lurking round every corner.

Well-meaning people were always trying to foist advice on me from suggesting macrobiotic diets to much more drastic treatments and regimes. Years earlier, when I had liver failure, I tried all sorts of quirky stuff including being massaged when naked by an eighty-year-old white witch in Devonshire (she

24

was fully clothed, I hasten to add) and paying her in fresh vegetables. (Robin Grant-Sturgis was convinced something beyond kinky was going on and was utterly appalled.) This time round I took a conscious decision to shun alternative practices and stuck to a rigid diet of egg and chips or, as a special treat, a tinned Fray Bentos steak and kidney pie with Cadbury's Smash mash and frozen peas. It so happened an old friend of mine, Jessamy Calkin, was features editor of GQ, the lads' magazine, and in 1993 she interviewed me for an article entitled, 'In the shadow of AIDS . . . Using a combination of morbid humour, fried food and good luck, Charlie has survived ten years with HIV'.

Charlie has been HIV positive for about ten years now. He doesn't know exactly when he contracted the virus – though it must have been sometime before 1984 – and he doesn't know exactly how he contracted it because he has the dubious accolade of possessing most of the qualifications; he's bisexual [me: or rather was], he used to be an intravenous drug user and he's had sex with prostitutes in East Africa. Now 41, his health is pretty good; he's not 'HIV well' but he's 'HIV and not too ill' and his T cell count (a loose way of monitoring the virus) is relatively high. Charlie is a very charismatic [me: possibly a matter of opinion] individual with a dry anarchic sense of humour. He is fond of calling everyone 'pet' and is generally philosophical about life, prone to saying 'Well there you go pet' about even the most serious of matters. To cope with his illness, Charlie maintained what is known in 'The Right Stuff' as an 'even strain'. At the Chelsea and Westminster Hospital, which he attends regularly, they are inclined to ask him why he thinks he's done so well. And he is inclined to answer, without being flip, that it is probably because he has always wanted to die and he never gets his own way.

I was always hugely grateful to Jessamy for rooting for me so strongly and humorously.

In the early 1980s, my general conduct left a certain amount to be desired. I have a vague recollection that once, when asked what I did for a living at a smart party given by the long-suffering Robin Grant-Sturgis, I disappeared into a shed, came back with a chainsaw and set about the art of converting two of my host's rooms into one. Just in case that failed to make a significant enough impact, later on the same evening, I set about eating a dead crow for a bet. I think my behaviour at the time can be no better summed up than by my no-nonsense rehab councillor, Mike Musson: 'You may like to think that you were the life and soul of the party,' he shouted in his highly distinctive nasal tones, his heavily perspiring face about one inch from my equally heavily perspiring face, 'but to everyone else you were just a fucking pain in the fucking arse!'

By 1984, I had had enough. There had also been too much weird stuff (and not in a good way) going on. On one occasion I had woken up at four in the morning in a state of brain/body disassociation and sheer terror, the like of which I had never experienced before. All I could do was to sit on the edge of my bed and chew Ativan (similar to Valium) like jelly beans until, an hour later, I passed out. I was both seriously depressed and desperate to give up alcohol and drugs, and I had found both to my surprise and horror that there was not a cat's chance in hell of my getting through even a couple of hours without some form of chemical support. I had by now not surprisingly lost my driver's licence for drinking and driving, so I attempted to get around on an old bicycle I had purchased for five quid. Given the fact that I was sweating profusely 24/7 and was shaking like a deranged pneumatic drill, this was not a big success and provided an interesting spectacle for other road users and pedestrians.

It was at Broadway Lodge Rehab Centre, through the haze and discomfort of withdrawal combined with the appalling prospect of facing reality sober, that I managed to get my head round the two-word mantra 'taking responsibility'. Looking back, that did in fact change everything for me and in a good way. Blaming others for all the things that had gone wrong was never going to achieve anything constructive.

There wasn't all that much side-splitting about Broadway Lodge but one thing did make me laugh. The offspring of super-wealthy parents or minor European royalty used to turn up with sets of golf clubs, tennis racquets and, on one occasion, polo mallets, asking where the swimming pool was. In reality, the place made the average borstal look comfortable. When you weren't being shouted at, peeling spuds, or bearing your soul, you dossed down in dormitories.

One night a Polish man, whom we all thought was Indian because he had actually changed colour due to extreme liver damage, was so disorientated that he got up in the middle of the night and mistook my bed for a urinal, which was somewhat distressing. When I mentioned this to the matron the following day she responded, 'Oh, don't be such a fusspot.

There's nothing wrong with the smell of fresh wee.' I thought, 'You try some pongy bloke pissing in your face at 2 a.m. in the morning and see how much you like it, love.'

Bizarrely, apart from the first week, my months at Broadway Lodge were as happy as any I've ever spent anywhere. It was a year and a half after I left treatment that I was given what, at the time, amounted to a death sentence. I am pretty sure that, had I received this diagnosis pre-Broadway Lodge, I would have switched into terminal self-destruct mode and ultimately drowned in a sea of self-pity and that frankly would have been curtains. For the record, I haven't taken heroin or any illegal drug since 1984, except for cocaine (which I hate) and raw opium in 1988. Over the counter and prescription drugs and wine are an entirely different matter.

One of the more agonising experiences was watching my good friend Nicky die. Nicky was a thirteen-stone wide-boy who seemed to encapsulate health and *joie de vivre*. He had loads of girlfriends, an entertaining disrespect for authority and an eye for the main chance. However, he had been an intravenous drug abuser and contracted Aids. I wrote to a friend at the time:

He completely disintegrated from the inside out. It was as if he had dry rot or something, he looked worse than any picture I've seen from Bosnia. The day he died he can't have weighed any more than five stone. It was doubly tragic because he was so angry; he had absolutely no acceptance of the disease whatsoever. It's fair to say if I was him I would have been the same, it's a very unpleasant way to go.

At Nicky's funeral someone came up to me and suggested that I must have been scared shitless visiting Nicky during his final weeks. I reluctantly agreed, given the implications regarding my own future, but I thought it so selfish to be frightened when he was in that state.

Come the 1990s I had survived so long that people wanted to know my secret. In response I'd say something along the lines of 'Over the past five years, all I've done is work my balls off, worry myself half to death, kept very odd hours, taken loads of pills and had a miserable time generally. But physically somehow I've kept it together. It's like anything else: there's a lot of luck involved.' My two biggest fears were that I'd die before my mother (I hadn't yet met Tim) or that I'd end up a living skeleton in some hospital unable to look after myself.

Until proper treatment came on the scene *circa* 1996–7 in the form of combination therapy, I made little attempt to prolong my life by the use of drugs, experimental or otherwise. That said, I did have a month on AZT (Zidovudine). I wrote at the time:

It's filthy shit basically. I don't know much about it but I do know that it made me feel really unwell and I was unhappy about taking it. Some people tolerate it OK but I felt like I was seasick during a force eight gale on a cross-Channel ferry having just been force-fed two jumbo pork pies. I hold and have always held that there is nothing on this planet worse than depression; that said intense and persistent nausea comes a fairly close second. Just the thought of stopping AZT made me feel better – it was like addiction in reverse. Nothing could induce me to take it again.

29

After that unsettling experience I made a conscious decision not to participate in any of the many random drugs trials on offer then, usually sponsored by global pharmaceutical companies, although for several years I took the antibiotic Septrin daily to ward off, successfully in my case, the life-threatening Aids-related pneumonia, Pneumocystis carinii pneumonia (PCP). There was at the time a great deal of pressure to take stuff; once a rather bossy doctor told me I was being irresponsible for refusing the hideous drug she was trying push on me. As a final, rather desperate sales pitch, she claimed it might prolong my life. I asked whether it had ever occurred to her that I might not actually want my life prolonged. I just object to doctors using power in that fashion. Thank God I met Mark Nelson, then a very young genius consultant. (Twenty-five years on, Mark is still my consultant, good friend and now a professor.)

I soon got bored of following the research into the origins of Aids and was frankly more interested in who killed Kennedy. I haven't had any 'road to Damascus' moments, although I feel that I have gone through a profound change of attitude to life. I like to think that I am possibly less angry and more compassionate now.

In 1994, almost ten years after testing positive, I told Jessamy, 'I've had some good days and not a few bad days but I've never been so depressed that I can't laugh at a *Carry On* film.'

3

D'accord with my Nidnod . . .
Life after Dad

It's September 1991 and my dad is in decline. His last horse-racing article sits half-finished in the rollers of his ancient typewriter. My mother finds the whole situation completely overwhelming. She calls me one morning in pieces. I respond: 'Mother . . . I really hate to say this . . . but you must prepare yourself as things are not going to get any better.'

My dad had always been the one constant for my mother. His sudden and very marked deterioration sends the family dynamic into a tailspin. For each one of us the spectacle of seeing the world-class intellect of my father disintegrate is a very personal, shocking and ultimately depressing experience.

One night, things spiral out of control and Dad leaves home for the last time. You might think that the arrival of an ambulance would bring a sense of relief, whereas instead it is the beginning of a whole new world of problems.

I go to see Dad the next day at the Battle Hospital in Reading. I find him just dumped in a ward and largely forgotten – as I guess in the eyes of a very busy hospital he is just old and on his way out.

A male nurse appears to check his mental state. He asks Dad if he knows where he is. There is a slight pause before my father responds, 'In the bloody black hole of bloody Calcutta.'

Two days later, still no doctor has seen Dad and I announce to the hospital that he is leaving. They say this is not possible for a range of ridiculous reasons.

Emboldened by my mother's anguish at what is happening, I tell the hospital they have thirty minutes to get my dad ready to go, in a wheelchair with his medication, or else I am carrying him out over my shoulder there and then.

All Dad wants is to go home, but there is no way in a million years that my mother can cope with nursing him at home only supported periodically by us siblings. So I take him to a care home ten minutes from my parents' house.

It seems like the miracle solution, whereas in reality the standard of care is dire, the place has an overwhelming reek of urine and my father is miserable.

The last time I see him is on the Sunday when I promise him that I will always look after my mother.

He dies two days later with my mother and his best friend Desmond Parkinson thankfully at his side. She never forgives herself that he was not able to die in his room at home.

Despite the fact it was expected, I am shattered when my mother rings to tell me how my father has died as she held his hand. This is a sobering experience like no other. Dealing with technicalities such as death certificates is frankly a walk in the park in comparison to my heartbreak at the obvious distress of my poor mother. Nothing really prepares you for this.

We have a small service at the crematorium followed by a thanksgiving service in Lambourn. In the afternoon my mother, my two sisters and I drive to the church to collect the ashes.

My mother, who has had several drinks, wig slightly askew, appears from the church as we wait in the car.

Believing, mistakenly, that the ashes urn is very fragile, I watch with my heart in my mouth as my mother totters (in only the way that my mother can totter) while clutching the urn to her breast as she weaves her way precariously between the gravestones.

The act of spreading ashes itself is a strangely amateur affair, particularly if you have never done it before. With my mother quoting (or rather misquoting) a poem, we throw my dad to the universe up on the Lambourn gallops.

Unfortunately, there is quite a strong wind and I get a substantial amount of my father in the eye and for a while think that I may have to go to A & E, and have to explain, 'I've got some of my dad in my eye.'

Several days later I return to London. Unpacking, I find the urn is still in the car boot. Casually I chuck the now virtually empty container in a dustbin – when suddenly I think, 'I can't do that. There's still some of my dear old dad in there'. In panic, I retrieve it and eventually drop it off Wandsworth Bridge in a one-man ceremony.

Three months later, Party Politics, one of Nick Gaselee's horses, wins the Grand National having been trained on the very gallops where we scattered Dad. We all like to think that Dad had a bit of a hand in it.

———◆———

That Christmas I stayed down with my mother and to keep busy we went on a small tour of close friends and relatives. My often repeated line as we stumbled from house to house: 'Mother's doing the drinking and I'm doing the driving.'

Once in the 1970s when my parents were going through a particularly rough patch my older sister Jane asked my father why he didn't he leave my mother. I cannot remember all of his response apart from his observation that my mother was simply not equipped with the emotional stability and life skills to survive on her own. My parents, *'au fond'* to use one of my mother's favourite expressions, adored each other and this rather pragmatic view from my dad was said in love. In truth, they could not have lived without each other. The promise I made to my father that, come what may, I would look after my mother, was a promise, given all my shortcomings to date, that I was absolutely determined to keep. Apart from anything else given my own illness status suddenly my biggest challenge was to outlive my mother.

My mother, Cynthia Sydney, the youngest of three sisters, was born in 1921 into a junior branch of the affluent Denison-Pender family. Her great grandfather Sir John Pender (1816–96) was Scottish and a hugely successful textile merchant in both Glasgow and Manchester. Most significantly, he was the leading financier behind the laying of the first transatlantic telephone cable in 1866. He founded thirty-two telegraph companies, including Cable & Wireless, and also financed numerous railway projects in the United States, as well as being a Member of Parliament for Totnes. When he died he was the equivalent of a multi-billionaire (at the time leaving £15 million). My mother, a few years before she died, bent my ear about how ghastly progress was, with mobile phones and computers coming in for particular criticism. I responded, 'Mother, I think that's a bit rich coming from you given your family's history and the fact you've all been living off the profits ever since.'

My mother, completely unfazed, merely replied, 'You do talk rot, my dear boy.'

To describe my mother's childhood as advantaged would be something of an understatement. She was brought up in a magnificent manor house in Dorset surrounded by adoring family, staff and animals.

'We had nine servants inside, two pantry, three kitchen, two upstairs but I never had any feelings of belonging to a privileged class, our staff were my friends,' my mother told authoress Anne de Courcy when interviewed for her book *Debs at War*. 'They didn't tell my parents when I'd done something wrong and for my 21st birthday they all clubbed together a bought me something special.'

Nobody could have loved her husband and her three children more than my mother, but despite this I don't think anything in later life really matched up to those formative years. My mother spent much time trying to recapture the feelings that magical period gave her. As my partner Tim used to often point out to me, despite her age, my mother never to her dying day lost 'the little girl within'. Tim enjoys recalling when my mother once showed him a photograph of her on the lawn of her home surrounded by masses of toys.

'What are all those things, Cynthia? Were you spring clearing the nursery or something?'

'Oh no, of course not, Tim, you silly boy,' replied my mother, 'It was my birthday and they were all my presents.'

Her father Harry Denison-Pender had been a highly deco-rated officer in the Royal Scots Greys for the duration of the Great War. He then enjoyed a rather quieter existence as Master of the Portman Hunt and gentleman farmer, putting in an appearance from time to time at the family telegraphic businesses. My grandmother Doris (née Fisher), was a gentle and delightful soul who together with her classically beauti-ful sisters Phyllis and Enid and much younger, somewhat wayward brother Peter was brought up in Warwickshire. Foxhunting ran in the family blood and Phyllis was married to legendary huntsman Norman Loder, who died prema-turely from a heart attack. Norman was at one-time Master of the extremely dashing and glamorous Galway Blazers and subsequently the Atherstone and the Fitzwilliam. It was upon him that Siegfried Sassoon based Denis Milden in his book *Memoirs of a Fox-hunting Man*. Sassoon, a close friend of my great-uncle since childhood, dedicated his poem 'The Old Huntsman' to him. Gallantly, for the duration of the Great War my great-aunt Phyllis, herself an excellent horsewoman, took over her husband's duties as Master of Foxhounds while he was away fighting. Horses and hunting were clearly in the family genes.

In 1939, everything was to change. Blissfully unaware of what was waiting just round the corner, on the final page of her diary for 1938 my mother summed up her thoughts and events of the preceding year:

> As is most appropriate on the last night of the old year I am writing my diary for the very last time a few minutes before midnight. What a year 1938 has been. I have had the most marvellous time in Paris which I shall never forget, it is strange to think when I started writing this diary I had never been there. In September there was a world crisis that nearly landed us in another war but God and Neville Chamberlain saved us from it. Then after only a few weeks in Paris I was brought home to have my appendix out. The New Year will mean a lot to me, I will be really coming out to the world, may I always do what I think right no matter how difficult that may be. I have also in the last year lost Timmy [her beloved dog] who has grown up with me and it seems that a small part of me is gone forever.'

The outbreak of war in September 1939 put paid to my mother's plan to become a picture restorer and she and her oldest sister Pamela joined the rather inappropriately named FANYs (First Aid Nursing Yeomanry). Aged only eighteen, she was not allowed to be sent abroad and the only option was to become a home-based Auxiliary Territorial Service officer. This held no appeal for my mother: 'I never saw myself as driving a lot of randy officers . . . and they were randy!' So in the autumn of 1940 she joined Westland Aircraft in Yeovil as a trainee draughtswoman in the jig and tool department, where she worked for two years until her health gave out.

For her years, my mother was rather naive: 'I was extraordinarily innocent . . . our sergeant was a lesbian but at eighteen I didn't know what a lesbian was.' She was also appalled to be subjected to a physical assault in the factory, something that she could never have imagined happening to someone of her background. 'On Christmas Eve the draughtsmen had all been out for drinks at lunchtime and when they came back they tried to push us to the floor and have their wicked way with us. We had to hit them with the steel rulers on our desks . . . thank goodness for those rulers. I was terribly upset by the whole incident. It was my first encounter with sexual "mores" different from our own.'

After a brief convalescence to regain her health my mother joined the Red Cross. 'We drove ambulances, private cars, vans, lorries, everything and helped with a mass evacuation of East Enders down to the comparative safety of Chislehurst Caves in Kent when the V-1s [self-propelled flying bombs] and subsequently the V-2s came along.' On one occasion a V-2 fell in front of an ambulance she was driving. 'I was transporting a whole lot of chaps who'd come back from fighting the Japanese, they all had beri-beri and were yellow. Out of nowhere a V-2 exploded about thirty yards in front of us and suddenly there was literally no road left . . . luckily, it was a hot summer evening and my windows were open so we didn't get broken glass blown in our faces. However the ambulance span round three times in its own length. By the end the men were green rather than yellow.'

Shortly after the war my parents met at the 400 Club in Leicester Square, introduced through my godfather Fitz Fletcher, who had been a POW with my dad. They became engaged after meeting only six times and married in December 1947. My father resigned his commission in the Coldstream Guards and began a long and very successful career as a racing journalist and author. They started married life in a charming Regency villa, 25 Launceston Place in Kensington. My elder sister Jane was born in London in 1949, followed by myself and Louise in 1952 and 1958 respectively at Barclay House in Yateley.

My parents enjoyed, or rather sometimes endured, a very loving but somewhat complicated and rather volatile marriage, best summed up by an incident at Budds Farm in the 1970s. My father had returned from Newbury races and had his feet up in front of a blazing log fire, surrounded by newspapers, a mug of steaming tea to hand, and the six o'clock news blaring from the radio. My mother had been fox hunting and a horse had trodden on her face following a heavy fall. She threw open the sitting room door and just stood there, a vision of mud and blood. My father casually looked over the top of the newspaper and said, 'Do you know where the biscuits are?'

Despite not having gone to university, my father had both a world-class intellect and wit whereas my mother was a very physical person who possessed, in her own words, 'a sense of the ridiculous'. My mother took loyalty to another level and at my younger sister's engagement party got into a fight with my brother-in-law's grandmother, who had had made a disparaging remark about me. They had to be physically dragged apart and locked in separate rooms. Writing was my father's release whereas riding was my mother's. Although not a great reader my mother absolutely adored poetry, particularly poems about foxhunting and the Great War, but her constant misquoting of it throughout my childhood had the very unfortunate effect of putting me off any form of poetry for the rest of my life.

My mother was hugely popular and possessed an absolute talent for getting things the wrong way round. In 1963, when I was eleven, we had lunch with Ian Fleming, who was a close friend of my godfather and cousin John Blackwell, at Royal St George's Golf Club in Sandwich. Ian asked my mother what she would like to drink. Determined to appear sophisticated she promptly replied 'A dry Martini, please,' before adding, 'stirred but not shaken.'

With the best possible intentions, she sometimes just messed up completely. When clearing out my parents' home after my mother died, I came across her old portable Grundig reel-to-reel tape recorder. The box included a tape with the label 'Stirling Moss. Goodwood 1958'. Intrigued, I put it on and pressed the play button to be instantly greeted with the unmistakably crisp and fruity tones of a young Stirling Moss: 'Madam, I think you'll find your machine would work a lot better if you turned the bloody thing on!'

To be fair, it wasn't just my mother who sometimes got the wrong end of the stick. In the late 1980s, I was having lunch with my mother and her first cousin Robin Denison-Pender at the Turf Club. Robin was a dead ringer for P. G. Wodehouse's character Gussie Fink-Nottle. At the end of the meal my mother turned to Robin and said, 'You do know that Charlie's got HIV, don't you?'

There was a brief pause before pin-stripe-suited Robin gave a huge guffaw, slapped his thigh and shouted, 'Well done you!' several times. He was clearly under the impression that HIV was a civil award. We didn't have the heart to put him straight.

It was exceedingly fortunate that, when I met Tim five years after my father's death, my mother and he took to each other immediately. Once, however, despite him recently being described in the *Tatler* as 'beautiful and boyish', she rounded on him out of nowhere: 'Let's face it, boy, you're no glamour puss.' Shortly after Tim's first visit to The Millers House in Kintbury, where my parents had moved in the mid-1980s, she wrote a rare letter to me. Her handwriting was unusual and often needed professional deciphering; legend has it that some of her correspondence is still floating around the postal system.

> Dearest CB,
>
> Maybe because although I often (always!) talk a lot I don't always say just what I feel. I admire you so very much and the way you have always dealt with this crippling health problem. You have never whinged and what is more important have kept going against the odds and also helped others to avoid, or survive, the drug menace. I admire all this so much. That is leaving out the wonderful son you have been to me and nephew to Aunt Boo!! I am so glad that you have found congenial companionship and you deserve any happiness in living that you can find. I am sure there may be a future longer and with a better quality than you think.
>
> All my love as always,
> Your Mother

(If there was ever evidence that a boy's best friend is his mother then this letter was surely it.)

Some years back, I had received a call out of the blue from my rather eccentric Aunt Boo, asking whether I might drive her to a hospital appointment. Thus began a rather unusual but hugely rewarding relationship in which I effectively became my aunt's carer (and her trustee) until she died some fifteen years later. Aunt Boo had stood, at one time or other, for every political party known to man (always losing her deposit) and was a leading light in 'Women against the Common Market'. I never received a letter from my aunt which did not have 'NO TO THE COMMON MARKET' emblazoned across it. Aunt Boo had the most wonderful set of mahogany steps from which she held forth – wearing a nylon, Jayne Mansfield style wig, which had clearly seen better days – regularly at Speakers' Corner in Hyde Park. Unsurprisingly, her immediate family, in particular her son (my first cousin Alex), found her quite a handful. However, as a nephew, I could enjoy and indulge my unusual aunt from a comfortable distance.

A few months after my mother first met Tim, realising the huge pleasure that he gave me, she took him aside for a tête-à-tête. 'I want you to promise me,' she asked 'that you will never leave my son.' She added, almost as an afterthought, 'Of course, my dear boy, you can have as many affairs as you like.'

My mother was never one to beat about the bush. When a close friend Piers brought down a new boyfriend to meet her, after a brief introduction my mother told the newcomer: 'It's all right that you are a Liberal Democrat, it's all right that you are a born-again Christian and it's all right that you are a vegetarian, but it's not bloody well all right that you are all bloody three.'

Mind you she had a particular downer on Liberal Democrats, having once in Newbury High Street publicly berated their parliamentary candidate as 'a crummy wet'.

Almost every Saturday evening for ten years, Tim and I would motor down to Kintbury, unceremoniously christened 'Cuntbury' by my mother. Very occasionally my mother would, to quote my father, have had her 'head in the Martini bucket' for a considerable period prior to our arrival. It wasn't her wig on the tilt that was the big giveaway but the fact that on these occasions she insisted on wearing my father's gold and crimson regimental sash. We soon learned that to be greeted with the sash was the precursor to a rather unpredictable and somewhat stormy evening. That aside these were happy days and it wasn't long before Tim knew more about foxhunting in Dorset in the 1930s than almost anyone else on the planet.

Tim and I both became experts on pubs in the Newbury area as every Sunday the three of us would try out a different one. My mother was herself already quite an authority on these places and was well known in several of them. She had the ability to order a can of Carlsberg Special Brew with the same style and panache as if she was ordering a champagne cocktail in the Rivoli Bar at the Ritz. On one particularly memorable occasion we were, I thought, keeping quite a low profile in rather a rough pub on the outskirts of Thatcham. To my dismay, as I went up to the bar to order, I heard my mother announcing, in a voice not dissimilar to the Queen's in an early 1950s TV Christmas broadcast, 'Well, the thing is, Tim, have you ever thought about having a sex change? Well, why not my dear boy? I've got the bloody money. You could go to Casablanca.'

43

To celebrate my mother's eightieth birthday in 2001, Tim and I took her to Paris on Eurostar for a couple of nights. In its early days Eurostar was fast, reliable and glamorous, and travelling first class was precisely that. On the way out, after several glasses of fizz, my mother managed to spill most of a cup of coffee all over another passenger's laptop. Failing to understand the ramifications, my mother whispered loudly to Tim, 'Absolute fuss over nothing' as she casually attempted to mop up with a napkin.

Within minutes of arriving in Paris my mother informed the Parisian lady who ran a flower shop near to our hotel that she couldn't speak French correctly. This set the scene for a very entertaining if sometimes rather fraught visit, the pinnacle of which was supper at an insanely expensive establishment called La Tour d'Argent overlooking the Seine and Notre Dame. This was the restaurant to which my grandparents had taken my mother on her seventeenth birthday in 1938, when she was a *jeune Anglaise* studying French in Paris under the auspices of the formidable Mademoiselle Fauchet. My mother had very generously offered to pay for dinner but was surprised to find that the prices had increased somewhat in the preceding sixty-three years since her last visit.

Back home in Kintbury my mother's health was now noticeably deteriorating. She had always looked much younger than she was – my friend Dean regularly referred to her affectionately as 'a fit old girl' – but now she was beginning to look her age. Despite the odd new hip, problems with breathing made getting around a real trial for her. 'I never thought that I'd end up like this,' she once confided to me, 'just a hopeless old bag.'

Physical activities, such as galloping her beloved horse Golly across the downs, that had once kept her on the button, were now completely out of the question. That didn't stop her from driving her sporty VW Golf GTI round the narrow Berkshire lanes with considerable gusto, as if competing in the final stages of the Monte Carlo Rally. She told me that now she couldn't go foxhunting, she got her kicks from driving past police cars at speed when well over the legal alcohol limit.

Little by little my mother needed more and more care. For years, local stalwarts Dawn and Keith Bailey had kept an eye on things. Keith looked after the garden and Dawn was my mother's friend, confidante and cleaner in equal measure. Keith loved to recall his first meeting with my father when he was interviewed for the job of gardener in the late 1980s. All had gone well until my dad asked him what his hourly rate was. Keith replied with something pretty modest like £3 an hour, and was amused when my father responded, 'Oh well, Keith, I suppose it is what it is. It will probably bankrupt me. Still, that's my problem not yours.'

Gradually my mother and I were obliged to seek outside help from agencies for live-in help to do the cooking and shopping.

Using agencies was not only breathtakingly expensive but inconvenient in that the girls were always changing just when we had made friends with them. Through an introduction via, of all things, a South African Christian group, we agreed to take on unseen, thus totally on trust, an Afrikaans lady about my age called Marinda. On the prescribed Sunday, I met Marinda at Kintbury train station and walked her up to the house. At first sight, being blond, tall and rather beautiful, she looked like a member of Abba. She was dressed in a pale blue terry-towelling jump suit covered in sequins depicting quite a significant variety of South Africa's wildlife. Accompanying her was BJ, her extremely handsome twenty-year-old son, who was a professional tennis player and had secured a job nearby. If Marinda's appearance didn't knock you sideways, then her strong Afrikaans accent surely would.

My mother was utterly horrified and immediately took to her bed, telling me in no uncertain terms that 'This glamour puss is completely unsuitable.'

'But mother,' I pleaded, 'give her a try. She's only just got here and seems very nice despite her rather unusual appearance and, in any event, there is no plan B.'

Poor Marinda, having travelled all the way from Johannesburg, didn't have a plan B either.

Things may have got off to a rather inauspicious start, but after some negotiation it was agreed that Marinda should stay for a couple of days and if, as my mother anticipated, things didn't work out we would cover all of Marinda's travel expenses to the UK and back again to Johannesburg. Just in case things weren't bad enough, it transpired that Marinda, a very respectable middle-class lady who had dedicated a large amount of her life supporting BJ's professional tennis career and had now fallen on hard times, had no nursing experience and had never washed up dishes in her life let alone made a bed or operated a vacuum cleaner. Tim and I left for London, dropping BJ at his new job off on the way, fearing the worst.

Almost predictably, quite the reverse happened and over the next two years, right up to the day she died, Marinda brought as much pleasure into my mother's life as anything I can ever remember. Her appearance injected into The Millers House a sense of life, melodrama and fun that had recently, as my mother's health had declined, been in short supply. As Tim said it was as if a middle-aged Mary Poppins had flown in with an Afrikaans accent.

It was also an education for me as up until then I had rather a disparaging view of Afrikaners generally. I now learnt first-hand how life wasn't exactly a barrel of laughs for anybody in post-Apartheid South Africa. From time to time BJ and his brother Teunis, whom we flew over from South Africa, came to stay to stop their mother from feeling homesick. I was both entertained and rather flattered to hear later that BJ had picked up an expression from me, which I gather I used frequently following some contentious comment or other from my mother: 'That mother . . . is a fucking understatement.'

Marinda always referred to my mother affectionately as Mrs M and I would receive regular texts, sometimes too regular, as to what was going on: 'I took Mrs M her tumbler of brandy with breakfast and a blue pill [Valium 10mg] but she wants still more brandy and two more blue pills!!!!!' or 'Mrs M still in bed and it's lunchtime!!!!She says unless I give her some more brandy and two blue pills she won't come downstairs!!!!' I never once received a text without at least five exclamation marks and the most I once counted on a single text was nineteen. It was clearly Marinda's way of getting her point across.

For a few months when her visa ran out Marinda's friend Marlu stepped in. Younger and fitter, Marlu was of the no-nonsense school. On one unforgettable occasion a tearful

Marlu confessed that in a moment of absolute desperation she had spanked my mother. Expecting to be sacked on the spot she was more than surprised that both my mother and I thought it was hugely amusing. My mother laughed as she later confided, 'That bloody girl is as strong as a bloody ox.'

After what had happened with my dad I was absolutely determined that my mother should die at home. This was easier said than done. On one occasion our GP, Dr Nick Yates, suggested that she be moved to a local 'cottage hospital'. I responded that unless it had a twenty-four-hour bar that was out of the question.

The real turning point came when my mother's adored Chihuahua Danny died following serious heart complications. I knew this would be a game changer and, in desperation, asked the vet if there was any way she could transplant a squirrel's heart into Danny. As things got worse for my mother I arranged for a hospital bed to be installed in her bedroom. Marinda filled the house with virtually every living piece of foliage from the garden together with scented candles that Tim and I bought in bulk from Price's candle factory in Battersea. About a month before she died, Dr Yates called in and unwisely asked my mother how she was. 'Well, how the bloody hell do you think I bloody am? I'm bloody well dying,' came the sharp response.

My two sisters, four grandchildren and endless friends trooped in to say their tearful goodbyes. My mother, on the other hand, was over the moon that the end was now finally in sight. Marlu was summoned from South Africa to help Marinda and gradually my mother slipped away.

The day she died was a blisteringly hot Sunday in early July

2005. I was on my way back from a shopping errand in Hungerford where, as well as essentials, I had for no obvious reason bought a cut-price ELO CD. As I played 'Mr Blue Sky' at ridiculous volume, I could have sworn that I felt her spirit fly away above my open sunroof, now free of all the hideous restraints that old age, depression and illness had brought upon her. When I reached the house I found Marinda absolutely desolate and being comforted by Tim and Marlu. Dealing with poor Marinda was a mercy as it took our mind off everything else.

Other than when my Aunt Boo had died a few years previously, I had never seen let alone touched a dead body before. Yet I found the experience of closing my mother's eyes, removing her rings and kissing her goodbye completely natural, more poignant than distressing, and made much easier by the knowledge that my mother was at last free.

Her body was respectfully removed my Mr Smallbone, the friendly local undertaker. The following day, by force of habit, I was almost tempted to ring him up to check if she had had a peaceful night in the mortuary.

At my mother's cremation service a few days later I was quite astonished and amused when Marinda insisted on taking group photos round the hearse and my mother's coffin.

For several weeks prior to her thanksgiving service we kept both my mother's and Danny's ashes on a sideboard in the dining room. It made us all laugh that Danny's ashes were in a tasteful little mahogany casket with an engraved brass plaque whereas those of my dear mother were in a mauve cardboard container with a typed label.

Giving the address at my mother's thanksgiving service

was one of the hardest things that I have ever done, and this time it was my turn to fortify myself with a blue pill and some Three Barrels brandy.

On many occasions after my mother had put in a particularly robust defence where frankly there was no credible defence possible, my father would turn to me in exasperation and quote 'A boy's best friend is his mother' and that was most certainly the case with my mother whose loyalty not only to me but to family and friends was second to none. That said it is not now my intention to embark on a long and emotional address during which I would probably break down, embarrassing not only myself but everyone else present here.

Instead, I intend to reflect on various light-hearted snapshots of my mother which all put together as a pastiche literally bring her to life; in particular her strength of character, originality, enthusiasm, sense of the ridiculous, fearlessness, generosity of spirit, ability to create drama out of nowhere, impetuosity and her extraordinary ability to get facts completely wrong and then make matters much worse by holding her ground. It was not for nothing that she was affectionately known within the family as 'the minister of misinformation'.

Several years ago my mother went shopping in Hungerford to buy a wok. She walked into a large hardware store: 'I'd like to buy a yuk please.' Response from shopkeeper: 'We don't sell yuks, madam.' My mother: 'In that case you're not with it at all', and promptly left the shop.

On another occasion she went into a local electrical store to buy a replacement light switch for the upstairs landing.

'Do you stock wall-mounted light switches, please?' asked my mother. 'Yes, madam, we carry a large stock. Are you looking for a one-way or a two-way switch?' 'Oh, two-way of course,' replied my mother confidently. 'On and off.'

Only a few years ago, after staying with several friends, she decided that in comparison to their beds her own bed at home was not very comfortable and thus she went into the Newbury Bedding Centre to buy a replacement. Young salesman: 'Can I help you, madam?' My mother: 'Well, the thing is I've been sleeping around a lot lately . . .'

On the way home in a car from my father's sister's cremation she remarked to my sisters and me, 'Do you know what? I think that's the most fun we've ever had with Aunt Joan.'

My mother's driving was legendary. She drove like she rode. With gusto. I remember she once called me after an accident in London explaining that she had 'ridden off a taxi'. Our neighbour Monica in Kintbury wrote to me saying she wasn't sure which was preferable – driving and being told how to or being a passenger. Once my mother's car aerial was removed by the closing barriers at a local level crossing . . . it was that close. Her grandson Piers once said, 'Granny, unless you slow down I'm not going to go in a car with you again!'

For myself, I was always grateful to my mother for teaching me to drive when my feet could barely touch the pedals. Apart from the day when my mother ran over a French gendarme's foot when we were late for a ferry at Dunkirk, my most vivid memory is about twenty-five years ago. I had met my mother up on the downs for lunch and the plan was to follow her to a pub. I had just at vast expense bought a Renault Gordini which was supposed to be extremely quick. My mother set off with me following. By the time she had gone sideways round a couple of bends I realised that the chances of keeping up with her were fairly remote and the last thing I remember seeing were her two beloved Chihuahuas, Peregrine van Nottenpool and the Baron von Otto, on the rear parcel shelf of her car desperately hanging onto the seat belt anchorage points with their teeth.

Any outing with my mother however mundane the mission had the habit of turning into an adventure. My father and I could hardly forget when, about forty years prior to the current war on terror, my mother decided while we sat on a crowded charter plane due to leave Corfu that a perfectly innocent fellow passenger, who later turned out to be a music teacher, had 'fanatical eyes'. She alerted the captain to her suspicions that he was in fact a terrorist and the aeroplane had to be vacated. It didn't make us all that popular with the other holidaymakers.

My mother also liked to contribute to any event she attended, often by asking 'interesting' questions. One wet Easter weekend she took her grandsons to watch a local falconry display. At the end the falconer asked if anybody had any questions. 'Yes, as a matter of fact I do,' gushed my mother. 'Tell me, is it possible to be d'accord with a bird?'

No tribute, however, would be complete without a few quotes from my father's letters to me. He often refers to her by her family nickname, Nidnod.

'If I believed in reincarnation I would like to come back as one of your mother's dogs.'

52

'Your mother is rather crotchety but luckily is off to Jersey tomorrow for a boating holiday. I shall lead a relaxed life here, having meals when I like and looking at the TV programmes that I like. Nor shall I be under any obligation to pretend I am deaf.'

'Nidnod departed for a beano at Inkpen. I think gin was in fairly abundant supply there and it had the customary effect of making your mother behave like Queen Boadicea on her return home. There are now three deaf people in this house ... Moppet [the cat], Pongo [the dog], and myself. Your mother is still convinced that a poltergeist whipped away a sausage she was cooking and I expect she will call the Reverend Jardine in for consultation.'

'Nidnod had her noggin in the Martini bucket for a considerable period and became totally unplayable in the evening which enabled me to go to bed early and read peacefully.'

'I did not much fancy Nidnod's driving on the way home. I prefer it when she is not being a female Fangio.'

'Nidnod talks of buying a revolver in which case she is certain to pot a member of her family before long.'

'Your mother managed to congratulate the wrong jockey on winning the Derby and then mistook Willie Whitelaw [the Home Secretary] for the caterer.'

'Poor Ian has been here trying to mend a radiator; he has failed to do so possibly because Nidnod never stopped talking and did not permit him to get on with the job.'

'Your mother had the time of her life today being the first on the scene at a motor accident near Kingsclere and therefore in an excellent position to boss the victims and apply first aid.'

'Yesterday a keen young man came and took about 119 photographs of me for publication on Sunday. As it was raining the whole time, my cap is too small for me and your mother was trying to cram the animals into the foreground, the result should be interesting. The photographer stayed till 3 p.m. that did not worry me as I left at 12.30 p.m. Your mother held him in riveting conversation.'

'Thank God our four geese were decapitated last week and not a day too soon. Unfortunately, Nidnod had allowed them too much liberty and they weighed far less than expected. We ate the first one last night and it tasted like a moist flannel shirt.'

'I won three quid at bridge last night with old Lord Carnarvon but your dear mother lost £4.60 at gin rummy and then expected me to pay which seemed a bit hard.'

'Nidnod tried to get into conversation with a grumpy old man in a pub, he thought she was trying to pick him up and turned his back on her and walked out.'

'Your dear mother is endeavouring to live on a purely liquid diet with unfortunate results. One evening she popped my dinner into her car and drove off with it saying she was going to give it to the poor. I was a little surprised, therefore, to find she had dropped it off at the Bomers. She is now known as meals on wheels in reverse removing hot dinners from the old and needy.'

'Last night we had dinner with Colonel B. His previous wife had gone off her onion. The last time we saw her she clasped Nidnod to her bosom and started to sing "Oh you beautiful doll, you great big beautiful doll." Nidnod tells me I was unkind to laugh.'

Of all the occasions when my mother really put herself in it, my personal favourite has to be when she was a guest in a box at Cheltenham races and was asked by her host if she would like a drink. 'I must say,' she enthused, 'I'm most awfully in favour of drinks companies that sponsor racing so I think I'll jolly well sponsor one of them.' She had a quick look at the race-card and, taking note of the sponsor of the last race, confidently replied, 'I think I'll have a large Massey-Ferguson please.'

I have since my mother died been overwhelmed by the number of people who have sent me their condolences who have never actually met my mother but said they felt they knew her intimately from all the stories that they had heard about her over the years.

My mother was under the impression that she was totally normal; she had no idea just how original she was. Had I suggested that she might be just a little eccentric she would probably have found the proposition insulting and dismissed it with 'You do talk rot, my dear boy.' Once, many years ago my mother, in a very concerned way, asked if my friends thought she was dull. I replied, 'Mother I can honestly assure you that my friends may think of you as many things but dull is certainly not one of them.'

4

The Turpin Years

Beyond any other single thing, the most defining moment of my life was when I was fourteen. Our wonderful mongrel Turpin, with whom I had grown up with from day one, was killed by a speeding cattle truck just yards from the safety of our home, Barclay House.

I was just a few months old when my parents ran over a black puppy near what is now Heathrow Airport. Fortunately, the dog wasn't seriously hurt and my dad took him to the local police station. Nobody claimed him and in due course he became ours. Given that we had found him in Dick Turpin Way we called him Turpin. For the next fourteen years there was literally no part of our family life that Turpin wasn't involved with, and he was as much a part of the family as any of us. Picnics, jaunty local car trips, horse rides, motoring marathons to Scotland and seaside holidays – Turpin was always right in the thick of things.

He was jet black with a white chest and stood at around

two foot. As my dad observed, he was 'very common and entirely lovable'. I guess he must have had a lot of spaniel in him as he had big floppy ears, a mass of curly black hair and a large tail which was constantly wagging in a somewhat enthusiastic manner. Not long after we collected him from Battersea Dogs Home, he came down with the often fatal disease canine distemper. My mother nursed Turpin devotedly and he got through it. Afterwards, Turpin proved to be the most faithful of friends and his loyalty to us would know no bounds, a thank you perhaps for rescuing him from the life of a stray. In reality, of course, it was us who should have been thanking him for bringing such joy into our lives. My father was moved to say that perhaps some of our luck and happiness vanished the morning he was killed.

Turpin was first and foremost our family dog but for me he will always be something much more important than that. My early life can be divided into two sections; life with Turpin and life after his death under the wheels of a 'B. N. Gray Livestock Transport of Eversley' lorry. The fact that I can, after all these years, remember the name of the transport firm says it all really.

My parents were always inspired when it came to choosing houses. In 1950 they moved together with my older sister Jane from a really charming Georgian villa to an equally delightful Georgian home, Barclay House, in what was then a classic unspoilt English village called Yateley.

To quote my father: 'We arrived at Barclay House in glorious autumn weather at the end of October 1950. I was forty, Cynthia twenty-nine and Jane about twenty months old. We were full of hope and short on money. I think our relations thought we were insane to move here from Launceston Place.'

The enthusiastic and thoroughly amiable estate agent who arranged the sale was Christopher Hibbert, who in later life became an extremely eminent historian. At the time Barclay House appeared on the cover of *Country Life* under the heading of 'Home, sweet home', a pretty accurate description as it turned out. Unusually for a fairly modest village house, Barclay House had extensive slate-roofed outbuildings including stables, a large greenhouse halfway down the garden and several fields. The house had been built *c.*1760 with a rather wonderful veranda and a large glass atrium that always leaked but allowed a decent amount of natural light to flood the central staircase and hall. Immediately beside the house there was a huge copper beech, which almost overshadowed it. For such a small estate, there was an interesting variety of trees and shrubs including willow, mulberry, elm, oak, apple, pear, greengage, various conifers, not to forget the vast rhododendrons that took up almost a quarter of an acre. It was into this truly charming corner of the planet that I was fortunate enough to have been born in April 1952, arriving some six weeks late in my mother's bedroom to, I gather, the delight of all.

At the time my father was horse-racing correspondent for the *Sunday Times* as well as being a post-race commentator for the BBC. There was still extensive rationing as it was six and a half years since the end of the Second World War, during which time my father had been held for the duration as a prisoner, having been seriously wounded and captured at the military disaster and subsequent morale-boosting rescue that was Dunkirk. Not surprisingly, the experience had a profound effect on his outlook on life. Before the war he had enjoyed hunting and shooting. After the war he never engaged in the killing of an animal for sport again. Not so my dear mother who taught me, aged ten, how to rough shoot.

Being a racing correspondent involved my dad driving thirty or forty thousand miles a year in a series of sporty second-hand Jaguars to various racecourses. When he wasn't driving he was writing, reading or gardening, all of which he loved. My mother was much more physical and sometimes gloriously irresponsible in her enthusiasm for life in general; she possessed a huge sense of fun. I can't imagine many mothers allowing their twelve-year-old son to drive them on the public highway. My mother was also a keen horsewomen and was determined that her children should follow suit. It would not be unfair to describe my dad as possessing a world-class intellect whereas mother, despite noble effort on her behalf, did not. In fact, she never, throughout her life, managed the transition from listening to the light service (Radio 2 and Terry Wogan) to the more intellectually challenging home service (Radio 4).

My parents loved their holidays in Brittany and Lake Como, and so it was that a few months after I was born Mrs Childs came to look after my sister and me for a couple of weeks while they were away. This worked out so well that, to the delight of us all, she came to live with us. Mrs Childs was a cosy-looking lady, probably in her forties, who was born within earshot of the bells of St Mary-le-Bow in Cheapside and thus a genuine cockney. From day one I was 'her darling Charles', and this affection was reciprocated in spades. However, I was clearly born into the wrong class. The benefits and privileges associated with my background have always held zero appeal for me. I enjoy my lot's existence as a colourful species, but I just don't care much to hang out with them. So even at an early age, I felt completely at home or as my mother might say 'd'accord', with Mrs Childs and her family. I wasn't a particularly social child outside our home, preferring instead all the attention I received as the baby of the family. Once, when my parents were away over my fourth birthday (my father was recuperating from a patch on his lung), Mrs Childs asked me what I wanted by way of a small party. 'Big cake, no people,' was my response.

Apart from the odd tantrum when I used to hit my head on the floor until I lost consciousness, the early years were incredibly happy ones. I was an enthusiastic singer, so much so that I used to rock my cot with such gusto that it had to be fastened to the wall. Downstairs, there was a sort of quasi-nursery/dining room, where our pet dove Lucy used preen herself in a large cage above the table with the result that it wasn't unusual to find feathers mixed in with the breakfast cereal. From there, it was a short flight of three or four steps down to the kitchen. At the top stair there was a small wooden child-proof gate, which I used to hang onto for hours whilst I sang to Mrs Childs, who clearly had the patience of a saint, as she busied herself preparing food.

What makes this all the more surprising in retrospect is that I cannot sing now to save my life and have no sense of rhythm whatsoever. This became very apparent when, aged twelve, I managed to persuade my mother to buy me a Premier snare drum in a stunning turquoise and metal flake finish from Boosey & Hawkes in Aldershot. It quickly transpired, perhaps because of my complete lack of co-ordination, that hard as I tried I just could not hit the drum with the two sticks at different paces at the same time. Six months on, my mother and I returned to the same retailer together with the drum. There, to my absolute horror, she took it upon herself to announce loudly to the entire shop, 'He's decided he doesn't want to be a drummer anymore.' It was possibly the most embarrassing moment of my entire life, and even today makes me cringe a little.

My initiation into kindergarten was a bit of a drama, to put things mildly. It was possibly the first time that I was obliged not only to do something I really didn't want to do, but to enter an entirely alien world away from the security of my family, mother and Mrs Childs, in particular. The local school was run by a Miss Tyler for children of four and a half to six years of age, and cost five guineas a term including stationery. Dropping me off on my first morning was easier said than done. I howled and clung to my mother like a limpet mine on an enemy destroyer. We were prised apart and I ended up, still howling, in a room full of strangers still clutching my mother's glove. In fury, I gave poor old Miss Tyler a really good kick as she bent down to pick something up. This was not a popular move.

On a physical level, although I say it myself, I was a very cute blond boy who was 95 per cent of the time full of joy. I rapidly got through another couple of junior schools before my parents stumbled across Major Mallock's Sunny Side Lodge in Fleet about ten miles away from Yateley. My two and a half years there were to prove the happiest educational experience I was ever to have.

The Major and his wife oversaw the running of this extraordinarily relaxed school in a large rambling Victorian house set in several acres of land, complete with their English setter. I made lots of friends and used to excel at the game 'kick the can'. My favourite dish, served up twice a week by kindly Mrs Mallock, was baked beans, mince and onions with mash. Other than perhaps an 'Olympic breakfast' in a Little Chef, I have never eaten anything to beat it. From time to time I still knock up my version of it on a cold winter's day. I only blotted my copybook once at Sunny Side Lodge when I was reported for repeating a mildly improper rhyme: 'Oh lady of Spain I adore you, please take off your knickers and let me explore you.'

Some of the parents used to share the school run, which was made easier by my older sister and some of her very talkative friends also going to a school in Fleet, called St Neots. I used to enjoy some of these rides, particularly when whiskered Mr Wolseley drove us in his 1920s Rolls-Royce estate car. It was an eccentric vehicle that looked like a sedate limousine that had one day skidded off the road through someone's garden, picking up a small wooden greenhouse en route. Other attractions were an opening front windscreen and a huge rubber and brass bulb horn, which omitted a long, low bellow. From time to time, I used to be taken to school together with my friend Michael Samuel by his family's fully uniformed chauffeur in a brand new, then highly fashionable, Citroën Safari estate. One day, despite his grandfather founding Royal Dutch Shell, Michael's parents decided to invest in a more economical mode of transport because of the rising cost of petrol due to the recent Suez crisis. So it was that one sunny morning the same fully uniformed chauffeur appeared at the wheel of a brilliant white Heinkel bubble car. Despite the fact that Michael and I were only aged seven at the time, it was still quite a squeeze in the front seat. Whenever we went over a bump, which seemed to be every thirty seconds, my head made painful contact with one of the door hinges.

At the time I was blissfully unaware of various family dramas going on around me, such as when my older sister Jane mercifully survived peritonitis and the night my mother, returning from a boozy dinner with friends Gerald and Helen de Mauley, turned her Hillman Minx over after hitting a tree. Afterwards, she swore that the steering box had failed, a claim met with some derision by my father. Early one morning, I missed the removal, under heavy sedation, of a barmy Spanish lady who had been employed to help in the kitchen. She had, among many other things, shocked Mrs Childs's very proper older sister, Hilda, by swallowing raw eggs and bacon. I was also oblivious to my father's illness from overwork, and my mother's double pneumonia.

It would have been hard to miss the celebrations that accompanied the triumphant arrival of my younger sister Lumpy in 1957, or to ignore the live drama being played out by our voluble and lovable au pair Fernanda and her romances with Major Barnett and 'Ron', which were a saga all of their own. Not to forget the fateful morning when our cross-eyed jobbing gardener, known somewhat inappropriately as 'The Merry Mason', announced proudly to my father, 'It's all right, Major, while waiting for instructions I thought I'd make myself useful so I gave the spaghetti a right good dig over to save you the trouble.' In under an hour, he had destroyed the mature asparagus bed so lovingly established by my father over the previous five years. My father observed years later, 'I never loved him after that act of vandalism.' One day that is hard to forget is the morning when by accident I virtually scalped our then gardener Williams's son, with a spade. Fortunately, Master Williams survived. My dad summarised: Charlie then denied the offence with such vigour that his mother believed him, though nobody else did, of course.'

I have particularly happy early memories of bucket-and-spade holidays with Mrs Childs in Littlehampton and family holidays in Brittany. Aged six, I watched as my dad's Jaguar saloon was deposited by a crane onto the deck of a ship in Southampton and then, unable to sleep due to excitement, looking at the harbour lights through a tiny porthole as they disappeared into the night while we steamed out towards France.

As a family we were fond of silly rhymes, such as 'Martha swallowed a jellyfish and Jane she got she got the cramp and mother-in-law began to jaw because the sea was damp . . .' Nicknames were part of family life: my mother was originally 'The Buzzer' and then 'Nidnod', my dad 'Twig' and later 'The Old Boot'. Picnics were a regular feature as neither of my parents ever had any qualms about taking their cars off down muddy tracks as if they were Land Rovers. Turpin was always a particularly eager participant, knowing that there was always going to be the odd cold sausage and saucer of warm tea up for grabs. Of all the places to picnic, I guess what we called 'The Robbers' Cave', buried deep in the woods up on Finchampstead Ridges, was a firm favourite. After food there was always hide and seek, followed by family races with my dad doling out 'rich prizes' to the lucky winners.

Unfortunately, all good things come to an end. Out of blue, horror of horrors, I was sent away a mere eight years old to Wellesley House, a preparatory school for boys in Broadstairs, Kent. It was such a surprise, because it had been agreed that I would be a day boy at a local school, but at the very last minute my eccentric godfather, John Blackwell, who was at that time a partner at Wellesley House, generously offered to fund that part of my education. My father told me that none of his experiences over five years as a prisoner-of-war was quite a bad as his first term at his preparatory school, Ludgrove. (Thanks awfully, dad.) Bizarrely I later discovered that my parents hated me leaving as much as I hated going. That was just the way the system for our mob worked back then, and they only wanted what was best for me. There was also considerable peer pressure on them to do the right thing.

I would concur with my dad that nothing thrown at me in later life was quite as awful as that first term, with the exception perhaps of clinical depression. Subsequent years at prep school weren't exactly a barrel of laughs either. To make matters worse, goodbyes were said on a public platform at Victoria Station before, clutching a tiny teddy called 'Sidney' as if life itself depended on him, I kissed my mother and boarded, complete with green trunk and wooden tuck box, the school train. I was determined not to cry – both my mother and I chewed gum, following a friendly tip. It was supposed to concentrate the mind and stave off any tears. I could at least take some comfort from the histrionics being played out on the platform by my soon–to-be friend Peter Hicks Beech (now sadly deceased from Aids) and his bejewelled and mink-clad mother, Diana Countess of St Aldwyna, dead ringer for Madame Bianca Castafiore, the 'Milanese Nightingale' from *The Adventures of Tintin*. In later years, the Countess would occasionally do an evening round of the school dormitories clutching boys to her vast bosom while distributing boiled sweets, a vision of extreme opulence and loveliness wafting around on a cloud of Chanel No. 5.

For the first three terms the 'new squirts' were sent to the junior school, North Foreland Court, run by a fairly humourless retired Army officer called Duncan Fraser and his equally dour wife. They were assisted by Colonel Craig, who sported a toothbrush moustache and the lovely Mrs Snow, who taught English. The bleak building was perched right on the edge of a chalk headland overlooking the Channel. Apart from the entire Isle of Thanet smelling slightly of rotting cabbage, my prevailing memory is that of being extremely cold and very homesick. Still, we all were in the same boat and I quickly made quite a few firm friends.

One day I was amusing myself in what was laughably called the model village, Wroxham, when an older boy threw my Dinky toys into a puddle and stamped on them. I was so incensed at this wanton act of vandalism that I marched straight up to a master and, pointing to the perpetrator, complained about what had occurred. The boy responsible was promptly removed and soundly thrashed. Now here's the thing, I clearly remember thinking 'there's something a bit too easy about this' and I was right. I was 'sent to Coventry' for being a sneak. It was a painful lesson in the ways of the world and one I was never to repeat, opting from that day on to deal with my own problems in my own way.

Every morning, there were prayers downstairs; these, of course, were compulsory. One time we were all kneeling down when in the distance we heard the distinctive 'clip clop' of leather-soled Cambridge house shoe making contact with the highly polished parquet floor as a boy ran down the corridor late for assembly. As he rounded the final corner at speed, I could see it was a freckled friend of mine, now the lean and distinguished boss of a major auction house, then more reminiscent of Billy Bunter in both build and style. Unfortunately, he had misjudged his lack of traction and, halfway round the corner, his legs slipped from under him. All we could see was this gigantic bottom coming towards us in mid-air. At that precise moment he let out a fart like a thunderclap. I laughed so much that I honestly thought I was going need medical treatment, my ribs hurt so much.

Meanwhile, back at Barclay House, the strangled body of a young girl guide had been discovered in scrubland a mere 100 yards away on Yateley Common. The poor child had been abducted and subsequently murdered by Arthur Albert Jones. My father, who took a keen interest in criminology, was delighted when the police set up their HQ in our kitchen; he was rather less thrilled when he was interviewed as a suspect.

The senior school, Wellesley House, was a rather different ball game. It had more than just a touch of Llanabba Castle, the school out of Evelyn Waugh's *Decline and Fall*, about it and I enjoyed a relatively happy and entertaining few years there. This was in no small part due to the extreme eccentricity of a large section of the staff and, in some cases, the pupils, many of whom turned out in later life to be gay. My only existing close friend from those days, Jonathan Hope, wryly observed to me recently, 'You could be popular even if you hated games', a fact that suited us both rather well. That said, I was caned by the headmaster John 'Baggers' Boyce, a distant relative by marriage, within a week of my arrival for 'flagrant and blatant disobedience'.

Years later, my godfather John Blackwell, who was most definitely in the 'eccentric' camp, confided to me that John Boyce used to beat boys naked.

'Well, he never beat me naked,' I replied, somewhat surprised by the somewhat unlikely allegation.

'Oh, you were all right,' he replied. 'You were family.'

On arrival we were immediately designated a school number and became a member of one of four competing teams – Vikings, Saxons, Romans or Danes – for the duration. I was number 74 and a Viking. We were all called by our surnames not only by the masters but by each other, the four Scott boys being Scott major, Scott minor, Scott minimus and my friend, Scott 4. Once, staying with my friend Charlie Hurt's family at their home, Casterne Hall, his father very kindly suggested that now they had known me for some time that I might like to be addressed as Charles or Charlie. I replied rather haughtily, although without intention, 'I prefer to be called Mortimer, Sir.' He fondly remembered it years later as one of his life's more memorable put-downs.

Wellesley House was primarily quite a handsome, purpose-built, late Victorian school building with a later wing attached. It stood in around thirty acres on the edge of Broadstairs town and housed around 120 pupils. It was almost entirely self-contained, with most sporting and other activities including squash, swimming, archery and rifle shooting taking place within the grounds.

Of the more unusual masters, three stood head and shoulders above the others. Topping the list has to be John Brooker aka Baz who like my godfather was also a partner in the school and taught French and Greek. He employed a colourful use of the English language to great effect. With his almost olive-coloured skin, dark hooded eyes and rich black hair curling tightly as it reached his collar, he had the opulent look of a well-built Spanish aristocrat. If you failed to keep attention in his classes, he would furnish the boy immediately behind you with a bayonet to prod you painfully at the appropriate moment. He regularly made an exaggerated gesture of wiping the sweat from his brow with his hand whilst reprimanding some trembling pupil, 'You make me want to puke', or, to me once, 'I wouldn't wipe your arse with a ten-foot bargepole'. He would often address the class as a whole as 'a bunch of dreadful little oiks'. He was a formidable and exceptionally classy character, hugely amusing, sometimes terrifying but massively popular with the boys. Bear in mind that this was still the tail end of post-war austerity, when the salary of most masters allowed them to purchase little more than an old banger or a bicycle. Baz, however, owned three cars, and what exotic cars they were: a black Ford Thunderbird purchased from Ian Fleming; a brand new 'Chinese eye' Rolls-Royce Silver Cloud III drophead coupé by bespoke coachbuilder Mulliner Park Ward; and a Mercedes-Benz 300S limousine. By repute, he also was a connoisseur of stamps and coins, a lover of Cuban cigars and a jazz aficionado.

Running almost neck and neck with Baz in the seriously-off-the-wall stakes was John Blackwell, aka 'JB', who was my dad's first cousin. He taught mathematics, golf and boxing, and liked boys so much, in a completely innocent way, that he, I thought rather pragmatically later, acquired a preparatory school of his own, Selwyn House. On his twenty-first birthday my father took him as a treat to a lady of the night in Soho. All went well until he discovered to his absolute horror that the woman had pubic hair and that was that, as they say. In the end it was left to my dad to do the honours.

John Blackwell was a keen amateur golfer and was for a while Captain of Royal St George's at Sandwich, where he regularly played a round of golf with his close friend Ian Fleming. He narrowly missed out on winning the Amateur Championship at St Andrews, claiming to his dying day that he had been fatally put off by his mother, my great-aunt Shirley, kissing him on the eighteenth tee. Subsequently he succeeded his brother Tom as Captain of the Royal and Ancient at St Andrews. Ian Fleming borrowed a number of names of Wellesley boys, including Goldfinger and Scaramanga, for Bond characters.

Like my father, John Blackwell was a POW and in retirement often regaled surprised guests with a rather elaborate story of how he was captured by a simply gorgeous Italian officer with a plume in his helmet. He went onto say that he had slipped the Italian his phone number at the Crosse & Blackwell HQ in Soho Square and was disappointed that he hadn't got in touch when the war was over. Like Baz, JB enjoyed motoring and gadgets. His convertible Bentley was fitted with a Philips record player that took 45 rpm singles. Not to be outdone by

Baz's Thunderbird, he acquired a gold Buick Riviera so wide it could barely scrape through the school gates. This was soon followed by another ex-Fleming car in the form of a Raymond Loewy-designed Studebaker Avanti with exhaust pipes the size of drain pipes, before getting hooked on Bristols. John Blackwell was popular on the golf course and popular with the boys, being something of an overgrown schoolboy himself. He and Baz were good friends and, when not playing snooker, listening to jazz and drinking vintage champagne, they often used to frequent the casino in Ramsgate where, John Blackwell once told me, if they won £20 they would then go out and spend £100 celebrating.

Running a distant third, not exactly top drawer although not quite in the Captain Grimes division either, came John Wilkinson aka Blenks, a dapper man in his forties with sandy hair and a slightly sadistic streak. I think Blenks spent a fair amount of his waking hours, when not throwing hard objects at pupils, working out how to emulate Baz and JB on a shoe-string budget. Where Baz would have a collection of rolled gold Parker 51 pens filled with different coloured inks and matching oblongs of ultra-thick blotting paper from Smythson, Blenks could only manage plastic Osmiroid fountain pens and blotters from WHSmith. When he finally scrapped enough cash together to upgrade his old Standard Vanguard estate to a Bentley, it was a ten-year-old R Type, with suicide front doors, that had clearly seen better days. From time to time, Blenks was allowed to join Brooker/Blackwell club but it was always on their terms and only as an associate member. He wasn't popular with the boys largely because his nasty side had a habit of appearing all too often.

Other notables included the headmaster 'Baggers' Boyce, a tall kindly old boy in his late sixties who had a long face that resembled a folded maroon-coloured face flannel. He was an enthusiastic pipe smoker who ran the school with wife Barbara 'M'boy', who was also tall and quite distinguished. They lived in some style in the school grounds in a large detached house called The Orchard. Then there was Miss Vickers 'Flo', who taught French and looked exactly like Colonel Rosa Klebb from *From Russia with Love*. She eventually retired to Yorkshire to live with her sister in their home, 'Chez nous'. Not forgetting ex-Spitfire pilot, the deranged Harry Dakeyne, who drove a sporty Triumph TR2 and taught science, and the awful Reverend 'Clipper' Crouch who was bald, drove a beige Rover 90 and suffered from halitosis. Ultimately he left under a cloud after a rather public outburst of anti-Semitism against a boy called Marks. Once during an argument, an exasperated eleven-year-old Jonathan Porritt (now a famous environmentalist) called Crouch 'a shrivelled up old mushroom'.

There wasn't much bullying at Wellesley House but what there was of it was extremely unpleasant. During my first year I was on the receiving end and I have never forgiven the perpetrators. Whereas I just accepted corporal punishment doled out by the staff as part of the rough and tumble of the place.

A tall, arrogant, older boy was captain of my dormitory, where nightly he dispensed arbitrary justice, to me in particular, by way of a painful punishment called 'bicep busters'. This involved the recipient having his arm twisted backwards while simultaneously receiving sharp karate chops, usually twenty or so, to the upper-arm muscle. On another occasion a blond boy suggested that I looked at something he had drawn. Unknown to me he had emptied most of the contents of a tube of Airfix glue on to the piece of paper. As I put my head down to take a look, he brought it sharply up to my left eye. This put me into the sick bay for a couple of days while various soothing dressings were applied by the kindly assistant matron. It was lucky that in 1961 super glue had yet to be invented.

On the whole, psychological torture was worse than the physical, and on that score two ghastly brothers were right at the forefront. Many years later, while working for Peponi Hotel on Lamu off the coast of Kenya, I gained a bit of a local reputation as a boat mechanic. One day I was asked if I would help a chap further down the coast whose outboard motor had broken down. I readily agreed until I found out that the chap was none other than one of the brothers. At that point I was undecided whether to pitch up and quietly sabotage the boat beyond repair, or send a message calling him a cunt and telling him that he must need his head examining if he thought for one nanosecond that I would willingly come within a million miles of him. In the end I chose simply to ignore the request.

In the bullying stakes I was luckier than some. Firstly, I toughened up pretty quickly and, secondly, I have never acquiesced to the status of victim without a fight. Not so my friend and contemporary Peter Hicks Beech who in 'Long Dorm' was beaten up mercilessly night after night by a little monster until his ears turned black and blue.

Real joy for me was the peace and quiet of sharing 'two dorm' with Harry Percy. He was a pleasantly eccentric boy with a shock of snow-white hair who was destined to become the Duke of Northumberland. In later years he became a hypochondriac with a predilection for honey sandwiches. Sadly he was to die aged only forty-two.

From time to time my mother would drive down with Turpin and stay with John Blackwell at his bachelor pad, a flint cottage called 'Minters' in the school grounds. On one such visit, my mother, having retired to her bedroom, was somewhat surprised when my godfather, who claimed to have no sexual interest in women whatsoever, peeked his head round her door. For one brief surreal moment, my mother thought he was about to make a pass at her (still waters running deep and all that). However, having pirouetted round the room a couple of times, it turned out he merely wanted to show off his new shorty pyjamas, all the rage at the time. My mother was always popular with my friends as she had an irrepressible streak of irresponsibility, like the day she allowed us to sit on the tailgate of my father's Fiat 2300 estate car with our feet dangling just inches off the road while she drove at some speed round Sandwich Bay. My parents seldom visited together.

Given how things panned out, I was surprisingly uninterested in sex and usually only got involved with the delights of mutual masturbation with other boys if I came across it by chance. I was never predatory and was never abused by a master; clearly I either didn't have the right look or I failed to give out the supposed signals. I was much more interested, together with my friend Charlie Hurt, in proving that I had all the credentials of a rocker. There was no better place to start than with our mutual adoration of Elvis Presley and castigation of Cliff Richard and anyone who claimed to be a Cliff fan. The only time that I knowingly tortured anyone was when I hung a harmless boy called Shailer upside down from a tree by his feet until he told me he loved Elvis, which he did quite quickly.

Charlie and I used to spend hours trying to establish how *hard* we were. The ultimate goal was to be as hard as nails, whereas we felt we were about as hard as warm butter. During the holidays, to my mother's absolute horror, my dad and I had gone into Camberley where he bought me a black leather jacket (well, faux leather) with a white fur collar (well, faux fur, too, actually). A piece of kit that was absolutely de rigueur for any self-respecting rocker. (I was twelve at the time.) Later on, I secretly acquired a pair of winkle-picker shoes embossed with tiny gold hearts. My mother was once somewhat astonished when, on the way back from watching Elvis star in *Fun in Acapulco* at the Odeon, Wokingham, Charlie Hurt, then aged all of eleven, demanded to be let out of her Austin Seven (Mini) following a mildly disparaging remark she had made about 'The King'. 'Following that unforgivable slur, Mrs Mortimer,' he said politely but firmly, 'I'm afraid I can't possibly travel another yard in the same vehicle as you.'

Although life at Wellesley House had its fun moments, it was as nothing compared to life at Barclay House and the village of Yateley. The excitement, commonly known as 'end of termitis' was always so intense the night before term ended that it was almost impossible to sleep. Two days later the feeling of waking up in my own bedroom at home on the first day of the holidays was indescribably wonderful. Had I been able to capture it in a bottle somehow it would have made heroin a non-starter in the addiction stakes. Given how life chez Mortimer would unravel, we were in the early 1960s a pretty contented and even more surprisingly fully functional family. Noël Coward's famous line, often quoted by my dad at the time, now seems almost prophetic: 'Cocktails and laughter, But what comes after? Nobody knows!'

During the holidays I used to make a bit of extra pocket money by doing a paper round on my bike and washing neighbours' cars. There was something truly liberating about getting up at 5.30 a.m., collecting my package of papers from the newsagent and finding that, apart from the milkman, I had the run of the entire village to myself. This would be followed by the bliss of a well-earned fried breakfast.

For some reason, I was fascinated by car crashes and would spend hours examining wrecks in Mr Blackman's garage, shamelessly seeking out gruesome evidence, such as blood and hair stuck to shattered glass, that the occupants had been seriously injured in the collision.

My best friend in the village was James Staples, a good-looking boy of my own age with dark hair, an engaging smile and, as far as I could work out, the same crewneck maroon jumper year in year out. 'The Capsule', as he was known, and I often shared paper rounds and both got a big kick out of bikes and cars.

James's home was not quite the free-for-all that ours was, but it had other attractions. His family lived in an enormous, rather down-at-heel Regency pile at the other end of the village, and they ran 'an armchair shopping service' (very modern in its day). James's dad was a retired major who took easygoing to new levels; his mother, who was slightly on the large side, shared with Hyacinth Bucket a keen sense of social order and was clearly the driving force behind the business. The focal point was a generous kitchen, painted deep red and fitted out with an Aga. There, endless mugs of tea and toast were on offer round the clock. We would spend many happy afternoons on our bicycles exploring the recently vacated American airbase at Blackbushe Airport and the massive car-breaker yards up there.

It was bad luck for me that all my best friends left Wellesley House the term before I did. Against all the odds, I passed my Common Entrance to Eton. By then my friend Charlie Hurt was already a pupil there. He called my mother from a phone box, 'Hello, Mrs Mortimer, I am afraid I have to tell you . . .' He then paused theatrically during which time my mother almost passed out in anticipation of some really dire news, '. . . that Mortimer has passed in!'

If there was a particular moment of the parting of the ways between my parent's hopes and aspirations for me and my own, then this was it. My becoming a pupil at the country's premier public school meant absolutely everything to them, and to my mother in particular, whereas all I really wanted was to go to a local comprehensive school and hang out in the village. As soon as I heard the news I implored my mother to drive down to Kent and collect me and my trunk three weeks before the end of term.

I was now twelve years old, a non-starter intellectually, although I loved Sherlock Holmes, useless at sport and completely unsophisticated. On a more positive note, I was always cheerful, but I was also impetuous and, in most matters, hopelessly naive. During my four years at Wellesley I only won one prize: a joint-gardening prize together with my good friend Charlie Cator. This was entirely due to his mother appearing a week before judging with a car-load of exotic alpine plants, which she then very kindly planted in our six-foot square plot and transformed it into a world-class rockery. The only sport I can say that I both enjoyed and excelled at was when I organized a mods versus rockers fight on one of the playing fields.

The best fifteen minutes of entertainment I enjoyed at Wellesley House was when the Samuels, the chauffeur/bubble car family, sent down a huge wooden crate of expensive fireworks for 5 November. Before the display organisers had a chance to unpack the contents, a random spark from the bonfire, aided by a brisk breeze, flew into the crate. Within seconds the whole lot went off like a direct hit by a shell from a Howitzer Cannon on a major munitions depot. Rockets flew absolutely everywhere in combination with a plethora of flashes, whizzes and explosions that seemed to go on forever. It may not have been a planned display but, as spectator events go, it scored ten out of ten.

The idea of heading off to Eton in a couple of months' time, kitted out like a glorified head waiter, filled me with horror. In retrospect, the easiest thing would have been for me to have simply flunked my Common Entrance exam while I still had the chance.

I decided at least to make the most of the intervening time I had at home. Thanks to my mother I learned to how to drive, the downside for her being that I was always taking her mini down to the fields to try out some handbrake turns. I think partly as a reward for passing into Eton and partly to take the pressure off her own car, she allowed me to persuade her into buying me a fully roadworthy 1951 Ford Prefect from Eric Baldwin, who ran the local garage. I would hang around the garage almost daily, trying to make myself useful in the tiny workshop. 'It's all right for you, Charlie,' Eric's sidekick Ron used to say, 'your bread's buttered.' Then, to drive the point home, he'd add, 'And it's got jam on it!'

From then on, all the money I earned doing my paper round and other odd jobs went on petrol at just over four shillings a gallon so I could drive my newly acquired Ford round our fields at high speeds. Turpin, usually an enthusiastic passenger on any motoring jaunt, soon lost interest as he preferred a more sedate ride. Being bounced around like he was in some giant cocktail shaker was clearly not much to his liking. My friends, however, eagerly queued up for rides.

Despite the fact that my dad had been there, I really knew very little about Eton apart from occasionally pitching up there with my dad in the summer holidays to use the impressive school swimming pool (a privilege afforded Old Etonians). I am hard pressed to think of any educational establishment on the face of the planet that was less suitable for me. I appreciate my parents' intentions in sending me there and the huge cost involved, but their laudable intentions did not play out as anticipated. Although not remotely left wing, I was extremely uncomfortable with privilege. Eton College, for better or worse, represents the absolute pinnacle in the privilege stakes. For me, gentrification was never going to happen.

Coincidentally, the term I started at Eton was also the first for the new headmaster Anthony Chevenix-Trench. He was quite a small man who was slightly curious in a number of ways. His demeanour was on the creepy side, he had a very distinctive voice often aped by pupils, and his left eyelid drooped severely. All this, however, was easy to overlook as it was rumoured that he had been tortured as a Japanese POW. Part of his remit was to help drag the school more into the twentieth century. Over the years I saw rather too much of him, usually as the result of some misdemeanour or other. Nevertheless, I rather liked him.

There were around 1,300 boys at Eton accommodated in twenty-five separate houses. I was destined for Warre House, which in school parlance was always referred to as CNCA after the initials of the house tutor Cecil Norman Christopher Addison whom I thought had the look of a rather officious tax inspector about him.

So it was, full of trepidation, I arrived one sunny afternoon with my parents in tow. All the new boys for my house assembled in my tutor's sitting room together with their parents for a good chit-chat and some tea and cake. Out of around six new boys I can only remember one, possibly because he became a good friend but more likely because he was cheeky, had bags of character and the air of being more self-assured than anyone else in the room including my tutor. He was of slight build with dark red hair, masses of freckles and a small snub nose. He had an uncanny ability to sniff out people's weak spots and then home in on them humorously but without mercy. Naive as I was I quickly decided that in this alien world into which I had unwillingly been dropped, this was a boy I needed to have on side. His name was Jeremy (Jerry) Soames.

Much of the school was still Dickensian. Although it was great to have my own room, it was heated by a coal fire in winter and with coal strictly rationed at best I could enjoy the bliss of a warm room on only two or three days a week. In the morning a nice Irish lady, called a 'boys' maid', would come round with a jug full of tepid water for washing and she would empty the bowl later. Baths were a luxury to be enjoyed only a couple of times a week. The main lavatories were situated in a block outside and in winter were bloody freezing.

The school uniform consisted of a black tail-coat, matching waistcoat and pin-stripe trousers with white shirt, detachable starched collar and mini white tie, which merely covered the collar stud. If a boy was really unlucky and didn't reach a prescribed height, for the first year he was obliged to wear a short cropped black jacket, not unlike a junior midshipman's from Admiral Lord Nelson's era. This rather unbecoming bit of kit was known as a 'bum freezer'. Some senior boys, in particular members of the super elitist, self-electing Eton Society (aka 'Pop'), wore altogether jauntier outfits with individually styled waistcoats often decorated with garish chinoiserie, damask or floral designs of many bright colours rounded off by sporty checked trousers that always reminded me of those worn by chefs in Wimpy Bars. On top of all this, there was a dizzying array of individual house colours displayed in stripes, quarters and hoops; and societies (as many as fifty) representing a variety of sporting and other more intellectual activities, from rowing, cricket and the wall game to law, literature and even beagling, which often entitled a member to wear a special striped blazer, sometimes with a matching boater. The floral boaters worn by the rowing eights during the annual river parade on the Fourth of

June (originally a celebration of King George III's birthday) were especially camp. How Liberace would have loved it all.

What wasn't quite so much fun was that, over the first few months, you were obliged to learn and be tested on all the Eton societies, associations, house colours, customs and, above all, what was acceptable behaviour and what wasn't. For instance, an umbrella (a 'gamp' in Etonspeak) must be carried unfurled. Only members of POP could carry furled umbrellas and to be caught carrying one was a punishable offence. Other bizarre privileges included being permitted to wear khaki shorts for games and being entitled to sit on 'Pop wall' on Long Walk.

Some customs were quite quaint, including capping (raising your hand with extended index finger) whenever you passed a master (known as a beak), and they would respond similarly. Other customs weren't quite so quaint, notably fagging and flogging. For the first year or so, like some sort of quasi-slave, you were allocated to a senior boy as their fag. If you were lucky, you would get a boy who was humane, such as the impossibly glamorous Bapji, Maharajah of Jodphur. He was also by any standards extremely handsome, captain of my house and a member of Pop. Prior to fagging for Bapji, I fagged for John Rickatson-Hatt, a long-suffering and amiable boy with a slight skin problem, aka (in the unkind way that school kids, Etonians or otherwise, have) 'Shagger-Hatt'. The house prefects, known collectively as 'The Library', had the right, if they wanted some errand carried out, to stand in a corridor and shout 'Boy' at the top of their voice. The instant we heard this we would have to stop whatever we were doing and run full pelt in the direction of the call. The unlucky sod who got there last would end up with some irksome fatigue, which could be anything from polishing shoes or making toast to running across town to another house with a message.

A disproportionate number of masters and boys had the right to cane or flog junior boys. Mind you, most boys would have paid good money to have been beaten by Bapji Jodphur. Birching proper, thankfully, had been dropped from the 'available corporal punishment menu'. Flogging still existed but was rarely practised, it was the ultimate punishment by the headmaster, usually as the only viable alternative to expulsion. Several years down the line I was one of the last boys to experience this particularly barbaric practice before it was outlawed and, believe you me, rather painful it was too.

As with the other schools I attended I started off as I intended to carry on and during only my second week I dropped a raw egg from a second-floor window onto another boy's head. Mercifully I was spared a caning and instead, when I was being *interviewed* by The Library, Bapji came up with the idea that I should write an essay on eggs. As it happened I rather enjoyed this task and to this day remember my rather arresting opening line: 'I like eggs, eggs are nice things . . .'

The fact that the school was in the Home Counties and not in some godforsaken corner of the Isle of Thanet had certain advantages, one of them being that with a fair wind I could comfortably cycle the 18 miles home in about an hour and a half. This I did fairly regularly. I never entered into the spirit of the big Eton annual days like St Andrew's Day and the Fourth of June as I found the self-congratulatory combination of privilege, ritual and theatre faintly distasteful, not to mention that these events were largely based around sporting prowess. Once, fuelled by the sort of exaggerated moralistic angst that teenagers have, I wrote a short poem about one such day which included the following rather provocative line: 'Pudgy hands smooth back greasy hair, there's a leper but what do I care? Why, boy, of course it's June the Fourth!' Given that level of underlying discomfort I sensibly used to let off steam by escaping for the day to some sort of normality.

My guess is that I certainly wasn't alone in these subversive thoughts, which were played out a couple of years later in the film *If*, starring Malcolm McDowell, that depicted a savage insurrection at a version of Eton. Given the drama that surrounds guns today it is amazing that they were so easy to get hold of, and the penalty for illegal ownership wasn't severe. I had a number of handguns, my favourite being a Browning .25 automatic with which I once missed killing a boy called Hextall by inches as he was studying his Latin construe. I had no idea that the wall I was using for target practice was quite so flimsy. Ian Fleming's son Casper did one better by owning a fully functioning submachine gun which he kept in his laundry bag to the surprise of his boys' maid one morning. Meanwhile, home life rolled along pleasantly. School holidays brought with them utter joy and school terms utter dread. My relationship with both my parents and my two sisters was excellent and family holidays and picnics were as much fun as ever. I was in many ways completely self-reliant and always happy to work to earn money to buy myself some relative independence. Even at that age I would rather be alone than hang out with someone I didn't much care for.

On top of his work for the *Sunday Times* and the BBC, my dad was busy researching and writing vast tomes on the history of racing. In order to help fund our education he had also become the rather unlikely PR officer for the Tote (the Horserace Totalisator Board). He would drive to a racecourse almost daily, often with family friend Peter Willett, also a racing correspondent, who lived less than a mile from us. At home, when not bashing away at his old Underwood typewriter, he would *relax* by undertaking marathon gardening projects.

My mother, on the other hand, fancied herself as a bit of a hostess also with varying amounts of success. After she died Peter Willett wrote to me:

> Your parents kindly invited me to one of their dinner parties at Barclay House. The last course was pate on toast. We all took a first taste and it was so revolting that no one knew what to do. Spit it out, swallow it in one gulp or just hold on for divine guidance? There was a long silence and then your father said: 'Darling, what did you do with that dead rat I found in the cellar last week?'

Then one morning everything changed. I woke up to hear animated conversation under my window with a stranger's voice repeating over and over, 'Jet black it is . . . jet black . . .'

I raced downstairs, little aware of the catastrophe that awaited me. Nothing really terrible had ever happened to me before and for some time I just couldn't get my head round the fact that our beloved Turpin was dead, slaughtered by a speeding truck. My first reaction was blind fury towards the driver responsible and I was glad he didn't hang around.

Grief took a long time coming and watching as Turpin was carted down the garden in a wheelbarrow seemed unreal. I clearly remember a small trickle of blood coming out of the side of his lovely old mouth, his muzzle now grey with age. We buried him, wrapped in a blanket, at the end of the lower lawn under a tree. I spent several days erecting a small memorial with his name on it. To this day, I still have his leather collar and bronze identity tag: 'Turpin. Barclay House, Yateley, Hants. Tel. Yateley 3195'.

With Turpin's demise everything seemed to change and, to use stock-market parlance, my family were on the happiness and contentment index about to enter a 'bear' market. I was now fourteen years old.

————•————

Eton then was geared up to churning out prime ministers and such like rather than accommodating awkward individuals such as myself. And it didn't help that I was chronically dyslectic and so uncoordinated it verged on clinical dyspraxia. I also had a strange thing going on in one of my eyes, which moved at a different speed to the other one. Luckily for me it was something spotted only by oculists and not pointed at with hilarity from the other side of the street by unkind individuals. In addition, I was on strong medication (Dexedrine, the equivalent of Ritalin) for attention deficit hyperactivity disorder (ADHD). I was always in the bottom three out of

1,300 boys in school exams and captain of the 'sine', the house team for those 'without' any discernible talent. I was, I think, the only boy in the school who bowled backwards despite expensive cricket coaching lessons at Sunningdale in the holidays. This failure was highlighted by my long-suffering father as one of life's outstanding flops. Seriously stressed out – hardly surprising under the circumstances – he wrote to me at school:

> I know there is a temptation for boys who fail to make their mark at work or games to try and gain a reputation as a law breaker and a defier of authority. I trust you will not give way to that particular temptation. If you do, judging from your past record of folly, you will end up with the sack from Eton or with goal. Doubtless you regard me as a monumental bore tolerated at times only because I fork out some cash, but senile as I am I probably know a bit more about you and your friends than you seem to realize; and what I know, I do not necessarily like.

And in a letter to my older sister Jane:

> Possibly we have brought up your brother unwisely but he can hardly claim to be underprivileged and unloved. He is not a bad boy and his little escapades are merely the attempts to gain applause and recognition of the merry little law breaker by one who has signally failed to gain distinction in other respects.

The problem was that the school and my parents seemed to be under the impression that I had some kind of control over my lack of performance both in the classroom and on the playing field. The fact is, with the best will in the world, I didn't. Eton in those days was not the ideal environment for a teenager suffering from the '4 Ds': disturbed, depressed, dyslectic and 'discoordinated'. You could perhaps add to that dirty and disheveled. An end of term report written by my Classical tutor 'Ordinary Faulkner' summed me up in classic Eton style: 'Nero was content to roll in the dust in order to collect his laurels, Mortimer however seems merely content just to roll in the dust.'

Beyond becoming class 'clown' and, to use my father's words, a junior lawbreaker, the options were somewhat limited. I did, however, have plenty of friends, not all of them disreputable.

Two friends and I were possibly the last boys to be flogged after being caught out following a late-night visit to Soho, and a certain Denise Bunny in particular. The fact that Miss Bunny refused to take a cheque rather put a damper on our ambitions of losing our virginity.

'But it's a Coutts cheque and Coutts cheques never bounce,' argued my friend Jerry, rather convincingly I thought. 'It's as good as cash.'

'Not in a Soho brothel it isn't, dearie,' came the sharp response.

It was rotten luck that we were caught out by a random fire practice. The beating involved being held down on a block by the school clerk – blimey, talk about child abuse – bare-arsed with trousers and pants round ankles, and then severely birched by the headmaster, Anthony Chevenix-Trench. He usually drew blood and, in my case, this required dressings by matron for several weeks afterwards. (People go to prison for far less these days.) Fortunately, it didn't bother me that much then or since. I'm also happy to confirm that I haven't spent my life trawling the small ads to relive the experience.

I wrote to my older sister at the time:

4 October 1968

Dear Girl,

Thank you so very much for your sweet letter. Very good of you to write. I'm very glad in fact that the whole incident is over and actually I'm quite pleased that I'm staying on here, for now anyway. Andrew luckily is also staying on for if he had left I would have felt v. guilty. My tutor was great over the whole thing as the headmaster had in fact sacked us but then good old 'Monty' [Field Marshal Montgomery], fortuitously Jerry's godfather, and Norman [Norman Addison, my house tutor] got us back in the school again. 'My word, Charles,' say Norman, 'can't have you gallivanting round Soho at midnight.' Think he was rather upset we didn't invite him along. Also during his questioning of me I said I bought Jerry and Andrew a drink on Paddington Station at four in the morning. 'My word,' says Norman. 'What did you buy – liquor?' I say, 'No, sir, we don't all buy liquor at four o'clock in the morning on Paddington Station.'

Actually as Twig [my father] said later what we did was foolhardy and irresponsible rather than wicked or vicious. Even so it was v. self-indulgent. But must keep up the old Mortimer adventurous spirit, eh what!!

'Quite candidly, my dear boy, the fact remains that you must really work like a black,' says Nidnod [my mother]. Oh well, I don't think it was anything like as bad as some of the antics that

Twig boasts that he did at Eton. Great cries of 'Twig for president!' echo in the background. Actually I am working v. hard now and I don't really fancy another flogging. V. painful! Michael K [Michael Kidson, my Modern Tutor] thought the whole idea of flogging was an anachronism and utterly revolting so was v. sympathetic afterwards. It's great to have someone as nice as he for a modern tutor.

Otherwise the term's great. Jerry, Andrew, Breitmeyer and Rodney etc. are all on excellent form.

Do you like 'A Little Help from My Friends' by Jo Cocker? I think it's really fantastic. I saw 'The Graduate' the other day and have bought the LP. Hope you are not too badly off from your car crash!

Oh well, looking forward to seeing you weekend after next. By the way, Twig will be over on the Saturday of that weekend.

Lots of love,

Titch

Some 28 years later, on 3 May 1994, I wrote the following letter, published in the *Evening Standard*. It sums up things and my attitude to the school pretty succinctly.

ETON HEAD WAS KIND TO ME

I was interested in Richard Hornsby's piece ('The Eton beating song', 27 April). I have not read the former Vice-Provost Tim Card's book 'Eton Renewed' and do not go out of my way to read stuff about Eton, a school for which I hold very little affection, but it was hard to avoid this article.

I was at Eton in the mid-Sixties, my short career there being notable only for its lack of achievement. However, as a junior law-breaker, I did rather well. The result was that I was regularly being hauled up in front of the head-master, the now infamous Anthony Chevenix-Trench, and occasionally the local magistrates court. My offences included poaching in Windsor Great Park, spending the night up to no good in Soho and riding a 500 cc Ariel motorbike at high speed when aged 15 through Maidenhead.

Despite these and many other indiscretions I was only beaten twice. The first time was by the captain of my house, the Maharajah of Jodhpur, and the second time with all the ceremonial trimmings by Mr Chevenix-Trench. The beatings had little effect on me then, apart from raising my peer-group credibility rating. What bothered me a lot more was the 600 lines of Latin Mr Chevenix-Trench set me as a punishment over the poaching incident.

If Eton under Chevenix-Trench was as harsh and barbaric as Mr Card and Mr Hornsby suggest then with my appalling record I would have been virtually flogged to death. The fact is I wasn't, and though I disliked the place a good deal my memories of various masters are good. In particular my Modern tutor (Michael Kidson) who put his job on the line bailing me out of a police station without informing the school.

With regard to Chevenix-Trench I remember him as an eccentric old boy who was usually good for a laugh and often surprisingly human and sympathetic. When I left the school, by mutual agreement aged 16, despite all my run-ins with him, we parted on good terms.

I have a clear memory of him giving me a leaving book, which I wasn't entitled to, and having the decency to wish me luck with whatever I chose to do or not to do with my life.

    C. M.

—•—

I think I first became aware of depression at school, aged about sixteen when, quite casually one evening, I decided to kill myself. There was no great drama about it. I merely thought that I had had enough. Without giving the consequences much thought, I swallowed over twenty powerful painkillers that I had nicked from matron's cupboard. To be honest, it was rather a liberating experience lying in my bed and thinking I'll soon be out of all this crap. What actually happened is that, not knowing much about pills, I just became rather pleasantly stoned, drifting in and out of consciousness until being rudely awoken by the boys' maid the following morning.

Clearly not expecting to see another day, I had failed to do my assigned task for early morning class and I did have quite a bad stomach ache, and so carted myself off to the school doctor (the kindly John Clayton, who became the Queen Mother's physician and famously saved her from a fishbone). Not thinking it was a big deal I mentioned that I had taken a few handfuls of painkillers, which was probably the cause of my internal discomfort. When the doctor asked me why I should have done such a thing I told him that frankly it wouldn't take a genius to work out that, given all my obvious shortcomings, I was a wholly unsuitable person to be educated at a school such as Eton. I had felt under such pressure to succeed there from all fronts (family especially) that ending it all seemed, at the time, to be the simplest and most pragmatic solution.

Little did I know, but this was a game-changer in terms of my school career and I left by mutual agreement not long

after. My concerned father wrote to my modern tutor, Michael
Kidson:

> I'm sorry I have not been to see you but first of all I had a nasty
> go of influenza and as soon as I could crawl out of bed I had to
> go to Cheltenham. As soon as I got back home, I was rung up
> by Norman Addison who wanted to see me. After hearing what
> he had to say and after learning the opinion of Dr Clayton, I have
> decided to take Charles away at the end of this half. He seems
> in a very confused mental state and Clayton wants him to see a
> London consultant.
>
> I don't quite know what has gone wrong. Charles has been
> very restless and has expressed desire to leave more than
> once. He seems very closely tied up with George Rodney who
> is also leaving. I wonder if they have both been experimenting
> with soft drugs.
>
> You have been a very good friend to Charles and I am most
> grateful for what you have done. I only wish you had had a more
> rewarding response. I don't honestly know what to do with
> Charles now but will wait and see what the consultant says.

No reference was ever made again to the pill incident and, as
if by magic, everyone from the headmaster down suddenly
became remarkably sympathetic. It was customary on leaving
Eton at the end of your time for the headmaster to give you
a leaver's book, which was a specially printed copy of poems
by Thomas Gray; but normally if you left under a cloud you
didn't get one. I not only received a book from Chevenix-
Trench but also a rare, handwritten inscription to me in Latin:
'Carolo Roger Henrico Mortimer . . . Non sine desiderio.'

('Charles Roger Henry Mortimer . . . Not without regret [at his departure]')

The term after I leave a boy in my house was caught smoking. When Norman Addison punished him he objected.

'That's not fair, sir. You allowed Mortimer to smoke.'

'Now,' said my old house tutor with suitable gravitas, 'there was a boy who really needed to smoke.'

5

Petrol in the Blood

Until fairly recently, Tim and I owned a couple of cars. For twelve years, we had a Nissan Skyline R32 aka 'The Coffin', which at the time held the world record for the fastest lap by a production car at the Nürburgring. Ours had been uprated to just a shade under 500bhp by Janspeed and was described by my mother as 'wig-raising fast'. We also owned at the same time a Mitsubishi Evo VII in mauve, a colour so hideous that neither Tim nor my mother would be seen travelling in it, and a 'Works' Mini Cooper S, which on country lanes Tim said was like going through a full cycle in a Zanussi washing machine.

When I say 'we', Tim doesn't drive and assures me that he has no intention of ever doing so (or doing the hoovering for that matter). Generally this has always suited me. I come from that generation of motorists who throw the Highway Code out of the sunroof the second they disembark in Calais. My deal with Tim then was as follows. We stop at the first services on the auto route to Paris where Tim consumes half a litre of *vin ordinaire* in conjunction with a Valium 10 mg (the blue one). With Tim now happily sparko I can get cracking and, in the words of my old friend Charlie Shearer, put TOF (toe on floor) and make my way towards Paris at a speed that today would land you with a six-month jail sentence and a confiscated car.

I purchased the Skyline in 1993 after Jeremy Clarkson had raved about it on *Top Gear*. I loved the fact that it was quite a modest-looking coupé that in performance terms was streets ahead of anything else on the road including motorcycles. At the time, my health, even by my standards, had taken a serious downturn and, in my weakened state, slipping into Skyline's low-slung bucket seat was akin to putting on a supersonic suit of armour. In an instant, on the highways at least, I became invincible. A few days after I took delivery, I was stationary at a set of red lights on the Cromwell Road, approaching Knightsbridge. A fully leather-clad motorcyclist on a Ducati pulled up alongside and gestured for me to lower the window. Unusually for a biker, he was slim and rather attractive, and I needed no encouragement.

'A fucking Skyline mate, fan . . . fucking . . . tastic,' he enthused. 'Can I wank over it?'

'I don't know about that,' I replied, 'but play your cards right and you can wank over me.'

Driving and all things associated were always a passion for me. During the first night I spent with Tim he mentioned his date of birth and I responded with unrestrained excitement that he was, in the rarefied world of registration plates, la crème de la crème: a '71 on a K'. I explained to Tim that registration plates in the UK were a petrol head's equivalent to the signs of the Zodiac. (The accolade continues, all these years on, to amuse him.)

When quite suddenly, a few years ago, I just sold our car and, apart from the odd hire vehicle, gave up on driving most of my old friends were dumbfounded. 'You without a car, it's unthinkable' was a common cry. There were, however, two very good reasons.

Firstly, I had deteriorated from being a very good driver, once nicknamed 'The fastest wheels in Fulham', to, in my opinion, a very bad one. To quote my dear mother, 'Although I say it myself I'm a bloody good cook' and I would say the same about my driving. I was an excellent driver largely because I loved driving, and there was barely a licence right up to and including an HGV1 (for big articulated trucks) that I didn't hold. What I drove didn't really bother me, I got as much fun out of an old banger as something more exotic, although by choice I loved 'Q' cars the best. To explain, these are ordinary-looking vehicles fitted out with insane engines, their mystery compounded by the fact that I always 'de-badged' them. My early 1987 BMW M5 being a classic example. It looked so mundane that once, when dropping off friends at King's Cross railway station, some people mistook it for mini cab and tried to get in, yet it would comfortably see off most Ferraris. The reason my driving fell apart was entirely due to poor health – my reactions and concentration lost their edge somewhat.

The second reason was the advent of speed cameras. In years gone by, both John Hobbs and I might, if depressed or stressed out, take a car for a spin to relieve the tension.

In those heady days, if you got back home without being nicked for speeding then that was then end of the matter. These days, a fast drive in the country can be followed several days later by an avalanche of buff-coloured envelopes containing hideous photographic evidence of a variety of motoring offences. All the fun has gone out of driving. It wasn't always so.

———•———

When I was twelve years old, my mother, who was always game for a bit of an adventure, bought me my first car, an old Ford Prefect for twelve pounds ten shillings (including road tax), which I drove at high speed round our fields. In time this car fell apart and was replaced. My dad described these bangers as 'Charlie's old wrecks that he drove insanely round the field'. My parents were extremely liberal about this sort of thing, and I would invest most of the money I earned doing paper rounds and other odd jobs on petrol. On one occasion my folks had a few friends round for drinks. Their children eagerly joined me for rides round my special track in the fields. The *pièce de résistance* came when my mother proudly assembled the guests on the terrace to watch me entertaining our junior visitors. Never one to shirk away from a bit of overt exhibitionism, I loaded all the kids into the car and in full view promptly drove my current car, a down-at-heel Rover 14 Sports saloon on this occasion, at some speed intentionally into a tree. One of the mothers shrieked and passed out and several of the children needed medical attention.

It reminded me of the time when Robin Grant-Sturgis, then

in his teens, took a group of friends up into the woods behind his house to watch him put an old Hillman through its paces. When he failed to roll it over, they eagerly shouted 'Chicken' at him. Twenty minutes later they piled in for a lift back down to the house for lunch. On the way, at high speed, Robin drove the car towards a bank with the intention of rolling it. All the occupants were now terrified and started screaming and pleading with him to slow down. As the car turned over for the first time (it actually rolled about three times), Robin cheerily shouted, 'Who's chicken now!'

Despite the fact that my dad had for the duration of the war both concealed and run the POW camp radio, known as 'The Canary', at home he pleaded utter incompetence on all matters practical. This clever ruse meant that it was always my mother who was obliged to sort out any practical malfunction round the house ranging from replacing tap washers to repairing fuses. Early on during the war my mother had been, along with the Queen, a FANY (a member of the First Aid Nursing Yeomanry) and was quite rightly proud of the mechanical skills she had learned during that period. It was, therefore, my mother who taught me, aged ten, to drive. We used to take her white Austin Mini up to the partially abandoned Blackbushe Airport. Within months I became competent enough for her to trust me to drive her regularly on a three-mile back road near Wellington College while Turpin exercised by running alongside. Come winter and the roads were packed with crushed snow, my mother would think nothing of attaching a huge tin tray with a rope to the back of her car and towing us three siblings, all wrapped up in duffle coats, woollen scarves and bobble hats, round the village with an excited

Turpin following on behind. These days the consequences for what would no doubt be perceived as gross parental irresponsibility would be dire. For me, looking back it was just part a near idyllic childhood for which I am truly grateful.

For my dad's part, he knew that there was nothing I enjoyed more than what I used to describe as a 'little disaster'. So the big birthday treat was to take his car, such as an Austin Westminster or Wolseley 16/60, down some unknown track in some local woodland until the inevitable: we got stuck up to the axles in mud. If we were lucky we would find a near-by phone box and persuade my friend James's dad, Major 'Freddie' Staples, to come to the rescue in his trusty Standard Vanguard estate equipped with heavy duty cross-country tyres and kitted out with ropes, sacks and spades. I suspect the Major, a hugely good-natured man kept well under thumb at home, enjoyed these excursions almost as much as I did. Mission completed it was egg, bacon, sausage and chips all round at Fred's Café. Pure joy personified.

The other big treat was to accompany my dad when every two years or so he purchased a new car. Of all these outings, the one that I remember like yesterday was going with him in 1964 to Jack Barclay's showroom on Berkeley Square. These days, half a century on, the same showroom only sells 'fully loaded' Bentleys to Russian oligarchs for six-figure plus sums. Back then, as well as some swankier marques it also sold Fiats, at the time considered rather exotic. We decided on a Pininfarina-designed light blue Fiat 2300 Estate with bright red leatherette upholstery, twin head lights, and capable of over 100 mph. Dad bought it there and then for delivery the following week. It sported a bench seat with a column gear change. On trips abroad I used to perch enthusiastically on the two front armrests between my parents, unthinkable today, whilst my two sisters, being mere girls, were consigned to the back seats. Hitting a ton (100 mph) was always a high point. His job as a racing correspondent meant that he got through a fair number of cars. All his vehicles, from the ponderous 'Alvis Luxury load carrier' to 'Reg Rover' (a 3.5 litre P5b Coupé) had nick names, 'Fred Fiat' was my firm favourite. My mother refused to travel in the bright red Rover, announcing that the colour was so brash it resembled a 'bookmaker's car'.

I was, somewhat bizarrely for one so disinterested in any form of sport and exercise, a hugely enthusiastic cyclist. I guess it was something to do with the freedom it brought me and I would think nothing of cycling fifteen miles to see a friend. My dad always said that after the invention of the bicycle the incidents of incest in the countryside dropped about ninety per cent as it allowed, suddenly, those keen on copulation to at least make it to the next village.

During the school holidays I would do my newspaper round on my bike. I wasn't, unlike my dad, a great reader of newspapers but I certainly remember a red-top headline in 1966 after Harry Roberts murdered three police officers in West London: 'Police comb Shepherd's Bush.'

I was very particular about my bike and built one to my own spec from various bits and pieces. Unusually for bicycles at the time it had no mudguards, and it had studded tyres and a fixed hub. Today, it would be classified as a cross between a mountain bike and a 'Fixie'. For years nothing would part me from my beloved bike until one day, just before I got my driving licence, it was stolen from outside a cinema in Slough. Since then, I have never had the remotest desire to get on another bicycle.

A form of transport that I wasn't quite so keen on, unlike my dear mother, was the horse. She was absolutely determined that my two sisters and myself should spend half our lives either on horseback or mucking out stables and cleaning 'tack'. My oldest sister Jane got off lightly. During her first ride on the family's newly acquired pony, Wendy, my mother accidentally sat on an active anthill. Being my mother she immediately whipped off her very white knickers and waved them about vigorously while shouting loudly. Wendy took fright and bolted. In time, my older sister either abandoned ship or was bucked off, and from that day forth swore that nothing on this planet could induce her back on a horse or pony of any description.

Unfortunately for me I was then, being some five years older than my younger sister Lumpy, right in the firing line. I was obliged to experience a dreadful ten days at Pony Club Camp. The pony club was then largely run by well-built women over sixty, all called Miss something or other and without whom we would never have survived the Blitz. It was at some ghastly pony club event that I endured one of my life's more humiliating experiences. My dad had pitched up and was reading peacefully in his car when he was disturbed by a pretty girl I was rather keen on, called Wendy (clearly a popular name back then) Dean.

'Excuse me, Major Mortimer, but you don't have a comb I could borrow do you?' she enquired of my dad.

My father made a show of digging around for a while in

the glove compartment before finally producing a really filthy plastic object with several teeth missing covered in grease, hair and what looked like dandruff. As he handed this unsavoury object over to Wendy, he said somewhat apologetically, 'No, I'm afraid I don't, but here's Charlie's.'

My mother, having grown up on a substantial farm in Dorset, was of that schizophrenic (my mother would pronounce it 'shit-so-phreenic') breed of British country dwellers who, on the one hand, would lay their life down for their dogs and horses while simultaneously getting huge pleasure from slaughtering other animals. Many of my relatives had been Masters of Foxhounds (MFHs), so it was in the blood. As my mother would frequently remind me, 'But of course, my dear boy, it's absolutely my world.' My dad on the other hand, found blood sports of any type faintly repulsive. He described pheasant shooting as 'overweight stockbrokers taking pot shots at semi-tame birds.' For my part, at the time I was more with my mother on this, but now I am most definitely with my dad.

There was, however, a consolation prize in all this horsiness. Sometimes my mother and I would follow our local hunt, the Garth and South Berks, in my mother's car, at the time an Austin 1100. The general plan was to predict which way the hunt was heading and then find a good spot to get out of the car and watch the proceedings from afar before moving on to the next location. My mother was nothing if not competitive on the hunting field and together (I must have been fourteen) we drove her car like demons possessed as if our one aim was to run over the fox before the hounds got to it. Although the car was a modest family saloon, albeit with front-wheel drive, we would drive it like a Chieftain tank in full-assault mode. On one insane occasion there was the poor fox running at full pelt across a meadow closely followed by my mother and myself in a car so covered in mud it must have been hard to make out what it was, pursued by the hounds, and then way back, the huntsman and the rest of the field. Any outing with my mother, however unpromising the mission, was always an adventure and this was no exception.

While on the subject of foxhunting, one of my favourite moments was an exchange at a pre-hunt ball (dreadful events) dinner between a bearded friend of mine called Bodkin, who had never been on a horse in his life, and the master of the hunt. Not one word had been uttered between them throughout dinner but, finally, as the port was being passed round, the master turned to Bodkin and in crisp tones enquired, 'Do you hunt?'

'Yes,' replied Bodkin through a haze of smoke from his roll up. 'I hunt cunt.'

Life with my parents at newly acquired Budds Farm had its ups and downs. Unlike our previous home, Barclay House, which was in a village, our new home was in the middle of nowhere and even given my ability to cycle large distances, there was nowhere much within twenty miles to which I actually wanted to cycle.

One fateful night I had a row with my mother, who had been listening in to my telephone conversation with a friend on an extension in her bedroom. It was always easy to tell if my mother was on the line as her heavy breathing rather gave the game away. I ran out of the house and jumped into her Mini Cooper with the intention of driving to the end of our drive where there was a public phone box. I could then, I thought, continue my conversation in private. Her car was up by the stables and as I zoomed past the front of the house my dear mother went way beyond the actions of a rational human being. Rather than just shout at me to stop she threw herself in front of the car. By then I was travelling far too fast to stop and, despite slamming on the brakes, I ran her over.

This was the second time an ambulance had to be called within a week. The first time, my dear mother had climbed on the roof and announced that she was going to jump off into the conservatory.

'Oh don't worry,' said my father as we started supper without her, 'she'll soon get bored and come down.'

My mother did get bored, as my dad had predicted, but being a very practical person decided to adjust the wonky TV aerial while she was up there. Unfortunately, while so doing she slipped on a loose slate and ended up falling bum first into the herbaceous border.

It also happened that my older sister was at home that week convalescing from an operation on her nose and consequently looked like she'd just gone six rounds with Cassius Clay. Coincidentally, she answered the door to the same ambulance crew on both occasions, who were polite enough not to laugh and decent enough not to inform social services.

I now needed my freedom, especially from Budds Farm. Luckily, I didn't have long to wait.

I got my driving licence within days of my seventeenth birthday. (I cannot ever remember feeling more excited.) It was without doubt the best year of my life. There was only one problem. A couple of years previously I had rather rashly agreed to drive a school friend's 500cc Ariel motorcycle from his home to Eton, a journey of some thirty miles. He couldn't do it because he wasn't old enough to hold a motorcycle licence and, as I was only fifteen at the time, neither was I. The only difference being that I wasn't particularly bothered about breaking the law whereas he was, and as it turned out with good reason. When the police stopped me I was speeding at, I gather, in excess of 60 mph through Maidenhead town centre with a friend, Andrew Clarkson, hanging on for dear life behind me. I still have a photograph of us setting off: I was wearing a cloth cap, a pair of 1920s flying goggles and a black silk scarf that I claimed (possibly correctly, as it turned out) one of my great uncles had round his neck when he shot himself.

Since I had neither licence nor anything as dreary as insurance, MOT or road tax the police took it all rather seriously. Eventually we were bailed out of Maidenhead Police Station by my stoic Modern Tutor Michael Kidson, who, and I will always remember him with huge gratitude for this, put his own job on the line by not informing the school authorities. I was already on my third 'final' warning, and had they known, I would have been given the push.

Some sixteen years later, I found myself back inside Maidenhead Police Station having, as a joke, overtaken a police car (which was at the time on an emergency call) on the M4 while not, a blood test was later to verify, entirely sober.

The result on both occasions was a subsequent appearance in the dock at Maidenhead Magistrates Court. On the first occasion, in 1967, I was banned from driving for six months, given two endorsements (today something like nine points) and a £10 fine. As I hadn't got a licence, the ban took effect when I applied for a provisional motorcycle licence the following April and when I finally received it six months later it was covered in angry red stamps. Thus my motoring career on the roads did not get off to a particularly auspicious start, and as a result insurance was terribly expensive. On the second occasion, in 1984, I received, not surprisingly, a twelve-month ban.

After the joy of hearing those magic words, 'I am pleased to inform you, Mr Mortimer, that you have reached the standard of competency as required by the Ministry of Transport', I could have kissed the examiner even though he smelt strongly of Virginia tobacco and stale beer and sported a full grenadier-style moustache. Now it was time to get cracking or more specifically get motoring.

It just so happened that all this conveniently coincided with my two sisters and I being left a modest cash inheritance by our paternal grandmother. As luck would have it, a condition of the will allowed me instant access to the lolly, a clause that I am convinced that my grandmother put in purely to annoy my father.

I went on a major motoring spending spree over the next couple of years and ended up acquiring, not all at the same time, an astonishing variety of oddball vehicles: ranging from a purple bubble car to a 1929 Rolls Royce 'Shooting Brake', and, on the more vintage sporty side, from an AC Ace Bristol to a 1932 Riley Special. More modern sports cars included a 1967 Ford Mustang Coupé and a fleet of Mini Coopers, Lotus Cortinas and Sunbeam Tigers of one form or another.

I also got a job. I was already earning some cash from my mobile disco, 'Make your party a happening with Boris

Discotheque'. My dad wrote in a letter to my sister, 'To make money the dreary old discotheque is again being circulated around middle-class homes in the Berkshire area'. But I wanted something a bit more substantial. I put in an appearance at Newbury Labour Exchange and announced that I was looking for work restoring vintage racing cars. Not surprisingly, they didn't have any vacancies of that nature available, though later on that day they rang to say that they had a vague recollection of someone wanting an apprentice for work of a similar type. They didn't have a name or even an address but said it was somewhere down the canal by Greenham Mill in Newbury.

The following day, I made my way to Greenham Mill. There was no one there, but there was a small sign about vintage car restoration. There was, however, no telephone number or anything. After arming myself with a few snacks and a bottle of cola, I sat under a tree and waited. Eventually my patience was rewarded. Mid-afternoon, a dark-blue Renault 4 pulled up and out got a young couple, Tony and Angela Simmons, who were about ten years older than me, with a small baby named Becky. Having established that Tony was the proprietor of the vintage car restoration company, I introduced myself and asked if he could employ me. Tony holds that I spun him some elaborate yarn that I had been offered an apprenticeship with Fiat Abarth, which didn't start for another six months.

Whatever the truth, the Simmons family, who took dysfunctional and eccentric to unchartered territory, became a constant and positive presence in my life for many years. My starting wages were agreed at £5 per week, cash in hand.

Before long we became partners of sorts calling our company, 'Specialist Sprayers'.

The very first thing I established, in the vast warehouse that constituted our premises, was 'The Trumpet Tea Bar'. Situated in a quiet corner, it consisted quite simply of a few comfy old leather car seats, a table and an electric kettle above which an old trumpet, which had clearly seen better days, was suspended by various bits of string. It was here while swigging tea and munching Topics or delicious handmade steak and kidney pies from the local butcher's that plans were hatched between us to expand the business. On many occasions the big plan was take the rest of the day off and go for a picnic. These were happy days.

I owned at the time an ex-Army Austin Champ Jeep (with a Rolls-Royce engine), and one day we set off to collect a vintage car for restoration. It was a massive, 1920s open-topped Lanchester saloon, which must have weighed about three tons. We had to collect it from the home of Francis Hutton Stott (renowned Lanchester expert) at Speen, only four miles away. As the Lanchester hadn't operated under its own steam for at least a decade, we decided to tow it back to our workshops. I drove the jeep, using it's very noisy low-ratio gearbox for maximum pulling power, and Tony the Lanchester.

We proceeded at a very stately 3 mph, largely because the Lanchester's brakes were virtually non-existent. At this speed, it took all of eight minutes to drive the length of Newbury High Street. Due to the noise of the Jeep's engine and gearbox I was completely unaware of what was going on behind, which was unfortunate since I had become the laughing stock of the entire street. Unknown to me, the rope had snapped as we turned into the High Street. Despite all of Tony's shouting and yelling from the stranded Lanchester, and the whoops of delight, laughter, wolf-whistles and, I am told, the odd shout of 'wanker' from a number of the pedestrians out shopping that day, I had continued to stare earnestly ahead, while now only towing a somewhat pathetic piece of rope, as if driving the lead vehicle in an important funeral cortege.

Another drama associated with the Lanchester was when I was dispatched in my 1954 Citroën 2CV van to London to collect a couple of large tins of bright yellow paint. The noble Lanchester was due to be sprayed in a pure cellulose (with yellow bodywork and jet black mudguards) that was true to the period. It had taken several weeks to have a not inconsequential quantity prepared by a specialist manufacturer. Unfortunately on my way back I took a sharp turn off Notting Hill, past what was then The Ark restaurant, rather too quickly. My somewhat elderly van rolled to an alarming angle like a small sailing boat in an unexpected gust of wind and the two huge tins of paint, which I had safely placed in the passenger footwell, toppled over. For the uninitiated, pure cellulose paint is about as far removed in convenience, and not in a good way, from good old Dulux gloss as gloss is from emulsion paint. To quite suddenly find myself literally up to my ankles in several gallons of the stuff was challenging. Luckily, the majority poured out through the many holes in the floor of my decrepit van. A kind waiter from The Ark helped me clean up as best we could with loads of newspapers.

When I summed up enough courage to phone Tony, reverse charges from a phone box, *persona non grata* didn't really cover my status. For many years afterwards a sizeable canary-yellow stain, in the shape of a small lake, remained on the road as a sober reminder to me whenever I passed that way.

The paint incident was trivial compared to when, several years later, while driving Tony's beloved 1965 7-Litre AC Cobra, (former owner, Robert Plant) into Newbury to buy an ice cream, the engine threw a con rod. In layman's terms, I blew the engine up, not a popular move.

Over the coming decades the Simmons family drifted in and out my life but they were always there in the background, a welcome port in the frequent storms that punctuated it. Of all the projects with which I became involved with Tony, the craziest was in the mid to late 1970s when he ganged up with some dreadful old gangster from Birmingham and bought, in auction, around 300 Army trucks as a job lot. The problem was that they were ex-German Army Mercedes Unimogs, all stuck, in various states of disrepair, in an extremely muddy wood somewhere in the middle of Germany. I worked out that if you spent just five minutes on each truck it would take up an entire working week, and to buy a gallon of petrol for each and every vehicle would require a sizeable mortgage. Not surprisingly, Tony and I made frequent trips on the Harwich to Hamburg/Bremen ferry where we discovered, among other things the delights of *Glühwein*. To relieve stress, understandable under the circumstances, Tony took to combing his hair obsessively and feverishly almost all of the time. Not much fun for him, hugely amusing for me.

It was while not entirely sober in the Harwich to Hamburg ferry's discotheque with my friend Charlie Shearer that I once ate my passport and then rather rashly produced a few tooth-marked remnants at passport control the following day, expecting the officers to take a sympathetic view. If there was ever a textbook example of poor judgement, that was it.

Charlie and I had gone to Hamburg purportedly to buy antiques to sell on to the Hobbs brothers in London. It so happened that Charlie's father, a highly successful business-man, was over there with his new German wife. Unwisely he allowed Charlie to borrow his 280SE 3.5 Mercedes Cabriolet, which in terms of expensive grand-touring motor-ing was, at the time, about as good as it got. Charlie and I used it to go on a pub crawl with the roof down and the volume up on the Blaupunkt stereo playing 'Magic Bus' by The Who. I have a very vague recollection, and believe me I am not proud of this, of standing up in the back of the car while Charlie drove like a man possessed, making vaguely obscene gestures and throwing beer cans at pedestrians. When we finally returned the car, there was smoke billow-ing out of both front wheels from the brake callipers, which were on fire. Charlie's father took one look at us and his priceless cabriolet, and with tears pouring down his face, he knelt in front of the Mercedes and repeatedly hit his fore-head on the tarmac.

It was during a rather unsatisfactory career as a squaddie in the Coldstream Guards in 1970 that I met Robin Grant-Sturgis aka 'The Squire' over a car deal. I had travelled down to Tiverton, Devon, in heavy snow, while on leave. I was staying with my old school friend Pete Breitmeyer (now Carew) and his family on one side of a deep valley, and on the other side were the Grant-Sturgises. For reasons now long forgotten, there was a feud going on between the two families.

I had enthusiastically driven down from Berkshire in a sporty but shagged-out Triumph TR3a, which clearly wasn't in a fit state to make the return trip to the Home Counties. It was with some misgivings that Pete mentioned that Robin, then aged eighteen, from time to time bought and sold unusual second-hand cars.

Robin had recently inherited Hillersdon House, a sizeable stately home that had clearly seen better days, and several farms. The Grant-Sturgis set-up was, for me, manna from heaven. Robin, with his mane of shoulder-length blond hair and always ready with a snappy sound bite, was huge fun and enormously charismatic. He was also very good-looking (mind you I would say that as for many years we were always mistaken as brothers). I ended up exchanging my knackered Triumph sports car for a massive maroon Mk9 Jaguar with a broken heater and an eccentric braking system. If you braked really hard the Jag spun a full 360 degrees, which made it interesting to drive. On the plus side it would not have looked out of place in the owners' car park at Royal Ascot, had four electric cigarette lighters (two in the front and two in the back), walnut-veneered picnic tables and about three cows worth of Connolly leather. As I gingerly drove down the potholed drive of the Grant-Sturgis mansion, I swore to myself that one way or another I'd be back. It was merely a matter of time.

I chucked in the Army a few months later. My departure was succinctly summed up in the colourful language of my platoon sergeant addressing my now ex-comrades: 'I've got some news lads, it's Mr Mortimer . . . he's gorn and thrown in his handbag.'

I was not flavour-of-the-month with my father, so I kept a fairly low profile, working for a small mews garage in South Kensington called BC&H Motors and sleeping on friends' sofas. My job largely consisted of picking up spare motor parts and riding on the garage's 1940s Harley Davidson. Eccentrically, it had a manual gear change on the side of the fuel tank. There was no requirement to wear a crash helmet in those days and cruising noisily through Hyde Park in the sunshine was better (almost better) than any drug. That said, I was never much good on a motorcycle as I possess little sense of balance. Several times I found myself flying across a road junction while sitting on the engine casing in a cascade of sparks. My only moment of motorcycle glory, or more accurately insanity, involved a Kawasaki 250cc. I had made a bet that I could drive at max throttle to Heathrow Airport and back at around 1 a.m., ignoring all traffic lights and stop signs, pick up a postcard from Heathrow (as proof of being there), and return to South Kensington in a prescribed time frame (thirty minutes). It was a kind of motorcycle Russian roulette that I won't be repeating again anytime soon.

After securing a highly unlikely position as the south-west sales representative of Metlon Products (manufacturers of metallic paints and aerosols), yet another of Tony Simmons's implausible business ideas, I telephoned Robin and arranged to rent a wonderful room on the first floor of Hillersdon House, complete with balustrade, and overlooking the deer park for the bargain price of just £4 a week.

Upon arrival I immediately acquired an early 1950s Mk1 Land Rover, which I sprayed in Metlon Stainless Steel paint, thus using up all of the paint samples. Not surprisingly a short time later I received a rather terse communication from Mr Bolton, Director of Sales, Metlon Ltd: 'I am very disappointed and surprised that after six weeks in the field, so far you have apparently failed to close a single order.' I fired back a suitably offensive response and was promptly given the boot.

I now embarked on a series of entertaining little business ventures with Robin, mainly revolving around motor trading and the 'glamorous' Exeter car auctions. Once, overcome with excitement at the prospect of making the princely sum of £5 on a Hillman Husky bought at the auctions for three quid, I rather rashly accepted a cheque in payment. As sure as night follows day it promptly bounced. The purchaser was spotted several months later sweeping the yard (as an inmate) of Exeter jail. In every other area life chez Grant-Sturgis was about as good as it gets and maybe for me as good as it ever got. The day I took a job working for Robin as a farm labourer, however, was not a big success.

After a particularly heavy night I was comfortably slumbering on my bed enjoying the view when at about 10 a.m. there was a sharp knock on my door. It was Robin's delightful mother, who was in no mood to trifle.

'My son has just called me from Ponsford [one of the farms] and informed me that you were due to start work there this morning at 8.30 a.m. Where were you?'

Absolutely furious to be addressed as a mere employee, I leaped out of bed and stormed off across the park in my company car, an aged International B250 tractor, to confront Robin. Given the somewhat terse nature of the message relayed by his mother I was more than a little surprised to find that he was still in bed himself. When I pointed this out, he responded quite loudly that as he was now my boss it was none of my fucking business if he stayed in bed till teatime and beyond if he so cared, and now I had finally had the courtesy to actually show up for work could I kindly get my finger out and clear the bloody yard? After I gave what I thought was a suitably pompous resignation speech, normal relations were once again resumed as partners-in-crime.

There were certainly some memorable moments: sowing a field with wheat being one, not so much the sowing but the harvesting. When the wheat crop was ready, we took a trip to a local scrap dealer and acquired an ancient and distinctly ropey combine harvester for, after some haggling, the huge sum of about £9. The harvester, a Massey Harris, was about as old as my dad. In fact, it was so old-fashioned that it ran on petrol/TVO and the harvested grain was fed into sacks on the rear of the machine, which meant that someone was required to stand there throughout the harvesting periodically checking the bags. When full each bag was unhitched, the neck duly tied up with baler cord and then replaced with an empty bag, all the while chaff would fly out the back like a small dust storm.

It took us around a week to harvest some twenty-odd acres of wheat. Our progress was not helped by the fact that half way through the job the Massey Harris's steering box broke. Spare parts not being readily available, we were obliged to compromise by tying some old horse lungeing reins to either side of the rear axle, which did all the steering, and I walked behind the wretched machine pulling the reins one way or another as excitedly indicated by a rather dictatorial Robin standing aloft, as if on the bridge of some ponderous old battleship. If all this was long-winded it was nothing as compared to the initial 15 mile trek back from the scrap yard to Hillersdon at approximately 2 mph, which took the best part of eight hours. It was at the height of the summer holiday season and so wide it couldn't be overtaken. It didn't take long to build up a very angry queue of frustrated motorists which stretched behind the harvester as far as the eye could see. The police became involved, and although frankly fairly unamused, they somewhat begrudgingly gave us an escort. Whilst on the subject of ancient farm machinery, my favourite bit of kit by a million miles was a 1940s David Brown Cropmaster tractor. What I loved about it more than even the eardrum-shattering backfires it emitted regularly was the fact it had two seats, side by side. Ideal for taking out a Friday night date.

Driving with Robin on the highways and byways verged on the irresponsible from time to time. It's crackers to think now that a really heavy, and I do mean really heavy, drinking session was considered by us to be the ideal precursor to a motoring jaunt. Robin had proudly acquired a second-hand Mercedes-Benz 280CE coupé from a local farmer, so late one evening, and not entirely sober, we took it for a spin. The car was fitted with cruise control, quite rare then, which allowed the driver to set the speed on a motorway without using the accelerator pedal. As we hit 100 mph on the Cullompton bypass, Robin shouted enthusiastically, 'Watch this, Sporty [his nickname for me]'. He set the cruise control and promptly did a backward somersault into the rear seat. This left us driverless at 100 mph with Robin laughing away in the back. Not to be outdone, I scrambled into the driver's seat, accelerated to 120 mph, set the cruise control, did a backward somersault and joined him.

Charlie Shearer was my other big motoring buddy. He was the only boy, as far as I am aware, to go straight from Eton College aged fifteen to borstal without a day's pause. Very sadly he died a few days before his thirtieth birthday in a helicopter accident when a chief of police (unlikely but true) in the Dominican Republic. Mind you, I'm not sure if flying at alarming angles under power pylons comes under the category of 'accident'.

Charlie, like me, lived and breathed cars. Our first joint adventure was in 1973 when we attempted to drive to Africa in his Range Rover. In order to fund this enterprise, we needed some serious lolly and Charlie convinced me that an antiques dealer friend of his called Chas owed him several thousand pounds. We concocted an ambitious plan whereby, masquerading as a casino owner from Bristol (of all places), I would confront Chas and tell him that Charlie owed me huge gambling debts and unless they were paid Charlie was going to get hurt. We were banking on the fact that Chas was genuinely fond of Charlie, then nineteen years old, and would go to some lengths to make sure no harm would come to him. Despite the fact that menacing is not really in my repertoire, the ruse, somewhat astonishingly, worked.

A few days later, having fitted out the Range Rover with all sorts of serious kit like a 'cow catcher', six massive quartz halogen spot lights and a pair (in case one broke) of cutting-edge eight-track Motorola stereos, we were on our way. Of course, we never made it to Africa having on the way discovered the delights of the seaside Spanish village of Cadaqués. It so happened that that summer Cadaqués was flooded with a mainly British crowd who largely resided otherwise in the Royal Borough of Kensington and Chelsea, many of whom already knew each other. Thus it was all rather social. For obvious reasons, Charlie and I were considered to be a bit OTT and so we tended to do our own thing out on the periphery.

At night we would drive up into the hills and spend the night sleeping, or more accurately attempting to sleep, in the Range Rover, Charlie across the bench seat in the back and me across the front two seats, having partially filled the gap between them with my battered briefcase. On one particular evening, I was woken up by a truly disgusting slurping and sucking noise, almost sexual in nature, emanating loudly from the rear seat. For a few moments I just lay motionless with my imagination in overdrive. Once I had plucked up enough courage to investigate, it appeared that Charlie, obviously still hungry, had managed to open about a quarter-inch aperture in a tin of sardines, before breaking the attached key, and was trying, with some enthusiasm, the absurdly impossible task of sucking out the entire contents of the tin through the tiny hole.

Every morning as we drove down to the village, playing Mott the Hoople or similar at some volume, a friendly barman would greet us with two large tumblers of rough Spanish brandy which got the day off to suitably decadent start. One evening we ended up with the artist Salvador Dalí and his eccentric wife Gala at their rather unusual home, consisting of three fishermen's cottages knocked into one, by the sea. It is relevant at this point to describe Charlie: he was thin, tall, with a massive shock of tightly curled hair and extremely sexual in a Mick Jagger sort of way combined with more than a hint of menace. He was totally alpha male with a fondness for older women (a year or two later he married Roberta, several decades his senior). At Dalí's, where all conversation was conducted in either French or Spanish, there there was a very pretty young German girl who was trying to persuade the artist to do a small sketch for some charity or other. Dalí responded that he would be delighted to make her a drawing, but the price would be $5,000, in cash, up front, which was the end of the matter. Several hours later, Dalí, somewhat transfixed by Charlie, took him to one side.

'I would like to paint you,' enthused Dalí. 'Come here in the morning.'

'I would be delighted to sit for you,' responded Charlie, 'but it will cost you $5,000 in cash, up front, for the privilege.'

Rather a classy response, I thought.

When the money ran out I flew back to London to collect another instalment from Charlie's antique dealer friend Chas and take it back to Charlie in Spain. On arriving home – I was currently sleeping at a friend's place in a corridor outside the upstairs lavatory – there were a pile of urgent messages from Charlie's father, whom I had heard about but had never met. I called him and arranged to see him the following day, at the offices of Thomas. R. Miller Insurance in St Mary's Axe. A disarmingly pleasant secretary ushered me into his massive office to find an expensively dressed gentleman, looking remarkably like the actor Patrick Cargill when he played the role of a rather arrogant doctor in Tony Hancock's *The Blood Donor*. He was sitting behind an antique mahogany partners' desk, gently stroking his nose.

Dispensing with all niceties, he said, 'I've only got three things to say to you, boy. Firstly, the senior partner in this company is a friend of your father. Secondly, it has been brought to my attention that you have a criminal record. Thirdly, it would seem you have knowingly perpetrated a fraud and unless you do precisely what I ask you to do I shall call the authorities and have you arrested. What do you say to that?'

'In that case, sir,' I responded without pause for breath, 'you are as big a shit as your son always told me you were.'

Well, that broke the ice. From that moment onwards we got on surprisingly well. Shearer senior was big on nicknames and I was soon christened 'Mort the Sport, connoisseur of fine motoring'.

It turned out the money I had obtained from Chas was not actually Charlie's at all but his father's. In the end, a sort of pax was agreed and I flew back to Spain to return a week later with Charlie and the Range Rover for a summit meeting with his dad. Under the circumstances, it was astonishingly friendly and all I really remember was Shearer senior giving his son the moniker 'The Expensive Gigolo'.

At one point I asked, 'With all these nicknames, sir, do you have one?'

Absolutely beaming from ear to ear he responded, 'Yes. They call me . . .' he said, pausing briefly for maximum effect and without a hint of irony, 'Goldfinger'.

Without doubt though the most disgraceful motoring performance put in by Charlie and me came some years later in 1978 when we were staying with his lovely, recently divorced mother Sylvia at her beamed seventeenth-century cottage in

East Sussex. Sylvia was, in her earlier years, the living embodiment of Miss Moneypenny. It so happened that there was a new Burt Reynolds film, *Hooper*, about the antics of a flamboyant stuntman showing in Tunbridge Wells that week. It also so happened that Sylvia had recently acquired an audaciously powerful and super-fast little saloon car called a Triumph Dolomite Sprint, rechristened by Charlie and myself the 'Dolly Olly Sprinteroo'. Somewhat reluctantly Sylvia lent us her brand new car on the condition that we were back from the cinema by 6.30 p.m. sharp as she was due at a bridge evening for 7 p.m.

Somewhat inspired by some of the more outrageous stunts in the film, we decided to try a few of our own on the way home. Clearly it was a big mistake to bet Charlie £100 that he couldn't take a series of S-bends at 100 mph. The car rolled three times but somewhat miraculously ended up on its wheels. It was, however, devoid of its windscreen. As the car was still fully driveable, we took a detour across country. This time I was at the wheel as we slithered this way and that, with the engine red-lining constantly and so hot that steam was pouring out from either side of the bonnet.

As agreed, at 6.30 p.m. sharp, we dropped the car back. It was no exaggeration to say it now resembled the winning vehicle in a Demolition Derby. Charlie breezed in to his mother's house without a care in the world and chucked her the car keys as if the Dolomite Sprint was exactly as it had been a mere four hours earlier. I heard the front door close to be shortly followed by a shriek as if she'd just discovered a headless torso on the gravel drive. In a state of utter shock, she ran back inside, exclaiming over and over again, 'But it doesn't have a windscreen!'

'Oh, don't worry mother,' responded Charlie cheerfully as he casually threw her his old motorcycle goggles, 'use these.'

When not trashing Shearer family cars, Charlie and I used to drop in on his aged grandmother who used to describe him as a 'Woolly Wahoo'. Conversations with her, since she was partially deaf, went something like this.

Grandmother to me: 'And what are you doing now, Charlie?'

Charlie responds on my behalf before I have a chance of answering, 'He's smuggling cocaine.'

Grandmother, somewhat surprised, 'Smuggling cocaine?'

'No, I'm struggling and in pain.'

———•———

In 1974, together with my good friend Colin Pool and with the backing of two highly dubious gentlemen of continental origin, we opened an estate agents, Tips Butler and Co., on Kensington High Street. Thanks to the miner's strike and the resulting three-day week, this turned out to be possibly the most unpropitious time in living memory to embark on such a venture. With much hope, enthusiasm and fanfare Tips Butler and Co. opened for business that February. Having managed to sell no more property than a single houseboat moored on Cheyne Walk, we shut up shop six months later. Largely to compliment my prestigious new position in the property world I had acquired a slightly down-at-heel Aston Martin DB4 for around £600. A few hours after taking delivery I blew it up racing Robin Grant-Sturgis in his DB5 on the Cullompton bypass. I subsequently sold it as a 'non-runner' for £120. Forty-two years on, Robin still has his DB5, which he informs me frequently, is now worth at least £750,000. Had I kept mine, even with a blown engine, it would be worth at least £400,000 today – and just to rub salt in no Capital Gains Tax is payable on cars.

It was now time to take stock. Rumour had it there was a fortune to be made working on the North Sea oil rigs. I had no fear of manual labour and so Charlie Shearer and I headed north to stay with some distant cousin of his while we looked for work. The cousin lived in some massive stone castle near Aberdeen, the only home I have ever been in that was actually considerably colder on the inside than it was outside. One evening, in the pub, we got somewhat inebriated whilst discussing the recent murder of Lord Lucan's nanny with an amenable Scot called Ian. By sheer luck it turned out, rather surprisingly given the amount he drank, that Ian was safety officer for one of the big oil companies and through him we secured jobs as roustabouts. The only proviso being that, given our reputations, we worked on separate rigs. Charlie lucked out and ended up on the *Ocean Victory* which was about a mile off Aberdeen. My rig, the semi-submersible *Ocean Kokuei*, involved in exploratory drilling in the Ninian oilfield, was situated halfway between Scotland and Norway. Therefore commuting to work was a slightly more arduous affair than jumping on a number 22 bus. I would catch a small propeller plane from Aberdeen to the Shetlands and then, weather permitting, fly by Sikorsky helicopter to the rig.

At the time there was more chance of being killed in an accident on the rigs than there was of being shot or blown up as a British soldier on a tour of duty in Northern Ireland.

Unbelievably, there was no training of any sort whatsoever and within a hour of arrival on the rig I was kitted out in overalls, hard hat and boots and outside working. A roustabout is simply a glorified deckhand responsible for hosing down, painting, checking the drill pipes and sleeves were straight and so on. The real problem out on deck was communication because of the incredible noise from the massive diesel V16 generators that powered everything on the rig, as a result it was totally impossible to hear anything. To shout a warning to a colleague in danger of being beheaded by a winch was utterly futile. Within days I had been promoted to the giddy heights of roughneck and ultimately assistant derrick-man. Roughnecks were the worker bees of the drill floor, working day and night under the queen bee, known as the toolpusher. When the rig was in drilling mode the toolpusher was boss, when it was on the move the bargemaster was. Shifts were twelve hours on/twelve hours off. Night shifts were a nightmare. At the end of a shift you were so knackered you could sleep literally anywhere. The food was as tasty as it was plentiful, with as many T-bone steaks as you could eat every six hours. I once eat four in one sitting. I opted for tours of three weeks on the rig and one off. The pay was incredibly good.

There was something really awe-inspiring about working up on the drill floor when dawn broke over the North Sea. It felt both surreal and exhilarating being a small cog in the midst of this vast, noisy and hugely complex industrial machine, about the size of five football pitches, standing some 40ft above the waves surrounded on all sides by an inhospitable sea for as far as the eye could see.

It didn't take long for me to acquire the nickname 'Jonah' since I turned out to be somewhat accident-prone. I made quite a few friends from every conceivable country and background. One time my flight off the rig was cancelled due to a force eight gale; I was on good terms with the Geordie radio operator and persuaded him to send a message to some friends I was due to go foxhunting with that Saturday saying I was delayed. He told me that he was once very involved with horses himself. I asked him how come and he replied with some enthusiasm it was when he was doing a milk round in Newcastle with a horse and cart. I enjoyed many of the stories about being 'on the milk' as he called it; however the one he insisted on telling me in some detail about his lower bowel prolapsing when straining on the lavatory one morning I found rather less entertaining.

Sometimes I found sleeping through the day if I was on the twelve-hour night-shift rota a bit tricky, so whilst on shore I visited an elderly local quack called Dr Arbuthnot.

'Any chance of a few Valium doctor?' I inquired brightly after a lengthy sob story.

Rather reluctantly he started to write a prescription.

'Oh,' I said, 'could you make them the 10mg variety? You know, the new ones, the blue ones.'

He stopped writing and looked at me quizzically.

I rambled on, 'I know they exist doctor . . . well you see . . . the thing is doctor . . . well all my friends take them.'

It was at this point that he put down his pen. Looking me straight in the eye, he proclaimed in a broad Scottish accent, 'Well in that case, laddie, if I were you, I'd change ma friends.'

Sound advice as it turned out.

A couple of years later, while recuperating from a lengthy stay in hospital following my liver failure, I enrolled via the local job centre on a government employment incentive run by Reading and Slough Road Transport Training Association (TTA). I enjoyed every minute of it and not only made several firm friends but walked away a few weeks later with a brand new unblemished HGV1 licence, my only serious qualification to date. (When I passed by the skin of my teeth, the examiner somewhat dryly observed, 'Mr Mortimer, if you continue to crane your neck in such an exaggerated fashion every time you check the wing mirrors, then may I suggest that you will soon end up with a serious neck injury.')

Now it was time to put my newly acquired driving skills to the test and get a job with a haulage company. This was easier said than done and, after a fair bit of shopping around, I ended up registering for part-time work with a down-at-heel drivers' bureau in Croydon. My first job was delivering crisps round various supermarkets in London. The articulated lorry was considerably more decrepit than anticipated and hot air from the engine had the annoying habit of blowing my delivery instructions and maps all over the cab. Of course, there wasn't satnav then, and a ten-year-old *A-Z* in large scale was about as sophisticated as it got. The result was that, on my first trip, I overshot several supermarkets and had to keep going as I still hadn't worked out how to turn my knackered old juggernaut around. It was easy enough manoeuvring a flatbed truck around an empty trading estate, but a huge container on wheels in central London was another matter altogether.

Finally, close to tears of frustration, I fell upon one of the designated supermarkets almost by accident. The loading bay was at the end of a very narrow access road, walled on either side. The protocol was that the delivery lorries queued up to wait their turn and, when called, reversed briskly down the access road to deposit their cargo. My turn came after about twenty minutes. Using all my newly acquired skills I gingerly, and I mean gingerly, began to reverse down the impossibly narrow lane using my two mirrors as the only form of guidance. After several minutes I had barely gone a few feet when out of nowhere a classic old-school jobsworth appeared in a tweed cloth cap.

'Bloody hell, mate, at this rate we'll still all be here for bleeding Christmas . . . for Gawd's sake, get a bleeding move on will you?'

I had set off at 7 a.m. with a list of twelve deliveries to make – it was now 12.30 p.m. and this was my first. Things were not going well and I was in no mood to trifle.

'What did you say?' I shouted back adding less loudly, 'You silly old cunt.'

'Get a bloody move on,' came the reply.

'All right then,' I responded, 'if that's what you want stand well back and watch me!'

With that I lined up the truck as best I could and reversed down the service road at some speed without touching any of the walls on either side. This was excellent, though what wasn't excellent was what happened next. There was suddenly a sound akin to that of crushing metal and smashing glass as my truck came to a juddering halt.

I jumped out of the cab and ran round the back to confront what was clearly going to be extremely bad news. It became quickly apparent that I had, unfortunately, crushed what turned out to be the supermarket manager's Ford Escort like an egg against a concrete bollard. The jobsworth was quickly on the scene and ashen white.

'Oh my Gawd,' he exclaimed with feeling, 'what we going to bleeding do now?'

Bizarrely, the accident had in a nano-second wiped out all the pent up anger and frustration that had been building all morning and I felt as relaxed as if I'd just had an intravenous shot of Valium.

'I'll tell you what we'll do,' I said with that sort of unnerving calm more usually associated with psychopaths. 'I'll drive the truck forwards a few yards while you go and round up anyone you can find in the supermarket. When they're all assembled on the loading bay give me a thumbs up sign and I'll do it all again in case they didn't see it the first time round.'

In 1982, I found myself back in Hamburg, this time in very different circumstances. With my HGV1 licence, I went on a series of mercy trips to Poland in support of of Lech Wałęsa and Solidarność. Mollie Salisbury was my unlikely driver's mate. It would not be an understatement to say that Mollie, then Marchioness of Salisbury, made the Queen sound like a bovver boy. (We were not obvious friend material.) On one occasion, we were loading the truck at Mollie's home, Hatfield House, and I was stacking stuff in the huge container with a good friend of mine called James P. (now sadly deceased). James, a very good-looking boy, was on some rather heavy prescribed medication at the time and we called him, not without affection, 'Slow but Sure'. Suddenly Mollie's cut-glass tones rang out.

'James, I've lost the Prince of Wales's coat!'

James showed no reaction whatsoever. In ascending volume Mollie repeated precisely the same sentence several times. Eventually James got round to replying. Quite slowly and deliberately, 'Don't worry, Lady Salisbury, I'm sure he's got plenty of others.'

Like all my previous trips to Hamburg we took the Harwich ferry. Mollie's old friend, Ginnie Beaumont, and her long suffering son Thomas were following our lorry in a backup van. An utterly charming and highly eccentric lady, who literally floated around on a cloud of extremely pungent Floris perfume, Ginnie managed to clear the entire dance floor in the ship's discotheque with her interpretation of the 'The Birdy Song'.

On that trip, I took Mollie to the ship's cinema to watch *Arthur* starring Dudley Moore. I had no idea the film was quite as bawdy as it was and certainly not entirely suitable for a sixty-five-year-old marchioness who had a reputation for upholding the strongest moral principles. At the first swear word, which I seem to remember was 'fuck' I felt myself go the colour of a bottle of Cockburn's Port. It was one of the most excruciating two hours I have ever spent in my life.

In Hamburg, with a few free hours to kill, James and I made our way to the city's notorious Reeperbahn red-light district. This made Soho look tame. Given all the evidence, it was surprising that I still hadn't worked out my sexuality. So it was that James and I picked up two astonishingly pretty girls. I have to say that any ardour that I might have mustered was pretty much killed off instantaneously when the extremely friendly young lady produced a very thin clear plastic sheet that she indicated had to remain between us at all times.

There was no actual body-to-body contact at all. Deep from the bowels, for want of a better word, of the warren of rooms that constituted this particular establishment of ill repute, I clearly heard James's very distinctive voice, rather more animated than usual, 'You must be fucking joking!'

One night on the road, Mollie and I were forced, as there were no hotels or convents in the area, to sleep on wooden pallets in the back of our truck. In the morning, I threw open one of the huge doors, expecting to unveil an attractive rural scenario, only to reveal a pot-bellied Polish lorry driver peeing, in full view, without so much as a care in the world.

By chance our very first trip to Poland coincided with the Falklands War and the day the Argentinean battleship *Belgrano* was sunk under controversial circumstances our heavy laden truck reached Warsaw. It was possible that there would be some anti-British feeling here and there. We were put up for the night at the British Embassy and Mollie, understandably, was very keen to get word to her husband Robert that she was safe and sound. For some reason all lines of communication were down except for the embassy telex. My then brother-in-law Paul Torday, sadly no longer with us, prior to his career as a highly successful author was boss of a marine engineering company in Newcastle. I looked up his company's telex number in a huge directory and sent the following message. 'Please call the Marquis of Salisbury and let him know that his wife has arrived safely in Warsaw.' The telex operator at Torday and Carlisle promptly called a pub of the same name and left the message with a bemused landlord.

Another entertaining trip came when my good friend Joe Gibbs' parents needed to move a large amount of furniture from storage at Camp Hopson of Newbury to their new, rather avant-garde house in Provence. Joe's dad was a field marshal and thus rather more organized than either Joe or myself. As he sat in a striped deckchair wearing a panama hat and holding a serious-looking clipboard outside the furniture depository, I don't think he expected Joe and I to round the corner in a juggernaut. He certainly wasn't expecting said juggernaut to remove the entire swinging sign from a pub and for it to be pursued on foot by a very angry landlord shouting obscenities. However furious the landlord was, it was as nothing compared to the Field Marshal who, with a face like thunder, gave me one of the many military dressing-downs I have received over the years.

Still all was not lost. Against the odds, Joe and I successfully delivered all the furniture to the south of France at a fraction of the cost of a professional removals firm. The delivery was somewhat hair-raising as the Gibbs's villa, affectionately nicknamed 'King's Thursday' after Margot Beste-Chetwynde's modern monstrosity in *Decline and Fall*, was situated at the end of an almost impassable track. Certainly it proved to be impassable for a heavily laden articulated lorry. The rear axle jammed on a huge boulder and we were forced to carry the entire load several hundred meters to its final destination, not a barrel of laughs in 35 °C. That evening, after paying a local farmer to drag the empty wagon back to the comparative safety of tarmac, we uncoupled the tractor unit from the trailer and headed for the pub, where a rather unsatisfactory individual asked us for a lift back to Blighty. Joe and I didn't fancy this at all so, after conferring, we gave him a lift back with us from the pub, with me driving the tractor unit like a

Lotus Super Seven in the hands of a lunatic. To our delight, he suddenly remembered he had other plans.

I am very fond of the Field Marshal's delightful wife Davina, an accomplished artist who once painted my portrait in their Army quarters in Knightsbridge. Sitting still really is not my strongest suit, and at one point I fell into a deep catatonic trance. Davina reminds me that I only made one request throughout the many sittings: 'Davina, could you very kindly obliterate at the stroke of a brush what would take me at least three weeks to accomplish with intensive use of a strong anti-acne cream?' The portrait now hangs outside the lavatory in my younger sister Lumpy's house in Wandsworth.

Very sadly Roland, the Field Marshal, died a few months before my dear mother in 2004. Davina very sweetly asked me to be an usher at his funeral. I wrote back: 'Possibly the least distinguished soldier of the twentieth century would find it a great honour to officiate at the departure of one of the most distinguished.'

6

Home is where the Heart is

In the 1970s, when I was leading a somewhat rackety existence, I was more than a little envious when a good friend, Patrick Fisher, and his lovely wife Kay, bought a vast house overlooking Parsons Green in London. Patrick had an unusual way of presenting himself which, I for one, found extremely entertaining. Mind you, the words 'acquired taste' also come to mind.

On a trip with him one morning to a very crowded Barclays Bank, I was surprised when Patrick announced in very loud and authoritative tones to no one in particular, 'Why on earth they allow any of these people to have bank accounts I cannot possibly imagine.'

In order to stop us being lynched I was obliged to mouth behind his back, 'Sorry, he's got issues.'

Another time he was stopped by the police for going about 4 mph over the speed limit. Patrick was asked by the officer to produce his licence which he duly did. The ensuing conversation was a class exercise in how to seriously irritate a police officer in under thirty seconds and ended up along the lines of:

'Are you or are you not Mr Patrick Fisher?'

'Well I'm not Mrs, am I?'

Patrick simply could not understand why he ended up with three points on his licence after this exchange.

His sense of injustice was compounded just a few days later. I had recently acquired a Renault 5 Gordini and was showing off to Patrick on the Westway by driving at break-neck speed. As we approached Shepherd's Bush roundabout, an unmarked 2.5pi Triumph police car pulled us up. I got out of my Renault to be greeted by a somewhat dishevelled police officer giving a passable interpretation of Jack Regan in *The Sweeney*.

'What sort of speed do you call that then, sonny?'

'Oh I don't know officer . . . around 110 mph?'

'Well, at least you're bleeding honest. There you are flying down the Westway like some sort of bat out of hell in your snappy little French hatchback . . . carve up the wife and two kids on their way to the supermarket . . . nip past a party of OAPs on the inside lane . . . Jesus, just what sort of driving do you call that?'

'Irresponsible, officer?'

The officer had now built up a head of steam: 'Do you know where you'll be in a week or two sonny?'

'No, where officer?'

'You'll be on your hands and knees pleading with a magistrate to give you your licence back so you can cling on to your grubby little job.'

'Yes, officer, that's exactly where I'll be if I carry on driving in this ridiculous fashion.'

'Oh go on piss off . . . I can't be bothered to waste the paperwork on you.'

Result: I escaped without so much as a blemish on my licence. Patrick, in a state of utter bewilderment at the unfairness of it all, proclaimed furiously all the way home, 'With your driving . . . you should bloodly well be in prison, and for a very, very long time.'

It didn't seem the moment to start a debate on the random inequities of life but I couldn't resist it. 'It's alright for you old fruit,' I said. 'You may consider it a gross injustice that you have three points on your licence, but you also have a mini mansion whereas all I have is a Renault Gordini and a suitcase, and most of the rest of the population don't even have that. One way or another, we are the fortunate few.'

Patrick's house was on the New King's Road and was in a poor state of repair. It had until recently been lodging rooms for Vietnamese refugees. On my first visit there, while Patrick and Kay discussed building works downstairs, I went exploring upstairs. I reached the attic bedroom where, the window being on the low side, I knelt to look out. Within seconds I was utterly transfixed. The view was just like the cover of a Ladybird book and presented a snap shot of life that was so calming and so safe it was like taking 10 mg of Valium. There was the green surrounded by leafy trees, a Zebra crossing, two red phone boxes, a red pillar box, a bus stop with old style Routemaster buses passing regularly in either direction, a traffic junction with cars, lorries, motorbikes, vans, bicycles all whizzing in and out as if choreographed, somehow missing each other by inches. And then there were the people. What politicians like to call 'real people', quietly getting on

with their lives surrounded by all the stuff that goes with sub-
urban existence from pets to perambulators. For me, this was
heaven.

After being glued there for a full twenty minutes, I made a
decision that one day this was where I was going to live. Over
three decades on, it is where I am writing this. I have lived
here now since 1988. It is a view that I have never tired of
and, when away, long to return to. Quite simply, it is home,
and I have no plans to leave unless nicely zipped up in a black
plastic body bag. Tim has very generously accepted, for some
time now, that this is the status quo and plans for moving are
no longer even discussed.

After extensive and expensive building works Patrick and
Kay moved in and threw the customary house-warming bash.
Of this I have a vague recollection of getting hopelessly jammed
in-between the glass panels of a huge double-glazing unit on
the first floor. Later, having been extricated from the window
by my old business partner (now sadly deceased) Colin Pool,
aka Murky Pool, we rolled the 100 yards down the road to
Tootsies Burger Café. Here we both received a lifetime ban for
something we considered fairly trivial whereas the manageress
clearly didn't. As I had already identified the area as my future
home, it was not the ideal start.

Over the years I rented various rooms in friends' houses
around Fulham and dropped in pretty regularly on Patrick
and Kay. Patrick at the time was attempting to write a rock
musical. My dad, who affectionately used to refer to Patrick
as 'The Toad', once commented to me, 'By the time The Toad
finishes writing that bloody musical, Rock and Roll will be
old hat.' Occasionally there were some interesting people

hanging out there – Patrick's ex, Tessa Dahl (Roald's daughter), and her friend at the time Gary Glitter all come to mind.

Sadly, Patrick and Kaye sold the house and moved to a vineyard in Suffolk. I went to stay with them just when my addiction problems were moving up a few gears. I was supposed to be staying the night and then shooting pheasants on a formal shoot at their farm the next morning. Setting fire to my bed did not endear me to anyone and somehow, despite being the only guest staying the night, I managed to turn up late for the shoot at 10 a.m. In terms of shooting etiquette this was almost a hanging offence and far worse than the fact that I was also fairly inebriated by the time I did put in an appearance. Over the day I embarked on a downward spiral of behaviour which, I gather, seemed to observers to be bottomless.

Transport from one drive on a shoot to another is usually facilitated by covered trailers towed by tractors with the 'guns' sitting in shooting gear on previously arranged straw bales. So it was that I ended sitting next to rather a self-important European aristocrat sporting a goatee beard.

'Tell me,' he said, 'have you ever shot this drive before?'

'No mate,' I replied, 'I've never fucking shot before.'

Unfortunately for all I ended standing next to Gerald Johnson (aka 'Good ticket'), another old pal who could have been teleported straight from a P. G. Wodehouse story, at the next drive. Having shared with him the explosive contents of my hip flask, I then proceeded to drill him, Coldstream Guards style, up and down the field.

My *pièce de résistance*, or what my friend Terry used to call his 'pierre de resistance', came when, after a boozy lunch,

I offered to drive an elderly nanny back to her home three miles away. With the benefit of hindsight, I am surprised that I wasn't physically restrained from going within 100 yards of nanny, let alone allowed to drive her anywhere. It seemed, at the time, quite fun to try a bit of auto-crossing, so I did. At one point I think we hit 80 mph across a field as I demonstrated how to change direction using the handbrake rather than the steering wheel. I do feel bad that nanny was apparently in shock afterwards and required professional assistance. I was subsequently *persona non grata* chez Fisher for the next twenty years.

———•———

In 1984, after several lengthy stints in various nut houses and drug treatment centres, I was lucky enough to benefit from a bit of family financial good fortune. Now thirty-two, suddenly I was in a position to buy a modest home. Never one to hang around, I found a flat overlooking Parsons Green within the hour. It was a few doors down from Patrick's old home; it was on the first floor and had a great view of the green. It took all of ten minutes to view the flat, put in an offer and agree a deal. I wanted to crack on so dispensed with anything as parochial as a survey or solicitor and exchanged contracts the next day.

Just after I moved in, my new neighbour Natalia knocked on my door to introduce herself. She was a very handsome and personable lady who, somewhat unusually for a woman, was a builder by trade. Some thirty years on we remain close friends. This was the first time in my life that I had ever had a place to myself and in many ways the new freedoms were beyond my wildest dreams. For most of my time there I had no fridge, no washing machine, no vacuum cleaner and, to my mother's utter horror and inconvenience, no lavatory paper. As it turned out I lived at that flat for just three years; however so much of consequence happened to me there it felt more like a lifetime.

When I wasn't lying flat out on the sofa 'dying' of Aids and watching free films courtesy of Johnny Vaughan at Video Shuttle, I was among other things starting companies, doing property deals, being burgled, cruising gay saunas, flying off to Morocco and Asia with dubious companions, buying old Mercedes cars, just lurking around and getting by as a mid-range spiv. Perversely, I found having a death sentence hanging over my head more liberating than constraining.

Then one night, along came the irrepressible Bazil. To say that I became fairly obsessed with Bazil from the moment I met him – in a basement club called Henry Africa's off Kensington High Street – would probably be understating matters. Bazil was twenty-one years old, mixed race, cute and mischievous, and never short of a snappy sound-bite.

Once, during the extremely lengthy, frustrating and ultimately unsuccessful (although not wholly) wooing process, I drove Bazil to Paris for Easter. We arrived around midnight and tried to book into a hotel near La Place de la Concorde. Unfortunately for me, it was very close to the Ritz.

'She likes the Ritz,' enthused Bazil.

In the insanity of lust combined with obsession I would have bitten the bullet and forked out for a suite just to keep Bazil on board, virtually bankrupting myself in the process. Thank God, it turned out that the Ritz was full. As I returned to the car to deliver the bad news and suggest perhaps the Maurice or the George V now Bazil had mastered the significance of five stars in the Michelin guide, he just turned to me and announced utterly deadpan, 'She doesn't like Paris'.

I knew Bazil well enough, even by then, to know that this was going to be the only and final edict on Paris. All I could do was to turn the car round and head home.

Up to this point I had never had anything that remotely resembled a full-on relationship with another bloke, largely because I had never met anyone for whom it was worth throwing caution to the wind. Except perhaps Stephen, an ethereal, timid boy from the Midlands. I met Stephen in a sauna in Covent Garden and promptly took him on holiday with me to Morocco. This didn't quite pan out as planned. He left me after three days and went to live in a cave. I never saw him again.

Casual sex, or as a friend put it 'gutter buggery', was one thing, setting up home and all that other stuff – that I had previously found the very idea of distasteful – was quite another. With Bazil now occupying my headspace round the clock, I simply couldn't contain my excitement about meeting 'someone', so I made out to several close friends that 'he' was a 'she'. (My friends were labouring under the misapprehension that I was straight.) This worked for a while and I was fully prepared for a certain amount of ridicule when I finally owned up to the truth.

I confided to my friend Caroline Brooman-White, 'Caroline, you know that girl I've been banging on about is actually a bloke.'

'Oh my God, how awful. How did you find out?'

By then I had known John Hobbs for well over ten years and even he hadn't suspected a thing. Nothing cheered up John more than a good personal drama, particularly if it involved human failings and character defects and my news was no exception. For months afterwards he would inform me with a certain mischievous pleasure: 'Literally every fucking day Carly [his brother] and I are sitting in the car and just out of fucking nowhere we dissolve into this uncon-fucking-trollable laughter apropos of nothing. We don't even have to look at each other because we know exactly what we are both fucking laughing about.'

When John asked me why I had never let on before, I replied, 'The fact is that since the day I met you, you've had this kind of mantra . . . "the thing in the world I hate the most are poofs" . . . well, it didn't exactly encourage me to open up.'

Perversely for John, many of his closest friends comfortably fitted in to that category.

Other friends had reacted differently: 'Oh, don't worry, we've always suspected that might be the case' was not a common theme. Joe Gibbs sat sternly opposite me in a café on Parsons Green and pronounced, ' But I always thought you were perfectly normal. I mean for God's sake, man, you even went out with my cousin Elizabeth for over a year. Really, Chas, I don't know what's got into you.'

I didn't dare reply about nine inches of fat black cock, actually. In any case, I was extremely fond of Joe and, to be fair, he was genuinely confused.

As for family, it was more hinted at than openly discussed. While waiting with my mother in a car wash in Hungerford, as usual getting all her facts completely upside down and inside out, she turned to me and asked rather seriously, 'Tell me, Charles, you aren't by any chance a "hetero-sexual" are you?'

'No, mother, I'm not.'

'Oh well, that's all right then. Of course, I've always been bisexual myself.'

What Bazil had failed to mention initially was that he already had a boyfriend, a very decent guy called Mark. However, all's fair in love and war, so to me this was just another hurdle to overcome. Mark was so much at Bazil's beck and call that my friend Mairead and I, rather cruelly as it turned out, christened him 'the handmaiden'.

Gay dating was a whole new ball game to me, and totally the reverse of straight stuff. In the hetero world you meet a girl, if you're lucky you get a name and number, and then a date and only then a shag if it all goes to plan. In the homo world you shag, then if you're really fortunate you get a name and number, and then perhaps another shag. I was rather tragically wandering round inviting boys out to dinner like they were some 1940s debutante.

Bazil introduced me to a whole new language of gay slang, double entendre and innuendo that, astonishingly, I had never heard before. 'She' was the standard description used by gay men for all men, irrelevant of their sexual leanings. I found this quite funny. Some of my friends didn't. Robin Grant-Sturgis, the epitome of an alpha male, was absolutely furious when I rang him after he had received a new passport and gone on a travelling spree and suggested jokingly, 'Now she's got a passport she thinks she's Alan Whicker.'

Bazil took it further than most. I was rather surprised, deflated and, I must admit, amused when, as I lit a cigarette after what I thought was rather a passionate twenty minutes in bed, Bazil turned to me and remarked, 'She thinks she's in the movies now.'

The one to watch out for was when Bazil, usually later on in the day, announced, 'She's tired now.' That was code for 'I'm going to make your life an unmitigated hell for the next two hours.'

When driving from London to Seville, the dreaded phrase was uttered and I found myself parked on an extremely dangerous hard shoulder while Bazil sat in the back of the car with the door open bathing his face in rose water for ten minutes. That, I am sorry to say, is the price of severe lust and obsession: you simply tolerate situations you wouldn't even dream of putting up with under normal circumstances. The first night in Seville I made the hideous mistake of choosing a mere four-star hotel.

'She doesn't like four-star hotels,' announced Bazil, who clearly had his focus firmly set on the sweat-inducingly expensive Hotel Alphonso XIII. I kept the peace by promising that we would move there the next day.

At about 5 a.m., the concierge rang our room to say that someone was trying to break into my car. I rushed down to find the rear quarter light had been smashed and set about repairing it with cellulose tape. A full fifteen minutes later, after gelling his hair and selecting the right colour of T-shirt, Bazil appeared.

'What are you doing?' he asked somewhat abruptly.

'Well, what does it look like?' I replied.

'I'm repairing the car.'

'Why?'

'So if there's an emergency we can leave at a moment's notice,' I responded I thought quite reasonably.

'Such as what?'

'Well, I don't know . . . I guess if my dad dies or something.'

'If your dad dies,' said Bazil, 'we'll be buying another car anyway so why bother?'

The next day we survived some looks of serious disapproval from Spanish aristos and ensconced ourselves in the fabulous Alphonso. Bazil never left the bed, let alone the room, for the entire week of our stay. On about the third day, his brilliant-white Calvin Klein Y-fronts came back from the hotel laundry not as brilliantly white as he required, so I found myself in the manager's office of one of the grandest hotels in Europe doing the 'Ariel . . . do your whites pass the window test?' with my boyfriend's underwear. It was mildly humiliating but not expensive, like the time in Jakarta when, unknown to me, Bazil took a shine to the bell boy's uniform and ordered two full handmade outfits from the hotel tailor.

Luckily, in a mad sort of way, I enjoyed Bazil's outrageousness and his razor-sharp repartee. One day in Earl's Court the police stopped him for no obvious reason and asked him if he had just come from Copa's, a well-known gay club.

'Why do you want to know?' asked Bazil.

'We're investing a burglary near here,' replied the officer.

'Well, make your mind up which one you're investigating, will you?' responded Bazil sharply. 'Burglary or buggery?'

Every Friday, Bazil would announce it was 'me' day as if he spent the entire rest of his somewhat pampered existence running the International Red Cross. I have to admit that there were times when even I felt an almost overwhelming desire to fall on my knees and bash my head on the floor until I lost consciousness just to bring to an end the sheer frustration of it all.

———•———

In 1988, Patrick and Kay's old house came onto the market. My flat, charming as it was, was around 500 sq. ft in size; their house was in excess of 4000 sq. ft. With dreary old Aids breathing down my neck I thought briefly that I just couldn't be arsed – to use a John Hobbs expression – even to contemplate the mechanics of borrowing insane amounts of money or, on a more simplistic level, carry my mattress 100 yards down the street.

Luckily, my neighbour Natalia gave me the necessary oomph to get cracking. Bazil played his role by insisting on turning up for our first viewing with rather stuffy local estate agents sporting bleached hair, bright turquoise contact lenses, a matching bandana and a faux-fur coat of interesting design. There then followed several weeks of spirited negotiation. This included a slightly stressful few hours when Natalia and I took an executive decision to use a prematurely received banker's cheque to enable contracts to be exchanged without either banks' actual authority. Finally, a few pounds lighter in both weight and our savings accounts, Natalia and I got the keys in May.

In the history of property development, I doubt whether a more casual and easy-going formula has been used than the one Natalia and I applied to dividing up our new acquisition.

I took the top two and a half floors, which of course included my 'Ladybird book view'; Natalia took the first floor with a mini ballroom overlooking the green, and we decided to fund the shortfall by developing and selling off the ground floor and basement. This could never have worked without mutual goodwill, which I am happy to report still endures. There was the odd hitch initially in that it took several years to discover that our 'architect' had no qualifications of any sort and Natalia's designer bath taps cost so much money they needed to be delivered by Securicor. In my section of the house more time and energy was spent creating 'Bazil's suite' than anything else. The room with the view became my dream bedroom/study complete with TV and stereo on a telescopic arm, a full-size fridge and an electric kettle. All paint colours were decided within less than twenty minutes; my room was painted dark Moroccan red including ceiling and windows, a scheme which remains to this day, and Bazil's suite was painted battleship grey, which doesn't.

There is however a price for brain damage and, after about a year of moving heaven and earth to change Bazil into someone he wasn't and was never going to be, I just woke up one morning and decided that painful as it would be to bring things to an end continuing what amounted to a car crash of a courtship, frankly, would be much more so. I think a couple of final straws were Bazil's friendly but unusual ex-boyfriend, who it turned out wasn't ex at all and came over every single weekend, and Bazil's 'new Hispanic friend' from Los Angeles who floated in one day on a vast suffocating cloud of extremely pungent eau de cologne and stayed for far, far too long before leaving behind a bankruptcy-inducing phone bill.

Meanwhile, Natalia and I sold the ground floor to a friend of mine who was so affronted when I told him not to waste my time by viewing the flat because he couldn't afford it that he promptly got the money from somewhere and bought it. This rash purchase by the now sadly deceased Johnny Toobad saved our bacon, but as it turned out he was obliged to sell up eighteen months later as he was skint. In a somewhat eccentric arrangement, Bazil and I, still friends, persuaded his 'ex' Mark to buy the flat from Johnny. Shortly afterwards, they moved in with two black cocker spaniels. That status quo remains and from time to time, sitting upstairs at my window, I am alerted by a loud wolf-whistle and look out to see Bazil, always dressed immaculately in white, with a huge grin waving at me merrily from across the street.

Post-Bazil, things calmed down a bit and I quite enjoyed living alone, although in truth I missed much of the previous two years' worth of theatrics and melodramas. For a while I rented Bazil's suite to an old friend, Boris, who only used the room about one night a month. Boris was a drummer who had had the misfortune to be in the band managed by me in the early 1970s. Since that highly entertaining (at least for me) shambles, things had picked up for him and he went on to join The Thompson Twins for a few years. At the time he was drummer with Robert Smith and The Cure, thus the downstairs bathroom literally overnight became littered with Brit Awards and other music industry paraphernalia.

Rather than pay me any rent, from time to time Boris purchased a bit of kit for the flat. One time it was a new washer/dryer. After he rang and told me it had been delivered I rushed home almost beside myself with excitement (I have a thing about white goods). Imagine then my disappointment to discover that the drummer with one of the coolest bands on the planet had replaced my lovely old Bosch with a fucking Hotpoint. I explained to a rather confused Boris that a Hotpoint had, at that time, about as much glamour as a Skoda. From then on whenever Boris played a concert in Eastern Europe he would bring me back some hideous plastic model of a Skoda.

As a kind of precursor to modern texting, in the1980s BT had a gadget the size of a small mobile phone called a Message Master. If someone wanted to make contact with me they could call a dedicated switchboard, quote my reference number and leave a short message. Seconds later, a loud bleep would announce the arrival in my pocket of said message. This had many advantages and just a few shortcomings. It allowed me to lead the life of a spiv without the expense of any office and yet keep in touch. It also gave me a totally unwarranted air of authority: if I was bleeped people would say 'Oh, is it important . . . do you need to use our phone?' 'How very kind . . . yes it is rather urgent.'

On the downside, I was in many ways too much in touch. One morning my then business partner Robin Grant-Sturgis was literally blowing a gasket with excitement as I was chatting away on my phone. After about twenty minutes, he could take no more and I received the message 'Would Ena Sharples kindly stop her waffle and ring her partner immediately.'

My Aunt Boo got the hang of it pretty speedily. To describe her use as incessant would be an understatement, and I would often receive upwards of ten messages from her a day. Every single message would begin with 'My Darling Charles' and end with 'With lots of love from your Aunt Boo'. The core of the message was often quite simple such as 'I'm feeling rather seedy today' or could be part of a lengthy drama of the type that Aunt Boo tended to specialize in. One night there was a power cut in her area at around 7 p.m. I decided that it was simpler to throw myself into her immediate problem with enthusiasm than try to persuade her that if she just went to bed that the power probably be back on in the morning. After twenty calls to the electric company and my aunt, I could safely confirm to her that power would be restored around 2 a.m. Feeling rather pleased with myself, I finally got off to sleep in the early hours. Suddenly I was roused from the depths of my slumbers by the bloody Message Master going off. I grabbed it thinking it might be something really urgent: 'My Darling Charles . . . I thought that you ought to know that my electricity is back on . . . Lots of love from your Aunt Boo.'

When some scaffolding was erected to carry out essential maintenance on the block in which she lived, it had the unfortunate effect of interfering with her TV signal. Over a three-month period, I received, and this is no exaggeration, over five hundred calls and messages from Aunt Boo. I did everything I could to improve matters but it was a happy day when the scaffolding finally came down and normal service could be resumed. Two days later I was horrified to get a message from Aunt Boo saying that the scaffolding had gone up again and what was I going to do about it. After some investigation and several Valium later it turned out to be a fake message sent by Boris, while on tour somewhere with The Cure. He clearly thought the ruse was absolutely side-splitting.

Somewhat bizarrely, while staying with him at his farm in north Devon, it was Boris who introduced me to the delights of supermarket shopping. Up to that point I had never, at least knowingly, set foot in a supermarket proper, preferring to buy all my daily supplies from Henry in Plaza Foods, my local corner shop. I still had a thing for Fray Bentos tinned steak and kidney pies together with instant Smash and frozen peas.

———•———

I had taken heroin for the last time in 1984 and coke four years later. Such abstinence, however, did not preclude legal highs, by which I mean booze and pills, largely on prescription but some just over the counter. By 1993 my intake of DF118, a powerful opiate analgesic, had spiralled out of control somewhat. (The name DF118 stood for Duncan Flockhart Ltd's 118th variety, otherwise known as Dihydrocodeine.) Much stronger than codeine phosphate, from an abuser's point of view it drew you in insidiously. It promised more than it ever gave with the result that it was hard not to increase the dose to chase a high that was perpetually elusive. The first few times were great but after that it never really delivered irrespective of the dose. I am told that other than John Hobbs, who used to hold his hand out and whisper to me in fairly inappropriate scenarios 'Give us a D,' that Williams Burroughs had been quite a fan.

In an effort to crack my particular collection of unhealthy chemical predilections I booked myself into the Priory, Roehampton. I left after a couple of months' treatment as clean as a whistle and back on the programme as a regular attendee of Narcotics Anonymous. It was at NA where I met

Dean, an utterly charming and extremely good-looking, twenty-five-year-old Romany. Dean was on his own admission an unreformed criminal who was at the time estranged from his family so I suggested he joined mine. As I announced when mildly inebriated some twelve years later at the christening of his son, Ethan (my godson), 'Once I worked out I couldn't shag him [Dean] I just tolerated him for the next ten years.'

Dean moved into Bazil's suite and lived with me for more than a decade. He turned out to be the nearest thing to an adopted son that I was ever going to have. From day one, the deal was that our home was a drug-free and criminal-activity-free zone. Self-appointed worthies from NA took a certain delight in warning me: 'You're totally fucking insane, he's a fucking crack addict . . . one day you'll come home to find the place stripped bare . . . he'll have sold everything you possess.' To which my regular response was, 'Thanks for the input love . . . but do you know what, if and when that happens I'll deal with it.' As it turned out, despite the unpredictable rollercoaster that was Dean's life, on the loyalty stakes I could trust him with my own.

The first time I took Dean down to meet my family at a get-together he slightly blotted his copybook by telling my uncle, the decorated war hero General Sir Kenneth Darling, 'Cheer up, Colonel, it might never happen.' The 'Colonel' got his own back by loudly announcing, from the depths of a sofa, 'Who the devil is that chap? Tell me . . . is he Charlie's new odd-job man?'

Many years later the tables were turned when Dean, during one of his rather unpredictable but insanely wealthy periods, employed an upmarket estate agent to find him a substantial investment property. I met him at one such potential purchase and was mistaken by the rather sniffy young agent as Dean's odd-job man. What goes round obviously comes round.

At home in London, I was amused that after a while we had unconsciously started trading certain expressions. I would hear Dean, when bartering with a rather bemused mate over some deal or other, starting to sound slightly colonel-like himself, with, 'You must be bloody joking'. I would surprise both myself and my bank manager at Coutts by, apparently from nowhere, coming out with 'You're having a fucking laugh, mate'. Dean's other sound bites included: 'Don't worry, it will soon be Christmas' when at a loss for something interesting to say and 'Hark at him' in response to perceived hypocrisy. 'My arse is red raw' (from diarrhoea) and 'It's brand new in the box' (to some poor unsuspecting customer), didn't make it on to the transfer list.

Dean had a habit, just when I least expected it, of disappearing. (As Tommy Cooper might have said, 'Just like that!') A few months after he moved in, I had a particularly virulent flu and was stuck in bed with a high fever. Dean stuck his head round the door and asked if there was anything I needed.

'Could you be really kind and get me some Lucozade?' I croaked.

After a short and moving speech from Dean announcing that there wasn't anything in the world that he wouldn't do for me, he went off. He reappeared some two days later, without the Lucozade. By then, I was feeling a little better and as Dean crept in surreptitiously – hoping to make it in unnoticed – he was surprised to find me in my dressing gown beside myself with fury attempting to change the locks on the front door. 'Right, Dean,' I said in a rather a patronising and self-righteous middle-class kind of way, 'this just isn't working. I want you to leave. Now.' Dean started packing his things and launched into one of the most pitiful monologues I've ever heard. I tried not to laugh but within minutes I was literally rolling on the floor in hysterics. Of course, Dean stayed and life moved on.

Part of our deal was that I took Dean along to all the NA activities that I was involved in at the time which were fairly numerous. Unfortunately, Dean's reluctance to embrace abstinence and engage with other recovering addicts were in a similar category of reticence to persuading my younger sister to be civil to someone she had decided she didn't like.

Whether asked or not, Dean held strong opinions on any potential partner that I brought home. 'Oh, he's nothing special' or 'You could do better than him' were familiar lines. To be fair, he was equally pernickety about the various 'birds' he brought back. One extremely lovely and charming girl was dismissed entirely out of hand because apparently she had fat ankles.

I got Dean a job as van driver with John Hobbs Ltd, where I worked as a director and had done for many years. John took to Dean although they had their moments. I let Dean have a set of keys to the huge, alarmed gallery that was home to the business and was usually stacked to the rafters with millions of pounds' worth of *objets d'art*.

One Monday, I came in and found things weren't as orderly as I thought I had left them the previous Saturday. Dean also had done one of his disappearing tricks. It didn't take long to work out that the state of the gallery and Dean's absence were inextricably linked. When Dean finally did put in an appearance his hangdog expression said it all. Absolutely shit-faced, he had decided, at some unearthly hour, to get all his mates along to the gallery for an impromptu party. I was so astounded that I started laughing. In reality, there was no damage done bar that to John Hobbs's already chronic anxiety levels. Dean was forgiven, though his keys were confiscated.

Around that time I joined a club – the only club I have ever joined, as it happens. My parents had always had aspirations for me to join the Turf Club in Piccadilly. It was a friendly, extremely old-fashioned club but not really my cup of tea. The fact that it had a strict dress code at all times didn't really appeal either.

The club I chose to join was called Attitude, located in a converted pub in Peckham. It also had a dress code, or more accurately an undress code, in that you were required to take all your clothes off at the door bar your underwear and shoes. Once inside, the underwear was optional. It was there that I met Renato, a handsome, thirty-year-old Brazilian, who had a slight look of a young Clark Gable about him. Although he didn't move in with me, he stayed a lot. Dean realized it was fairly serious when I took Renato down to meet my mother. 'Oh, but of course bring him down. I just simply adore foreigners,' she gushed. Renato's mother came over from Brazil for a few weeks and stayed with us for a while. When she finally left the UK, she had I gather learned just two words of English picked up from me, 'Extremely unsatisfactory'.

Renato was very keen to promote all things Brazilian and many of his sentences began with 'In Brazil we . . ' before he launched into an observation about Brazilian culture that sounded like a page out of a travel brochure. He decided as a special treat to cook Dean and me the Brazilian national dish, which involved a lot of black-eyed beans and various other unappetizing bits and bobs. It was a noble effort but sadly destined to end in failure. If my taste in food was conservative, it was nothing to Dean's whose main diet at the time was a 'full English' followed by endless packets of Walker's crisps washed down with Capri-Sun. When Renato wasn't looking, Dean caught my eye and pulled a face as if he was eating a dead rat.

Being South American, Renato was quite feisty; he was also rather bossy in a finger-wagging sort of way. Once on holiday I asked him if he had ever seriously considered becoming a travel warden. This was a big mistake, and boy did I pay for it. Another time, after he castigated me for wearing corduroy trousers rather than shorts on Bournemouth beach, I referred to him as 'Miss Bossy Pants'. He turned on me furiously and demanded, 'Who this Bossy Pant?' However, the biggest explosion of all came from me. We were driving in my Nissan Skyline through Richmond Park when I asked Renato what his favourite film was. Without hesitation he said it was *Mary Poppins*. 'Mary fucking Poppins,' I shouted incredulously and promptly drove off the road into a ditch. It turned out that there was a lot about gay life that I had yet to learn.

It was while I was seeing Renato that my T-cell count dropped into double figures. That, in Aids-speak, indicated that I had developed full-blown Aids (at least according to American medical criteria). Whatever the prognosis, I started to feel really rough. At the time I wasn't drinking alcohol at all and thus found going out in the evening fairly challenging. After about 8 p.m., I found it almost impossible to stay awake. One night, despite having drunk several cans of Red Bull, I fell asleep on a massive loudspeaker at the Fridge in Brixton (which takes some doing); another time, a slightly surprised Renato found me kipping under the dinner table at his friend's place, where I had managed to crawl unseen between courses. The more tired I felt, the more grumpy I became. One night there was a minor drama when I refused to give some of Renato's Brazilian friends, to whom I had taken quite a dislike, a lift home.

In 1995 Renato and I went for a week's holiday in Cairo. He had ambitions, God alone knows why, to become a Trolley Dolly (i.e. a British Airways steward), an aspiration which years later he succeeded in achieving. On the plane out, there was a fair bit of finger-wagging as if he was already a member of the cabin crew, and he struck up friendships with anyone whether they wanted to or not. (Following the excellent example set by my dad, and not my dear mother, I am not matey to total strangers.) When I pitched up grumpily while Renato was in mid-flow, I think people thought, 'My God, what is that utterly delightful young man doing with that miserable old git?'

It was while in Cairo that I had a brief epiphany one afternoon: I felt so overwhelmed with fatigue that I just knew things were now going to go downhill, rapidly. Unknown to me, or anyone else at the time, the first really effective Aids treatment was only months away. Had this not been the case, it would have been curtains for me before Tony Blair and New Labour won the election in May 1997, which as it turned out was a fate worse than death.

Renato and I gradually parted company on the best of terms and in a friendly gesture he managed to get Dean one of his more unlikely jobs as a towel boy in a gay sauna in Covent Garden. It was in a grubbier gay sauna that was to become the unlikely setting for a profound life-changing experience.

———•———

As well as having the dubious distinction of being right-hand man to John Hobbs, from 1996 I was a junior partner at Simon Finch Rare Books Ltd, an antiquarian book business based in London. Simon and I had met twelve years previously and we often bought and sold things together.

He was also the worst timekeeper in the world. Thus it was, on Tuesday, 10th December 1996, that I found myself waiting impatiently for him to pick me up. He was already forty-five minutes late. We had both been invited by the Royal Bank of Scotland to a formal lunch with placed seating before watching the Varsity rugby match at Twickenham. Since we owed the bank a not insubstantial amount of money and needed a lot more, it was vital that we made the right impression. We finally pitched up looking somewhat dishevelled just in time for coffee and petit fours. The bank's beano was being hosted by the area manager who had a striking resemblance to a Toby jug. If he was pleased to make Finch's and my acquaintance, he concealed the fact remarkably well.

I am not a sports fan. In my teenage years my dad used to take me to the races with him in the vain hope that I might show some interest and learn a thing or two. As it happened, the only thing I learned is that the best time to get a drink at the bar without hassle is when a race is on. Rugby certainly was not within my field of expertise and beyond uttering a few inane remarks, I sensibly kept pretty much schtum throughout the match. It's a pity I didn't continue to keep my trap shut.

When the match ended I turned to the Toby-jug character and said, 'Great. Now we've got the best bit.'

'What on earth do you mean,' he replied somewhat bemused, 'the best bit?'

'Well, surely you've got tickets for the players changing rooms and showers . . . haven't you?'

He gave me a look otherwise reserved for the lowest form of life and strode off looking even redder in the face than usual. As positive PR outings go, I don't think it was right up there.

By the time Finch dropped me back I was absolutely knackered. Dean was up to no good somewhere so rather than stay home alone I had a vague plan in my head to a pay a visit to my regular sauna, a friendly but sleazy little number called the Locker Room in Kennington. I was very good friends with the boy on the desk and the arrangement was that he let me in, in return for the odd bottle of vodka and an occasional carton of duty-free fags. However, having been stuck in traffic for hours with Finch I thought I'd try somewhere a bit closer to home. This left only once choice: Star Steam, described in ads as catering for both straight and gay customers on Lavender Hill, Battersea.

Words cannot describe just how seedy this place was. I had ended up there once or twice before and had always sworn never to return. Not only did most of the blokes look like John Prescott (my apologies, Lord P) but it was filthy. To use one of Dean's most damning descriptive words it was 'rank'. In fact, had you asked me to make a list of the most unlikely places to meet the future love of your life, Star Steam would definitely have made it into the top three.

Later on that evening, sitting in the stinky mist of what masqueraded as a steam room, I noticed a slight elfin-like figure seated on my right. It was Tim. He looked about fourteen, had a shaved head and liked a good chat. He may have looked like an angel but there was nothing particularly angelic about his behaviour in Star Steam that night.

One thing about the gay world is that it is so transient that you can give a really good line in old bollocks and get away with it as the chances of seeing a sauna-shag again are pretty much zero. Tim holds that I affected a fake cockney accent and, when I dropped him and his friend Geoff home in the John Hobbs van, that I claimed to work in a yard. A turn-on for him, apparently. For his part, Tim claimed to be Dutch as well as a number of other things, all of which he now vigorously disputes.

Falling head over heels can, in my experience, be bitter-sweet but in Tim's case sweet outweighed bitter by about a thousand to one. Given the yarn I'd spun, the first night he came round to mine he had expected to find that I lived on a council estate. He was therefore slightly surprised not so much by the flat but by Aunt Boo. At about six o'clock in the morning the voice of my aunt, sounding like the last remaining member of the Romanovs, resonated round the bedroom as she left a lengthy message on the ansaphone. Tim shot up in bed.

'My god,' he said, absolutely transfixed, 'who on earth is that?'

As time went on he was going to hear much more from the two Denison-Pender sisters, namely my dear mother and Aunt Boo. At our first breakfast we had a lively chat about the fundamentals of life, which culminated in me commenting, 'You're a little nutcase.' 'Takes one to know one,' responded Tim cheerily, and that just about summed it up for our future life together.

Dean, not known for his conversational skills, met Tim and gave his verdict: 'Talks a lot . . . don't he?'

Dean and I, despite his regular trips to various drug treatment centres round the country, had quite a cosy little set-up so introducing Tim into the equation was always going to have its moments. I asked Dean if he minded if Tim and I could have the flat to ourselves one evening.

'Oh, that's rich . . . that's very rich,' announced a very aggrieved Dean. 'On top of everything else now you're throwing me out of my own home.'

Rather than endure anymore 'poor me' speeches, I took Tim to Luxor for ten days.

'I know the most wonderful guide in Luxor,' enthused my mother before we left. 'When you arrive at the airport just ask for Mohammed . . . absolutely everybody knows him.'

We ended up in a Sheraton with a huge balcony overlooking the Nile and, bar one disastrous trip to the Valley of the Kings, we never left our room for the duration. It was while having dinner on the third day that Tim agreed to move in permanently when we returned to London.

Tim was living with his close friends Kerry and Matt and

their dog, a huge Weimaraner named Silber, opposite Battersea Dogs Home. I went over there one evening to get the once-over from Kerry, a New Zealander, who had a slight air of Ma Barker about her and whose swearing made John Hobbs sound like a choir boy. All was going rather well until I was left alone with 'Silber' who suddenly got all territorial and attached himself to my right arm, with his teeth. Eager not to appear like some drama queen I pretended nothing had happened, but fuck me was it painful and I had the tooth marks for months afterwards.

Determined that this relationship should be something different and lasting, Tim and I cobbled together our own ceremony, including a declaration of commitment. The first paragraph read: 'In the absence of any existing lawful means by which one man may marry another the following is our covenant until such time as British law permits us to formalize our commitment to each other.'

Prior to this it was meet-the-family time. Tim's parents are devout Pentecostals; his father is a preacher, and a very enthusiastic one at that. Over the years Tim had sprung many surprises on them, being on the cover of *Euroboy* as the gay porn star of the year being just one of them. Nonetheless, the announcement that he was moving in with a man almost twenty years his senior was a whole new ball game. God only knows what his parents expected I was going to look like, but when we met them at Parsons Green tube station they were literally shaking. Tim had probably told them I was some sort of tattooed and bearded leather queen.

Astonishingly it all went rather well. 'Too well,' remarked Tim later. So while I was off making tea in the kitchen he informed them in a matter-of-fact way that I had Aids. 'Aids!' exclaimed his mother with total incredulity. 'But that's contagious.'

There was only one non-negotiable and that was that we went down most weekends, ultimately every weekend, to my mother's to keep her company and to keep an eye on her. Fortunately my mother and Tim took to each other in a big way and a pattern was quickly established that I did all the practical stuff and Tim the emotional. When we arrived after work on a Saturday evening, I would check out what repairs needed doing round the place while Tim and my mother would, within an hour, polish off a litre of cheap white wine together, talking, as my dad might have said, 'complete balls' with unbridled enthusiasm. Tim adored my mother and she him: it was win-win all round.

With Dean now fully on board, Tim and I went ahead with our ceremony in the living room on 1 May 1997, the day Tony Blair swept into power, and left for a honeymoon in Bali the next day. One of those really weird things about mental illness is that I remember vividly sitting in the bath just before our ceremony feeling almost as depressed as I've ever felt in my life, whereas the reality of the situation was that I have never been happier. Bonkers.

The honeymoon was a great success and we stayed in a beach hut on Bali. Well, not exactly a beach hut per se, since it was part of the Bali Oberoi Hotel and thus had everything from air conditioning to an extensive twenty-four-hour room service delivered silently by electric cart festooned with garlands of local flowers. The Oberoi also served up amazing green cocktails (a mixture of rum, Curaçao and other things), two of which were guaranteed to obliterate an entire afternoon as effectively as being anaesthetized with a mighty dose of propofol (the drug that dispatched Michael Jackson) or clubbed with a chunk of lead piping. The only memorable drama of our ten-day stay was the moment when I asked Tim, 'Do you think we've both made a ghastly mistake?' Clearly we hadn't, and I have never had the stupidity to ask such a question again. The reality of it is that we have formed between us a rock-solid survival pact based around everything that is probably strictly prohibited in a co-dependency therapy manual. Anyway it endures and we're happy. Both of us are extremely neurotic in very different ways but we never belittle or mock each other's shortcomings. Many times Tim has been obliged to wait an hour or more while, with my OCD well and truly in overdrive, I would check the flat at least fifty-eight times before locking up and leaving for even a couple of days. Tim has his own very personal and particular range of time-consuming foibles, of which taking endless photographs of himself to check if his face is fat is just one. My heart sinks if anyone casually mentions to Tim something along the lines of 'Haven't you put a bit of weight on since I last saw you?' They might just as well have said that half his family had just been wiped out in a car crash.

Home life fell into something verging on routine. Dean announced he was going to become a fitness instructor, which seemed a surprising choice of career given his predilection for crack cocaine and Walkers salt and vinegar crisps. He also thought he might become an actor and, with that in mind, bought a paperback, *The Complete Works of William Shakespeare*, which still remains unopened on a shelf downstairs. Tim, when he wasn't being an artist or helping me run the Hobbs gallery on a Saturday, worked three days a week on the front line at the local job centre. He said he loved the gossip in the tea-room, had absolutely no plans for promotion and has recently completed twenty-five years in the role. He is possibly the most unspoilt and unambitious person I have ever met. He is under the impression that he was put on the planet entirely to smoke, drink and social-ise. Although not a natural when it comes to domestic chores he makes up for it, he feels, with his strong mystical beliefs, in par-ticular that 'the universe' will take care of everything (including the hoovering) and as a result the entire flat is full rare and exotic rocks and crystals. (Many a time have I had a painful encounter with one when padding round the place in bare feet.)

On the chatting front, one of Tim's best phone pals is Akhtar, who lives in Udaipur, India (thank God for cheap calling plans). We met Akhtar about six years ago when staying in Devi Gahr. He was then a very good-looking nineteen-year-old Muslim lad, who took guests on a tour of the local village. From the moment Akhtar told Tim that he looked like Princess Diana I knew we were in for trouble. They immediately formed a mutual admiration pact and left me for dead. About two hours later, huffing and puffing, I finally caught up with them. Tim implored me to give Akhtar a tip.

'Okay, Akhtar,' I said, 'here's a tip . . . two poofs it's always the old one that's got the money.'

Despite this inauspicious start we have remained good friends ever since, and Akhtar is now married with two children. Last year we bought him and his family a goat for Eid. The village children christened the poor goat 'TimCharlie' and then ceremoniously cut its throat.

165

When I was out, Tim and Dean would from time to time get up to all sorts of delinquency. It was only years later that they told me that they were alerted to my imminent return by the very distinctive two chirps emitted as I set my car alarm in the street outside. Thus by the time I got into the flat all mind-bending substances and paraphernalia had been stuffed back into some hiding place or other. At the time, I was still very much into macho stuff like guns, fast cars and *The Sweeney*.

So when I got back one evening to find a medium-sized teddy bear, with a very comfortable round bottom and a red bow round its neck, sitting on our bed, my immediate reaction was 'What in the fuck is that?' Tim explained that it was promotional gift from the Jobcentre and it was his intention to give it away to a suitable child. A day or so later, I came into our bedroom and exclaimed in horror, 'So where the fuck is Teddy?' Teddy was retrieved and became a cornerstone of our existence and still is. (Teddy made four you might say.) This was surprising, not least because of our age, my age in particular, and the fact that I hadn't shown the remotest interest in teddies since 1959 and then only in passing. In due course Teddy came to represent everything that was wholesome, decent and lovely about life and at some point we split the world into two very defined categories: 'friends of Dean' and 'friends of Teddy'.

Dean had some suspect friends, one of whom, Kevin junior, had a conviction for armed robbery. When Kevin junior fell out with Dean, he threatened to come round and shoot me 'just to piss him off'. And when he did turn up in a particularly menacing manner, I explained down the intercom, 'With the best will in the world, mate, I've got just about enough on my plate right now without having to deal with you as well. Not only do I feel like shit with some hideous Aids-related thing going on but I've got my barmy aunt [Boo] threatening her neighbours and calling me up every fucking minute and my mother having some crisis or other which I'm meant to be sorting and calling me up every other fucking minute.'

Astonishingly he seemed to think this was all quite funny and that was the end of the matter. 'Be lucky son,' were his parting words and we never heard from him again.

Other friends of Dean's, all of whom I liked, one by one ended up getting very long jail sentences for a variety of extremely serious offences. When introducing Dean to family or friends, I would kick off along the lines of 'This is Dean who lives with us. He's a professional criminal.' He always seemed quite pleased with this and saw it as some sort of accolade. That said, over the years Dean also had some notable legitimate business successes: his waste-transfer site (Wasteworld) and his vintage movie poster shop in the Fulham Road being two of them. At one point, Dean became so affluent that there was talk of him acquiring a small country estate. Tim and I would be provided with a small cottage and in return I would mow the lawns. During these heady times any girl Dean dated was instantly whipped off to Bond Street to be dolled up at Dean's expense in Gucci, Prada and Burberry and other snazzy gear that he deemed suitable if they were to be seen out on the town with him.

I persuaded Dean that books could be a great investment and over the years he amassed quite a collection of modern first editions. These were mainly Ian Fleming (all the Bond books) and other titles that had become classic films such as

The Godfather and *Psycho*. I sold him an amazing collection of Evelyn Waugh, all generously inscribed to his commanding officer, very rare and a great buy, I thought. It was only when Dean came to sell them some years later that he discovered that Evelyn Waugh was actually a man and not a woman.

Dean also managed to squeeze in a brief career as an extra in *The Bill* and other TV soaps. He ended up being represented by some professional agent and a photo of him with a deep sun tan appeared in their books. Shortly afterwards he was sorely miffed to be offered a number of Bollywood roles by film companies that had mistaken his origins as being Pakistani.

'That's all I fucking need,' moaned Dean.

On a trip down to see my mother, who liked to call Dean 'Digby' for some obscure reason, greeted him with, 'You look very brown and handsome, Digby. Have you been on holiday somewhere nice?' Dean said he'd been to Morocco where everything was 'filthy' and the food was 'rank'. My mother had an old friend staying at the time who was also a JP. She ushered my mother discreetly into the kitchen. 'Oh, Cynthia,' she whispered, 'how can you be so stupid? Of course he's brown. He's Pakistani!'

I think Dean used the fact that he lived with a gay couple to his advantage. Tim assures me that many girls, particularly those in the fashion industry, love a gay, so our living arrangements made Dean, very much a bloke's bloke, seem multi-faceted and metro-sexual. There was, however, one little problem. Tim is very much 'Hello, darling, what's your star sign?' whereas with the best will in the world I am not. So when Dean, as he did regularly, brought a girl home, once memorably a female gangster from Dagenham who was also an expert in kickboxing, the result might unravel along the following lines. Dean and young lady are sitting at the kitchen table enjoying toast and coffee. In flounces Tim and immediately launches into an enthusiastic introduction of himself to young lady, followed by the usual gay chitchat. Dean says nothing but grunts occasionally. Ten minutes later I stumble in semi-clothed. The look on young lady's face says it all: 'My God, you've got to be kidding me. This decrepit creature is the adorable Tim's partner. It's sick. Yuk!'

Some twelve years ago, Hannes, a charming young German investment banker, together with a massive grand piano, moved into the flat directly beneath our kitchen. Although he never lived with us, at times it felt like he might just as well have. For the following three years, we suffered Hannes learning to play the piano from scratch. It was a painful process, and largely because Hannes is very personable we stuck with it. Mind you, Hannes is pretty tolerant himself. One night, during a dinner party, I became obsessed with unblocking the kitchen sink and poured no less than two litres of caustic acid down the plughole which, as fate would have it, showered Hannes who was in bed asleep. He had to spend the next thirty minutes cooling his burning skin under a cold shower. Over the years his piano playing has improved significantly and these days, when we have friends over, I occasionally slip a requested play list under his door.

Our bedroom is a good walk away from the kitchen and has the advantage that even if a small riot is taking place in there, I can discreetly resort to my sanctuary and not be able to hear a thing. That was to change one morning when I heard an unfamiliar noise that penetrated the entire flat. It was quite sharp and sounded like a bizarre mixture of Orville the Duck and Scary Spice. I rushed down to the kitchen to find to my amazement that the source of the voice was Dean's staggeringly beautiful new girlfriend, Tricia. Much as I grew to love her, you would not want Tricia issuing instructions if you had a hangover, even if you were hidden deep in the bowels of Hitler's bunker and she was a good kilometre away at Checkpoint Charlie.

Tricia is Mancunian through and through. She is a highly successful model and whatever life has ended up throwing at her over the years, she couldn't spell the word victim if she tried. Over time Tim and I got to know all her delightful family and ended up liking Mancunians so much that we now do loads of art projects up there. Her dad, a keen gambler, looks not unlike Sean Connery and like all folk from Manchester they like a party. When Tricia first took Dean up North to meet his future in laws, I joked, 'It's absolutely unbelievable but they actually think you're class up there.'

It was a sad but inevitable day when Dean finally left and set up home with Tricia. A void was left that we choose not to fill and for many years Dean's room remained exactly as he left it, still cluttered with *Thunderbirds* posters and James Bond memorabilia. 'The happiest days of my life,' he would reflect when he popped round from time to time to see us before disappearing into his old room for twenty minutes of quiet contemplation on the vagaries of life.

On 21 December 2005 Dean and a very heavily pregnant Tricia were the only witnesses at Tim and my civil partnership service at Chelsea Town Hall. Due to the couple in front of us spending so much time organizing Will Young to sing and their pink Jaguar cars, we slipped in and thus have the honour to be the first registered civil partnership in Kensington and Chelsea with certificate number 0001. The four of us celebrated afterwards with a bacon sandwich in the sadly now closed Picasso Café on the King's Road. A month later Tricia gave birth to their son Ethan Charles at Chelsea and Westminster hospital. An event that Dean described, in a rare emotional moment, as 'a life-changing experience', which indeed it was; but as it subsequently turned out for all the wrong reasons.

7

The Fine Art of
Dealing Antiques

It was 1987 and the novelty that I might die in the next ten minutes was receding. Since meeting John Hobbs back in 1973 I had hung out with him on a fairly regular basis. Very occasionally you can be lucky enough to meet someone who, in a positive way, changes the entire course of your life. For me it was John Hobbs. Around the time I met him my father commented that I was about the most naive person of my age, then twenty-one, that he had ever come across. After a few years hanging out with John I became about as naive as Bernie Ecclestone. In the early years of our friendship John was endlessly trying to have one over on me. His mildly malevolent and eccentric old dad Sid once wrote to me, 'You watch out for that son of mine, John, he'll nick all your money and then just tell you to piss off.' But in a strange way my child-like innocence to the ways of the demi-monde inhabited by John, certainly in the early days, worked to my advantage.

One such time was when John encouraged me, in a moment of madness, to buy from him a full-sized Victorian fairground carousel for rather more than the price of a flat in Battersea. John was rubbing his hands with glee having pocketed a size-able profit. Two days later, he was staggered when I doubled my money by selling it to some Swiss punters.

'I can't fucking believe it,' John moaned, 'we stitch him up with overpriced old crap and the wanker fucking doubles his money. It's fucking unreal.'

Several other big deals fell into this category including a massive seventeenth-century cupboard made in Frankfurt, in which I lived in for a while.

All this was to change and change to our mutual advantage. One day, when I was in the Hobbs' shop in Chelsea's Furniture Cave, John took me aside. 'You know a bit about property, Charlie boy, don't you . . . We want you to do us a big favour.'

He went on to explain that although the business was doing very well, they were still mainly selling to dealers who then resold their stuff for large profits to private clients. Thus they wanted a prestigious retail outlet of their own in a good part of town so they could start selling direct to wealthy customers.

'Well, the thing is, this huge shop has become available in the Pimlico Road, Belgravia. If we could get it, I fucking promise you we'd becoming fucking millionaires over fucking night!' he gushed. 'There's just a couple of problems. The landlords, the Grosvenor Estate, will not give consent for it to be used as an antiques shop and Crowthers [the fireplace firm] has already exchanged contracts on it. What can you do?'

Astonishingly I knew within seconds what to do. 'You know I don't normally come out with something like this but on this occasion I want you to do exactly what I am going to tell you to do.'

Even more astonishingly he agreed.

That year I was running a boxer short company 'Raffateer Ltd (slogan: *Would you be caught dead in anything less?)* with my then business partner, the extraordinarily pretty nineteen-year-old John K (aka Toyboy). Johnny Vaughan was our super salesman, and we were enjoying some modest commercial success.

However, this project was altogether more pressing and the following three weeks was more reminiscent of the TV show *Lovejoy* than a serious business enterprise, and John and I worked all hours to achieve our goal. It was more than fortunate that Toyboy had an excellent contact in the Grosvenor Estate office. By using a mixture of subterfuge, inducement, slight mischief, luck, together with some world-class legal advice, we eventually won the day and the shop was ours.

For my efforts, I became a director of Hobbs and was rewarded with a pair of fine Russian chairs subsequently sold for a small fortune. I officially became part of the Hobbs's inner circle as the company's meteoric trajectory from mere runners to the highest echelons of the antiques trade continued at an unprecedented rate. As John predicted the new shop was absolutely pivotal to their plans.

The shop at 46a Pimlico Road opened a few months later. It was decked out with an ornate parquet floor bordered with palm wood and painted (ceilings included) in dark green with Moroccan red skirting. Rumours abounded that the brothers were drug barons and the shop was merely a front. John's most often used phrase, until the relationship between them soured, was 'my brother is a fucking genius'.

John and Carlton were a strangely incongruous duo. It was generally thought that the shy, socially-awkward Carlton was the easy-going one of the pair, whereas the handsome, charismatic John was the utterly ruthless one. What the brothers did have in common was a prodigious talent for dealing in world-class antiques. They also crucially secured the invaluable assistance of the Kent-based enigmatic genius (and I don't use the word lightly) restorer Dennis Buggins and his team of some sixteen craftsmen. It cannot be overestimated just how critical Dennis's role was then. In the early days, antique Russian furniture was a firm favourite because it looked great, sold for fortunes, was very fashionable.

The first time I met Dennis was in 1987 when he was in his late twenties and was summoned to check out a suite of Russian-looking furniture extensively veneered in Karelian birch with ormolu mounts, which had been bought in Sweden. This may sound rich coming from me, but it took me all of ten seconds to work out that Dennis was a raving nutcase.

Within minutes he had whipped off several ormolu mounts and turned everything upside down and inside out before giving his opinion.

It's not old,' he pronounced, 'probably 1920s or 1930s but definitely not period [i.e. late eighteen/early nineteenth century].'

This resulted in a moment of mild panic in the Hobbs camp. The dealer in Sweden who had sold the suite as period was immediately contacted and told it was coming back and a full refund was required. Surprisingly this was agreed with little fuss.

However, prior to shipping, the suite was left in the shop and a few days later in wandered Rudolf Nureyev's decorator. To the Hobbs' surprise, he was very taken with the suite, or more accurately with the armchairs that formed part of it. It was explained that the suite was owned by a Swedish dealer and the brothers would get in touch with him to see, firstly, if he would split the suite up and, secondly, how much he would then want for the armchairs.

John rang the Swede who agreed to split the suite and then quoted some outrageous price for the armchairs, in fact several times more than had been paid for the entire suite just days earlier. To the brothers' utter dismay the decorator consulted with Rudolf who readily agreed and the brothers were left deflated, having effectively thrown away a huge profit.

'You couldn't fucking make it up,' John was to mutter for years afterwards. In those heady days it was almost unheard of for anyone to get the better of John in business, backgammon, poker . . . well anything really. It was generally agreed that he was possessed of a 'star quality' and as a result he would never take any sort of defeat lying down. John, on his own admission, would feel extremely resentful if he felt someone had had one over on him. That said, he would invariably transform a negative into positive by learning from the experience and turning it to his advantage in the future.

The extremely close friendship that I continue to enjoy with Dennis wasn't always quite so cosy and for years he accused me of 'guard-dogging the Hobbs', something which at the time I actually took as a compliment. (Dennis takes the description 'Marmite' to new levels – love him or loathe him.)

Dennis is the most gifted restorer of his generation. He is rather handsome – think more Piers Brosnan than Arthur Negus. He is also chronically dyslexic. I can usually understand what he is saying, though most can't. He calls it 'Dennis speak', with ideas coming so thick and fast that he just cannot turn them into words and spit them out quick enough. Dennis is also possessed of a gritty determination that knows no bounds. I was quoted as saying, 'Charlie Mortimer says fondly of Dennis that he is elementally Saxon. That as some Dark Age battle took place, Dennis would still be standing, swinging his mace as the arrows poked out of his chain mail, a Kentish Saint Sebastian who would never say die'. Once on a trip over from Turkey, where he now lives engaged to a lovely local girl less than half his age called Burcu (I am booked in as best man), he insisted on showing me a brief video on his iPad. In the footage, taken by his extensive battery of security cameras at his home in Bodram, I could clearly see a stocky young thug climb over the garden fence and surreptitiously make his way through the house until he reached the top floor. 'This,' said Dennis in a state of high excitement, 'is when he makes his big mistake. He comes into my bedroom.'

In the footage I could see the burglar going into Dennis's bedroom. Seconds later the intruder is seen flying out of the bedroom, closely followed by a naked Dennis waving a cutlass, exiting the house at something approaching warp speed and launching himself over an eight-foot garden wall as if attached to a rocket.

'Nobody comes into Dennis's bedroom uninvited and gets out unscathed,' concluded Dennis with evident satisfaction.

At the time I had a deal going with the brothers that I would make myself useful and try to learn the business and, in return, they would allow me to fund the odd purchase and share the profit. John assured me, 'The only fucking problem you're going to have is how much fucking tax you're going to fucking pay.' Despite good intentions on both sides it didn't really work out that way. I really tried to understand antiques but it became very obvious very quickly that I had no natural aptitude or flair whatsoever. John Hobbs would later say, 'I've known Charlie fucking Mortimer for over twenty years and he still can't tell the fucking difference between something in Peter Jones window and the fucking Hermitage.'

On our initial trips down to see Dennis at his extensive Hurst Farm workshops, despite my best efforts to learn the business, John had called Dennis, 'Charlie hasn't got a fucking clue. All he wants to fucking do is sit in the kitchen with Mary [Dennis's wife], eat toast and take Solpadeine.' All true I'm sorry to say. The first purchase I made with them as a joint project didn't really work out either. The deal was that they would find the object, restore it if necessary, and then sell it. I would fund the purchase myself, and we would split any profit.

One day John said, 'We've found just the thing for you, Charlie boy. It's the most magical fucking chinoiserie over-mantle mirror I've ever fucking seen and it comes from a private.' To acquire heirlooms direct from a family was gold dust as they had not been offered in the trade or at auction before and the eventual price could reflect this lack of exposure. The more distinguished the family and the more prestigious the provenance, the higher the eventual price achieved. This particular mirror had reputedly been a gift from Edward VII (Bertie) to his mistress Alice Keppel.

When the brothers showed me the mirror, with huge enthusiasm, I had to hide my true feelings as I thought it was hideous. It looked like something originally destined for King Ludwig II of Bavaria's fairy grotto but had been rejected on the grounds that it was too camp. It was a lesson to me to follow my own instincts in future despite my lack of knowledge or feeling for antiques. Depressingly, the mirror cost me about the same as my flat in Fulham and two years on lay unloved, in pieces in a restorer's workshop in Brixton, while a debate raged on about exactly how it should be restored. Restoration is not unlike translating a comedy from one language to another. Do it unsympathetically and all the humour is lost.

John always behaved very honourably to me and several years on he felt so bad about the way things had panned out that he repaid me in full plus interest, which was fortunate as by then I had had to put my flat up for sale. It took him at least a further five years to sell the wretched mirror and then at a loss. The brothers were always incredibly generous towards people who introduced them to lucrative deals. They were also men of their word and the respect that both Dennis and I held for them, in our separate ways, was absolute.

In 1989 I decided I needed a qualification beyond my humble single O level and HGV1 licence and thus enrolled on a mature students' programme to do a law degree at Ealing Poly (now Thames Valley University). At the time the ordinary criteria for doing a degree course were waived for older students and suitability was assessed on a series of interviews.

During one such interview, I was asked what I would think if I walked into the lecture theatre and it was full of eighteen-year-old Asian boys. In spite of answering, somewhat frivolously, 'Christmas?' I passed in.

Despite throwing myself into the course heart and soul, it turned out that chronic dyslexia was as big a hindrance at thirty-seven as it had been at seventeen. It seemed a shame that I regularly achieved marks over 90 per cent on my practical work yet when it came to exams everything just fell apart, catastrophically. Yet, as John often used to say, when talking of his father Sid, 'In the land of the blind the one-eyed man is king', so the very fact that I had at least completed two terms of a law degree gave me a certain kudos and legal standing in the Hobbs firm.

Sid Hobbs was a real character in every sense of the word. Reputedly he had joined the Home Guard during the war so he could nick cigarettes from bombed out tobacconists and sell them on the black market. John told me his dad spent the entire war stealing things. He was, however, kept well in his place by his formidable wife Kitty. Originally from, to quote John, 'Fucking Bradford, the arsehole of the world', she was tough and looked after her kids as a lioness might her cubs. On one legendary occasion in the 1960s Sid managed to wind Kitty up so much that she stabbed him almost fatally. Kitty was hugely popular, loved and respected in equal measure. Sid was really a most mischievous, albeit handsome and somewhat charismatic, old villain, who surrounded himself with proper gangsters. He loved to hold court in his Chelsea junk shop 'Odds and Hobbs' to local hoodlums and lowlifes.

Sid, like John and myself, used to suffer from 'nut pressure' and was a regular inpatient at Springfield Mental Health Unit in Wandsworth. I used to go up and see him with John. On these visits John, voyeur that he was, used to do 'wards rounds' emulating a psychiatrist and engaging with patients who took his fancy whilst I chatted away to Sid.

After my brief spell as a law student came to an inglorious end I persuaded John to take me on doing some basic admin for the company as clearly antiques and *objets d'art* were never exactly going to be my forte. One of the few positives of dyslexia is that suddenly you can find yourself quite adept at something for which you never considered you had the remotest aptitude. Just by luck within days of my new appointment, while trawling through the accounts, I uncovered the fact that the company was paying for three separate fax machines whereas in reality there was only one. Had these contracts continued for their duration the firm would have ended up shelling out the price of a fully loaded Range Rover. Thanks to this little discovery, and the fact that I found I had a natural flair for tax planning, my future was at least temporarily assured. For the first time in twenty years I became a paid employee on PAYE. As John would mutter from time to time, 'I thought the wanker wouldn't last a fucking week'.

Quite often in the morning one or other brother would pick me up from my flat and drive me to the gallery. If it was Carlton he would be in a pristine Mercedes and wearing an immaculate suit with some obscure piece of baroque music playing quietly in the background. If it was John he would be in a filthy VW Corrado V6, once described by Duncan

McLaren as the fastest ashtray in the world. He would invariably be wearing an ankle-length leather overcoat and on the stereo would be Roy Orbison's greatest hits at volume setting nine out of ten.

Both brothers were in their ways super-stylish dressers, having their suits made by Fulham tailor Dimi Major, who made extremely natty numbers for customers as diverse as Tony Curtis and Ronnie Corbett. That said, sometimes things didn't quite go as planned. Quite often Carlton and I used to go for lunch in Peter Jones. Carlton had had a suit made by Major with a slight hint (hint is giving the suit the benefit of the doubt) of green about it. It wasn't my favourite and I couldn't hide my amusement when on several occasions he was mistaken for a salesman and asked the technical details of some domestic implement or other.

Many times I would end up as the butt of a John Hobbs joke but very occasionally I got the opportunity to get my own back. We were having lunch one day at Coutts and Co. in the boardroom. John was wearing a dark blue suit with red pin-stripe. Frankly, I thought it made him look like he worked for the postal services in one capacity or other. Towards the end of lunch, our host senior director Terry asked John if he wanted some more pudding.

'I would, Tel,' replied John with feeling, 'but I'm as fat as a fucking pig. Do you know what? I've got about eighty fucking suits and I can only fit into one of them.'

'Isn't it a pity it's that one?' I chimed in cheerily.

One of my great pleasures in life was just hanging out with John. He was a great story-teller and I can safely say that whatever mood I was in there was never a day I didn't enjoy being in his company and listening to colourful accounts of his antics with notorious thugs like John Bindon (whom I rather liked) and the incredible ups and downs of life as a knocker with the infamous Jack Leach. There was little I didn't know about the Fulham underworld in the 1960s. For many rather desperate years, whether it was Aids getting me down or, worse still, depression, John was an absolute lifeline.

Despite being a lousy antiques dealer, from time to time a serious drama came along into which I could really get my teeth. When this did happen, John and I would make quite a formidable partnership. One such occasion was, for want of a better description, 'The Rothschild Vases Saga'. In the late 1980s Jacob Rothschild used to enjoy drifting around the antique shops on the Pimlico Road and, for a while, became a sporadic client of ours. (I think he genuinely admired the brothers' style.) Unfortunately relationships were soon to deteriorate.

What had started off as a relatively straightforward exchange deal with Jacob – involving a unique pair of Regency console tables belonging to the brothers being swapped for a pair of fabulous Egyptian Porphyry vases that he had recently inherited and a carved Russian sofa – soured after he pulled out of the deal. John and Jacob fell out catastrophically, and God alone knows how much money was spent by both parties on legal fees over the next four years. Rumour has it that Jacob was forbidden from mentioning John's name by his wife, Serena. It was hardly surprising that my invitations to the Rothschilds dried up. However, I did become something of an expert on family trusts. Not the most scintillating of subjects.

Sadly, I knew that with writs flying around that my friendship with Jacob's daughter, would probably hit choppy waters. As I explained to her at the time, it was like supporting opposing football clubs: there was no middle ground.

Following discovery it seemed almost inevitable that the dispute was heading for a full trial in the High Court with Charles Hindlip, chairman of Christie's, and a selection of other seriously eminent figures being subpoenaed as witnesses. In the end a deal was brokered. Instigated through a mutual friend, James Hepworth (aka 'the man from the ministry'), a council of war, consisting of Charles Hindlip, John and myself, was set up in the kitchen at John's massive new gallery adjacent to Chelsea Barracks. You don't become the chairman of Christie's by accident, and Charles had that rare ability to make you feel like you were the only person in the world who mattered when he spoke to you. What happened next is one of the reasons that despite all our ups and downs I remained 100 per cent loyal to John. The fact is, when all was said and done, I was only an employee and these weren't my assets on the line. Nonetheless, John made it clear to Charles that I had lived and breathed this dispute and had really gone the extra mile, so he was leaving the final decision on whether we accepted the proposed solution or not entirely to up to me. Reluctantly I gave Charles's proposal the thumbs up and, finally, after working our way through several firms of lawyers, spending hundreds of thousands in legal fees and now some four years on since the original deal, it was over. The great and the good of the fine arts world collectively heaved a sigh of relief and life moved on.

While on the subject of the Rothschilds, John Hobbs's brother-in-law Thodal was one of life's more entertaining characters. In the 1960s, during a period of unaccustomed affluence, he acquired a Bristol 409 coupé with push button gears, which at the time was the height of sophistication. He fancied himself as a bit of a ladies' man and used to impress girls by driving them in the coupé to stay in a motel out in the country. En route to their destination, Thodal would stop at a telephone box and call the motel reception pretending to be Lord Rothschild leaving a message for himself. Quite how they fell for this, given their very different styles of speaking, I have no idea. Thus when he arrived the receptionist would say, 'There's an important message for you from Lord Rothschild. He says it's extremely urgent that you contact him immediately.'

In front of the girl, Thodal would reply, 'Oh, he never stops bothering me about something that silly old fucker.'

On one particularly memorable occasion Thodal's sixteen-year-old son Oz had got into some sort of trouble. I gave Thodal my word that I'd do whatever I could to get matters resolved and spent the next ten hours doing precisely that.

To say that Thodal was over the moon with my efforts would have been an understatement; he was profuse in both his thanks and gratitude for what I had managed to achieve.

'If there's anything, absolutely anything, I can ever do for you, you only have to say the word,' he enthused.

'Well, there is one thing . . .'

'Just ask.'

'Well, the thing is in all the earlier panic over Oz I left my car in Fulham and I was just wondering if you could possibly give me a lift home?'

'What in this traffic?' responded Thodal. 'You're having a laugh, you cunt.'

———•———

Due to my lack of knowledge and confidence I wasn't usually allowed loose on clients. I was also a fairly hopeless salesman. John was the front man on the sales floor, having the confidence and charisma to deal effortlessly with some of the richest people in the world. Even he committed the odd faux pas: one day in July he greeted an American billionaire, who was surrounded by a small platoon of personal bodyguards, with: 'Hello, Mr F . . . you over here for the shooting then?'

One day, however, I was the only one around when a customer walked in, a handsome guy in his forties, dressed very smartly in an American preppy sort of way. I found him extremely agreeable and spent a couple of hours showing him over our two sizeable galleries. Literally falling over myself with excitement that I now had a client, I gave him a folder with photos and descriptions of all the things he had liked and recommended that he next visit Christopher Gibbs in the West End. John had known Christopher since the early 1960s when he hung out with the likes of Mick Jagger, Cecil Beaton and Paul Getty. Christopher was a great ally to us, though occasionally John would mock him mercilessly. One time he wandered into John's office with huge wicker basket hanging off his shoulder. Barely looking up, John greeted him with,

'Hello, Christopher, you don't half look a cunt with that fucking basket.'

Several hours after I had dispatched my new client to Christopher, he called me up.

'Charlie, it really is very kind of you to think of us but do you have any idea exactly who Andrew Crispo is?'

'I think he's a big art dealer from New York who has some great clients.'

Christopher couldn't believe that I'd never heard of him. Within the hour he couriered over a book, called *Bag of Toys* by David France, all about Andrew Crispo. It turned out that my lovely new client was notorious in New York and not in a good way. Andrew Crispo was a vastly wealthy 57th Street art dealer who was a chief suspect in the gay sadomasochistic 'Death Mask Murder' of Eigil Dag Vesti, a handsome young fashion student from Norway. He was never charged although his side-kick Bernard Le Geros was found guilty and sentenced to twenty-five years to life. Le Geros admitted pulling the trigger but claimed that he was acting on the explicit instructions of his boss Crispo. Soon afterwards, Crispo was sentenced to seven years (later reduced to five) for income tax evasion. He owed $4 million in back tax.

Other than administration and litigation my only other notable contribution prior to the Hobbs' split was the gallery catalogue. I was at the time also involved with Simon Finch Rare Books and I noticed that in the book world catalogues were compiled and sent out to clients several times a year. I put the idea to Carlton and we got cracking, the aim being to produce something really spectacular in a thoroughly restrained sort of way. Not like the idea once floated to us by an Indian design company to have a piece of pink tinted tissue paper between every page with swans drifting around randomly printed words such as 'elegance' and 'sophistication'. The catalogue got off to quite a slow start as Carlton and I were going to do the photography ourselves. To this end, I borrowed a Hasselblad from a friend only to discover that neither of us could work out which end of the camera you looked into and which end you pointed at whatever you wanted to photograph. It was, in retrospect, a crackers idea. Having sorted out the photography professionally, Carlton, his girlfriend Stefanie Rinza and I would spend hours after work writing, rewriting and then rewriting the descriptions of the thirty-odd pieces painstakingly selected for inclusion in the catalogue. To describe Carlton as particular would not begin to cover his absolute obsession with minutiae. Stefanie was a very pretty German who, a quarter of a century on, is still Carlton's business partner in New York. She had obtained a degree in Russian and had, at the time of compiling the catalogue, been working for the absurdly elite McKinsey and Company. Like all Germans she tended to be quite methodical, and Carlton said she had even devised a system for watering his mother's lawn by dividing it in equally sized 100cm x 100cm segments. Ultimately no expense was spared: the catalogue was printed by an exclusive, certainly expensive, Italian printing company and bound in black silk.

The brothers had no problem with expenditure when it came to raising their profile. No better example of this was when it came to antiques fairs. In 1990, we exhibited at the prestigious Grosvenor House Fair. Even then it felt like some huge top-heavy old battleship about to sink under the weight of its own self-importance. Our few appearances at fairs were designed for maximum impact rather than for sales, and always involved 'trophy pieces' displayed on parquet flooring in front of opulent, folded waxed linen curtains in either very dark blue or green. This was a direct copy of the formula used in our gallery, known as 'The Black Lodge', inspired largely by David Lynch's *Twin Peaks*. Despite being the lead salesman, John did not enjoy being on the stand and did so only occasionally and with the greatest reluctance. One afternoon a rather attractive young lady whom he knew vaguely passed by and got into conversation with him.

'I feel really, really hot,' she said.

John, unusually for him mistook all the signals, and launched into a lengthy moan that it was unbearably hot because the organizers were far too mean to invest in air conditioning.

'No,' she replied with a wink. 'I just feel really hot!'

My experiences were not quite as lively. The fair was opened by the Queen Mother who, together with a sizeable entourage of lackeys, wandered from stand to stand. I had previously rather unkindly described the Queen Mother as a 'purple apparition with black teeth'. As she approached our stand, suddenly you couldn't see the Hobbses for dust, which left only me and a suite of Viennese furniture (*c*.1820).

'Tell me about this most interesting looking suite,' enquired the Queen Mother.

'Well, ma'am, it's very rare and comes from . . . ' This was when things rather fell apart as I tried without success to say 'Schloss Wetzdorf' several times. In the end I capitulated and merely came out with something rather less challenging, 'It comes from Austria ma'am.'

'How fascinating,' continued the Queen Mother. 'Is the gilding original?'

My response, sounding like some East End car dealer: 'All our gilding is original, ma'am.'

The stand at Grosvenor Fair was as nothing when compared to our only appearance at Paris's highly prestigious Biennale at the Grande Palais. This cost about the price of a small house in Chelsea. Dennis Buggins worked with a small army of fifteen craftsmen for just under three weeks to build the stand, and I handled all the admin having at least a very basic understanding of schoolboy French. Whenever I visit Paris and attempt to communicate, the normally rather snotty Parisians just fall about laughing. I am told that in their eyes I am like a Jacques Tati caricature of an Englishman. On one occasion it took me all of five minutes to order in French two cups of black coffee with hot milk on the side, after which, the entire restaurant stood up and applauded.

The first requirement for participation in the fair was for the company to be accepted as members of the 'Syndicat National des Antiquaires' under the formidable leadership of Mme Elisabeth Gautherot. This hurdle successfully cleared, Mme Gautherot and I got to know each other quite well in the subsequent weeks. Dennis as always really pushed the boundaries and as a result I ended up almost hourly in Mme Gautherot's office either pleading, complaining or demanding. It was our intention to have the best stand at the fair, better even than the legendary French dealer Bernard Steinitz, who had great style but was in reality the most dreadful old crook, and Carlton generally got what he set out to achieve.

It's sad to think that motoring in Paris, or anywhere for

that matter, has changed so depressingly for the worse since 1992. I had exclusive use of a rather powerful customized Mercedes 560 sedan and would amuse Dennis by hitting well over 100 mph down the Champs Élysées. We bet Peter Jones, who was supplying the parquet flooring for the stand that there was no way he could top that in his cherished Ford Sierra Cosworth. Pull that sort of stunt today and you'd not only end up banged up for six months but most likely your car would be confiscated before being auctioned off by the local gendarmerie. Over the few weeks spent constructing the stand, I stormed all over Paris collecting stuff for Dennis and his band of merry men. I cannot remember parking legally on a single occasion and in all that time I received not one ticket; the only time the Merc was towed away it cost me a paltry twenty quid to get it back. I had the time of my life.

A couple of days before the grand opening, the vetting committee (a collection of appointed experts who check the authenticity of the exhibits) questioned the age and description of several of our more significant pieces. Convinced that that they were not acting with the best of intentions, I marched into Mme Gautherots crowded office.

'Mme Gautherot,' I exploded, 'this vetting committee is an absolute joke. It's entirely made up of Little Hitlers.'

Mme Gautherot rose slowly to her feet. 'Monsieur Mortimer, there are currently well over a thousand people working in Le Grand Palais. These people all have between them the same goal and that is excellence, to be the very best in the fair. They work quietly and diligently to achieve their aim. Let me tell you this, that among these good people there is only one Little Hitler, and his name is . . . Monsieur Mortimer!'

In a mad sort of way I took it as a compliment. Thanks largely to Carlton's vision combined with Dennis's genius the Hobbs's stand was generally agreed to be the best in the fair.

———•———

In 1991, John had the very traumatic experience of going round to visit Sid in his flat one day only to find him dead in a chair. The following year, Kitty died from liver cancer. Soon after her death the relationship that had held so firm between the brothers literally fell apart at the seams. Within a year they had split their company in two and each gone their separate ways. It is inconceivable that such a thing could have happened had Kitty still been alive. The feelings that Dennis and I had during this topsy-turvy period were not dissimilar to those of two young siblings caught up in an acrimonious divorce. John never forgave his brother for forcing his hand, and he never once visited him in his new premises in Great Peter Street. It was, however, with some excitement and optimism that the newly formed John Hobbs Limited moved into a massive 12,000 sq. ft. gallery, the interior having been designed and built by Dennis. Every single window had been blacked out and an elaborate, theatrical set built within, complete with parquet flooring, computerized lighting system and air conditioning. Boasting an astonishing array of furniture, marble *objets d'art*, sculptures, paintings and chandeliers, the two words, despite being rather unoriginal, most uttered by new visitors were 'Aladdin's cave'. To use an equally clichéd description, it definitely had the wow factor.

Prior to all this, John sat with me in his car and asked me to be 'the backbone' of his new outfit. It so happened that I was suffering one of my fairly regular bouts of depression at the time and the very idea of that kind of responsibility made my blood run cold. I replied that as long as he was aware that I existed on a 'knife edge with some sort of sanity on one side and insanity, obsession and depression on the other' that I'd give it my best shot, but not to expect miracles. I can't think of any other company on the planet where a response like that would seal you the job of managing director. Mind you, with John job titles were fairly meaningless. If there were problems with angry creditors and such like, he'd always say, 'You'll need to deal with my managing director, Charlie Mortimer. He handles all these things. I don't have anything to do with the day-to-today running of the company.' If some of our more glamorous clients came in, such as the Saffras, Valentino, the Santo Domingos, Bill Blass and so forth, it was an entirely different matter. I suddenly became the teaboy. 'Charlie, make Mr and Mrs Santo Domingo a coffee, will you? And after that go and buy me some fags, there's a good lad.'

He once had the audacity to write me one of his infamous letters, which started in true John style:

Charlie . . . you are the most fucking arrogant piece of shit that I've ever fucking met . . . I've been told by some people that when they come into my fucking gallery they think that you are the fucking owner and that I fucking work for you.

To which my response was:

Oh that will be the Santo Domingos will it? Given the fact you treated me like your personal butler it seems somewhat bizarre that they somehow came away with that impression, don't you think?

The hierarchy at the new firm consisted of John, his son Rupert and me. I have known Rupert since he was two years old and we have always got on incredibly well, sharing a very similar and fairly silly sense of humour. He loves to remind me of when I taught him how to drive. 'Lesson number one when driving in London is never, ever give way to a bus or a black cab.' John became rather frustrated by us laughing at his more eccentric outbursts and he frequently referred to us as 'the chuckle brothers'. On one occasion, John employed a PA, whom he knew Rupert and I couldn't stand, purely to annoy us.

There was nothing John loved more than constructing an abusive letter or fax. Often his first words of the day to me would be 'Have you written to that fucking piece of crap yet?' To which I would invariably reply, 'And which fucking piece of crap are we alluding to this morning, Hobbs?' (In later years I usually called him Hobbs rather than John.)

I guess my favourite John fax moment happened after Elton John came into the gallery one morning with a very pleasant young Italian man. Rupert and I showed them round for an hour or so. The Italian showed interest in quite a few, mainly neo-classical, objects, which came to about £300,000. I told him I would courier photos and descriptions of the pieces round to where he was staying.

'I'm sorry, I didn't quite catch your name,' I said.

He responded but still neither Rupert nor I could make it out, so I asked him to write it down, which he did very politely. He turned out to be Gianni Versace.

Later on, I sent him a package which included a list of our best prices on all the pieces he liked. Sometime later on, I received a fax from him making a rather lower offer for the pieces than our £220,000 price. (He was offering around £190,000.) I told John.

'Give me a piece of fucking note paper' was his instant reaction prior to him scrawling out a fax in biro. Now bearing in mind that John had never met Gianni Versace and we could, at that moment, have really done will some sales, both Rupert and I were somewhat surprised by John's fax, which he told me to send pronto. It simply read: 'Piss off you cheap Italian cunt!'

Unbelievably Versace clearly found it quite amusing and ended up buying a few things.

Elton John was a great client as he usually wrote out a cheque on the spot. He was also very kind when John disappeared to various addiction clinics from time to time, writing him good luck cards.

I once took John down to an addiction treatment centre in the West Country, called Clouds, for an assessment interview. (I often used to accompany him to doctors.) After twenty minutes of fairly mundane questions and answers, the counsellor said to John, 'Well, I guess that just about covers things then?'

'Covers things? You're having a laugh!' I exclaimed with incredulity. 'Blimey we haven't even started yet.'

Dr Tony Greenburgh was John's GP. He was as loved as

any doctor could be by his patients, many of them residents of Belgravia and other 'society' characters. My first impression of Tony was that of a small man behind a large desk whose features were almost completely concealed by a wall of vodka and tonics and a heavy cloud of cigarette smoke. John adored Tony, and it was easy to see why. Conversation turned to medical matters, and I eagerly joined in. Towards the end of the appointment, Tony mentioned that he wasn't feeling too well himself.

'Have you tried these, Dr Greenburgh?' I enquired, chucking him a pack of four Solpadeine that I always carried with me.

A glass of cold water was produced and he sampled a couple. As we left he enthusiastically shook my hand saying, 'Thank you for those, I feel much better already.'

I responded, 'My pleasure, Dr Greenburgh, my invoice will be in the post.'

Apart from trading antiques John also acquired a brothel in Slough, which specialised in voluptuous, middle-aged housewives. As you can imagine, this purchase livened up life a little. There were always dramas of one sort or another going on in Slough but they were far more entertaining than had we ended up acquiring a tobacconist's. John had always had a certain predilection for girls with huge tits and bums.

His best buddy at the time was Austrian billionaire and industrial mega-thug Jeffrey Steiner, who seemed to own houses the size of hotels in major cities and resorts all over the world. John and Jeff had an appalling influence on each other and their conduct together was unbefitting of two senior citizens. I once flew to Switzerland as a favour to Jeff to complete some rather bizarre business deal on his behalf. Things didn't go quite as planned and I ended up receiving, quite unjustly on this occasion, all the blame from a very angry Jeff. He could have been the bad guy in a James Bond film without even passing through the make-up department. He could also be highly intimidating in rather a menacing sort of way.

Completely undeterred, and taking a leaf out of John's book, I sent him quite an abusive letter. It ended along the lines of 'I'm not on your payroll, Jeff, and was merely doing you a favour because of your friendship with John. To be honest I've got enough on my plate just now dealing with my dear old mother, Aunt Boo and Aids without you jumping on the bandwagon . . .'

Jeff immediately called John in utter astonishment that one of his employees should have sent such an insulting letter. John always very protective in a situation such as this saw it as a great opportunity to wind Jeff up: 'You must have really, really upset Charlie, you know, Jeff. I've never known him ever write anyone such a letter as this.' As if I didn't write several on a daily basis, mainly on his behalf. The end result was that I received an utterly charming letter, verging on an apology, from Jeff. It was like getting a bunch of flowers from Darth Vader.

John once claimed to me that he was getting married purely to give his partner of many years 'more credibility when she dealt with the builder'. I didn't believe a word of it. He was, *au fond* (as my mother might say), very much a family man and would often move heaven and earth on behalf of his kids. He was always quite staggeringly generous to his two wives and girlfriends.

From time to time my friendship with John was miscon-strued. Laura, an Italian/American girlfriend of John's, once suggested that we were having a gay relationship. I took her aside and explained that her suspicions were absolutely absurd. Firstly, John was about as 'un-gay' and as alpha male as anyone I'd ever met. Secondly, I explained that, in the same way that perhaps her ex-husband liked to talk about golf with his friends as a form of recreation, John and I liked to talk endlessly about mental health and prescription drugs as our form of recreation.

In 2001, the year before I resigned as a director, John's business antics had become increasingly hair-raising and he thought nothing of using such unethical practices such as 'phone-hacking' with the same casualness as a red-top journalist. I brought up the subject of my pay, never a popular topic, and weighed in with, 'Look, old fruit, I am the only other director of John Hobbs Limited yet you treat me like a taxi driver with the fare on the meter whereas in reality I am the get-away driver and the fare's negotiable.'

There was a brief pause before classic John response, 'Do you know what Charlie? Nobody but a complete cunt would ever be a director of my company.'

Never, as it turned out, has a truer word ever been spoken.

———◆———

John died tragically and unexpectedly on 13th March 2011 in the wonderfully eccentric and glamorous flat that he had created for himself at vast cost. During the early hours, he suffered chronic heart failure while in his bathroom and was found later on that day by his sister, Linda. I rushed over as soon as I heard and spent several hours in a state of shock talking with Linda and his nephew Oz until his body was taken away.

'I wish he hadn't died in the bleeding khazi,' said Linda with feeling.

'It's only the great ones that do die in the khazi, Linda,' I replied, also with feeling.

The obituary in the *Daily Telegraph* began, 'John Hobbs, who has died aged 64, emerged from the demi-monde of post-war West London to become one of the most successful antique dealers of his generation . . .' In every generation of antique dealers there is always one character who in the charisma stakes stands out head and shoulders above all the others. In this case it was John Hobbs. As John liked to say, fairly frequently, 'You can't fucking buy charisma!'

In an ideal world I would have liked to have been Elvis Presley's right-hand man during his Las Vegas period, but it turned out being John Hobbs's side-kick came a pretty close second.

For John's funeral the crematorium at Mortlake in south-west London was packed to the rafters. Despite John's explicit instructions, the occasion was, unfortunately, not entirely wanker free, but I felt at least the gesture of his last wish had been made if not precisely executed. The majority of the congregation, however, were colourful enough with several well-known local Chelsea characters from the 1960s, such as Jack Leach, putting in an appearance in heavy cashmere overcoats and dark glasses.

About a week earlier, whilst on holiday in Rajasthan, I

received a surprising text asking if I would be prepared to give John's eulogy. I immediately said yes. That part was easy enough. Three days later, realizing that I had only managed to write about two lines, I woke up in state of some panic imagining myself trying pathetically to put a few notes together in the car park of the crematorium. I owed John more than that and for the next twenty-four hours I sealed myself in the hotel's business centre (eccentrically named 'Good morning sir! Multi functioning office services'). For better or for worse here is the (slightly edited) result:

John Edmund Hobbs (1946–2011)

Firstly, my sincere apologies to the minister here (who, thank God, is a humanist) since any meaningful tribute to John must surely include one or two expletives. Secondly, to make it clear that in the short time I have I could never begin to do justice to this most colourful, charismatic, complicated, charming, stylish, talented, flamboyant, generous and ultimately most tragic and self-destructive of men.

It would be impossible to be indifferent to John Hobbs. John was passionate in every area of his life and consequently everyone who came into contact with him felt equally passionate about him.

I promised John that if I were ever asked to speak at his funeral I would repeat the following. Several years ago, when he was suffering from suspected cancer of the kidneys, I asked John if the worst came to the worst whether he had any specific final wishes he would like me to carry out on his behalf. He thought for a moment and simply replied (in only the way that John could), 'Make sure there are no fucking wankers at my funeral.'

When I first met John in the summer of 1973 he was without doubt the most interesting and magnetic personality I had ever come across with a humorous and thoroughly disrespectful attitude for any form of authority and in particular the background I came from. Our seriously wild mutual friend Charlie Shearer described him then as being possessed of a star quality.

Around that time we went out for dinner with Charlie's rather self-important father who decided during the meal to give John a lecture on Old Etonians. 'Which,' he said 'come in two types. Either they are the most loyal, trustworthy and dependable friends or they are complete shits.'

John waited for a few seconds before responding, 'And into which category do you put yourself then, Mr Shearer?'

John was the absolute master of the art of the 'wind-up' and I, like every member of his family, would be a regular victim of his mischievousness. Nothing amused him more than if we went to a serious business meeting for him to introduce me in the following way: 'This is my managing director, Charlie. He's a poof . . . and he's got Aids.' Or to terrorize some poor accountant who unwittingly drank his coffee out of my mug in the gallery. 'Oh, you're in big trouble now. You've just drunk out of the Aids mug. It's very contagious you know.' The colour would drain from the accountant's face, and I would be left to try to console him with medical fact. On the plus side I will always be grateful to both John and Carlton for employing me when I was unemployable and giving me a chance when no one else would.

I remember a John classic. He had just been sitting around in the kitchen at the gallery with some friends from Alcoholics Anonymous. When they left, I asked him how come he seemed to be the local doyen of AA and yet he was still drinking. 'Oh,' he said, 'you don't understand; it is just the DESIRE to stop drinking that is the requirement for membership.' He then continued, 'And do you know what my favourite moment is? It's sitting in my car outside the Walton Street AA meeting and while I'm rolling myself a joint I keep thinking to myself that even if I was the richest geezer in the whole world no money could buy the entertainment that I'm about to have for the next hour and a half'.

John also had the knack of becoming the quasi-victim in really bizarre Pinteresque scenarios. Such as in his twenties when he feared for his mind and consulted a psychiatrist, who promptly fell in love with him. The psychiatrist persuaded him to drive him around as a form of therapy and then subsequently confessed to John that he had murdered his wife. Only this sort of thing seemed to happen to John and regularly did.

Going anywhere with John was always an adventure however unpromising the mission.

There was the evening in the 1970s when John and half a dozen or so others, including Charlie Shearer, were enjoying a late-night poker session in the Salamis Restaurant, Fulham Road, when a man with a gun and a grievance charged in. Within seconds at least seven fairly well-built blokes had managed to barricade themselves into a lavatory on a landing designed for one medium-sized individual.

The Fine Art of Dealing Antiques

When living in Tite Street, I guess around 1968, John quite innocently lent his Saab to Nicholas van Hoogstraten for a weekend. The following week much to John's surprise he was arrested on suspicion of conspiracy to murder. It subsequently turned out that the now infamous van Hoogstraten had used John's car to fire-bomb two Rabbis in Brighton he had taken against.

Some history. John was born in 1946 and lived, when very young, in St Albans before the family moved to Fulham. To describe his parents, Sid and Kitty, as characters would frankly be an understatement. Their father Sid had a shop on the King's Road which sold all sorts of old things called 'Odds and Hobbs'. This and knocking with Jack Leach (proprietor of the infamous Gasworks restaurant in Chelsea) was John's introduction to the antiques business, and he soon became very adept at using his youth, looks and charisma to charm wonderful objects and furniture from grand homes, clubs and offices in the West End. To quote society favourite, Christopher Gibbs, 'He was then a youth of striking beauty who looked as if he'd strayed from a band of angels in a Quattrocento painting'.

Very fashion-conscious, he was also somewhat of a ladies' man. However, I will not attempt here to delve into John's rich personal life as it is not my place to. (I'd like to get out of here alive.)

When I met John he operated entirely from a 1968 Maroon Peugeot 404 estate. A car that to this day still holds the world record for unpaid parking tickets.

It took some time and several false starts for John and Carlton to form the unstoppable partnership which propelled them in a few short years from 'running furniture' to being major antiques dealers on the world stage.

In those more carefree days all was fair in love and war, and it was not long before they acquired a base together in the Furniture Cave. It always amused both John and Carlton that having met them once for all of ten minutes my father summed them and their company up as follows: 'In my opinion,' he said, 'one day you are all going to be taken away in a Black Maria.' My mother, on the other hand, had a very soft spot for John and he for her, stemming perhaps from the fact they both suffered from extreme self-destructive tendencies and periodic bouts of black depression.

It was also around this time that John embarked on a decade of psychoanalysis. I clearly remember asking him why he was doing it. His answer – I guess referring to his wild days hanging out with John Bindon – was classic John: 'For years, I thought I was so clever fucking everyone else and then I woke up one morning and realised that the only person I was really fucking was myself'.

I think these early days of success at the Cave were perhaps John's happiest. It was a very different place to what it is now, being then more like a club. John absolutely loved to hold court at the Furniture Cave playing poker and backgammon almost always dressed in an ankle length leather overcoat with the collar up. He once flew to Dallas with Fletcher [a close friend] and somehow managed to relieve poor old Fletch of a six-figure sum playing backgammon during the flight. My memory is that you never wanted to bet against John because he had an uncanny habit of always winning.

It was often said of John that he was born lucky and the brothers complemented themselves in so much as John was always the front man, the showman, whereas Carlton preferred to stay in the background.

I think it was the next level of success, when in 1987 they moved to Pimlico Road, that sat so uncomfortably with John. By 1990 the cracks in the relationship between his brother and him were all too apparent for those of us working closely with them.

In 1993, almost immediately after Kitty's death, John and Carlton split the company into two halves in a demerger. It was Carlton who forced the issue and I'm certain that John never forgave him.

With the split John moved into the huge gallery in Dove Walk where he could indulge his own fantasies and whims unrestrained. Rupert and I worked with him and we had a lot of fun. We even managed to acquire a brothel in Slough.

John Hobbs Ltd was a world-class success on every front. A spectacular gallery displaying amazingly glamorous pieces in a truly dramatic and theatrical way . . .

The clients were as ritzy and as exotic as the furniture and works of art and included amongst many, many others: Valentino, Hubert Givenchy, Bill Blass, Gianni Versace, and Elton John. They were all mesmerized by John.

Of all the clients nobody loved John more than his great buddy and billionaire client Jeffrey Steiner who had wandered into the original Pimlico Road shop one Saturday afternoon in 1988 and breezily spent over £1 million. I used to describe them as two old men behaving disgracefully. Frankly they were as bad as each other. Once at Jeff's mansion in the south of France John was persuaded to give an elderly and very straight-laced guest a joint. The guest, who was also in the billionaire club, promptly collapsed and it was assumed he was dead. Jeff went into total panic shouting, 'If they find a fucking corpse here I'll be ruined. Just get rid of it. I don't care how.' In a plan worthy of a Peter Seller's farce someone produced a Mercedes limo and John and Jeff tried to heave the body into the trunk of the car only to crack it's head on the boot lid. At this point the lifeless came to life and not unreasonably enquired 'What the fuck is going on here?'

I think that this was a fairly typical John and Jeff evening. Jeff sadly died several years ago. If he hadn't I can assure you I wouldn't be telling this story. I have quite enough on my plate sorting out John's lawsuits without being sued for defamation by Jeff as well. The highest point of financial success at John Hobbs came with the sale at Phillips in New York in 2002 where all the genuine stock was sold and John received a massive multi-million pound payoff which he promptly, in true John style, spent within weeks.

John had a very human and compassionate side to him and I know that there are several people here who have received unprecedented acts of generosity from him over the years. However, tributes to John as a father, former husband, former partner, brother, grandfather, uncle and brother in law are entirely a family matter and thus I will leave them entirely to the family . . .

I can however say that from my perspective John was always good to his family and for all of them there will be a huge void left in their lives.

The Fine Art of Dealing Antiques

For myself and I suspect many others life and the world will be that much less entertaining, that much less colourful and let's face it that much less crazy without John.

8

Letters to Johnny
(J. R. Vaughan, JA4307)

In the early days following my Aids diagnosis in January 1986, few places were more important to me than the Parsons Green branch of Video Shuttle, conveniently situated not 50 yards from my flat. I was at the time rather reluctantly adhering to the strict principles of Narcotics Anonymous so I wasn't drinking or abusing anything worth of a mention. I was, however, feeling distinctly rough and one afternoon stumbled in there for another couple of films.

There was a very chirpy, good-looking boy behind the counter, whom I hadn't seen before, chatting away merrily to another customer. When it came to my turn, I was slightly surprised when he addressed me as follows: 'You always pissed then?'

Quite quick for me, particularly under the circumstances, I instantly responded, 'Only when I'm driving as it happens, if it's any fucking business of yours.'

Somehow this brief exchange became the cornerstone for an unusual friendship that still endures on. Johnny, who was about twenty at the time, possessed an intense curiosity and an opinion on absolutely everything. This was combined with unparalleled enthusiasm, and what I can only describe as a humungous zest for life.

I began to rather look forward to my visits to Video Shuttle purely for the entertainment value that I got from a half-hour chat with Johnny. The conversations were so fast, so intensely stimulating and so insanely varied that I left feeling pleasantly exhausted. When I got to know him a little better, I would occasionally take him for a spin in my latest motor. Johnny would jump in, park himself expectantly on the passenger seat and announce with some gusto, as if we were doing a television documentary, 'Motoring with Chas!' Johnny talked even faster than I drove, which frankly was quite an achievement.

On every level, he really was a lot of fun and certainly as far as I was concerned, during a period when I was generally considered to be some sort of social untouchable hovering somewhere on the threshold of life and death, a breath of fresh air. There was the added bonus that I got all my videos for free. Prior to this, I was once so determined to avoid a £12 overdue fine that I induced a friend to call him up and explain that I'd had a bad fall down the stairs and thus had been unable to return the films on time. What I hadn't expected was that Johnny was so concerned that he promptly locked up the shop and came storming round to check if I was okay.

One day, entirely based on my rather vivid description of my eccentric political activist aunt, Johnny thought he spotted her in Fulham Road Post Office. He bounced up and excitedly announced, 'You must be Aunt Boo'. By some insane coincidence, it was indeed my aunt and, after a somewhat lively conversation, Johnny insisted on carrying all her shopping home. It was an encounter that she was never to forget and from then on she always referred to him as 'My darling Johnny'.

The owner of Video Shuttle was, even by my standards, a total nutcase and a rather challenging individual to work for. After Johnny had one of his regular run-ins with him, I came up with the genius idea that he should come and work for John K (Toyboy) and me as salesman in our fledgling boxer-short company Raffateer Limited (slogan: *The boxer shorts for men that women like*). Despite arriving thirty minutes late for his interview he got the job and was instantly promoted to head of sales at £100 a week.

Raffateer manufactured 95 per cent of its stock in Thailand (Bangkok) and Indonesia (Jakarta, Yogyakarta and Bali). Neither Toyboy nor I had any previous experience of the rag trade whatsoever, his family business being shipping. So it was an interesting learning curve for us at times. The previous year we had embarked on a six-week buying trip in Asia. It got off to a rather poor start. In the taxi from Bangkok airport the enthusiastic driver launched into, 'You wanna fuck my sister . . . brother . . . mother?'

All these kind offers were politely declined, though he suddenly had a eureka moment as we pulled up outside our hotel.

'I know,' he exclaimed to me, excitedly pointing to Toyboy (who looked all of about fourteen years old), 'you fucking baby.' To say Toyboy looked utterly appalled would not do his expression justice.

We spent a week in Bangkok and ended up ordering 10,000 pairs of silk boxers. We were both delighted, until we tried to sell them. The unfortunate fact was that Toyboy was about 26 inches round the waist; I was a mere two inches larger; and Thai men aren't exactly giants. The result was that our carefully worked out sizing programme, in which I was a 'Large' and Toyboy a 'Medium' was for the rest of the population rather on the small size. The shorts were unsalable other than for people of extremely restricted growth or children.

We moved on to Jakarta, where we obtained a list of potential manufacturers from the British Consulate. We trudged round them, while I became increasing sweaty and grumpy. We eventually found ourselves sitting in the corridor of what appeared to be an old aircraft hangar masquerading as a factory, when a friendly Indonesian came bouncing up and stuck his hand.

'Happy?' he said.

I replied rather brusquely, 'No, actually I'm not. Why should I be?'

Embarrassingly, it turned out he was merely introducing himself as his name was Epi. Rather ashamed of my colonial-style rudeness, I profusely apologised.

Back in the UK the company did quite well and we sold to Topman, Harrods, Next, Liberty and so on, fortunately with the right-sized shorts. I pulled off a bit of a coup at London Fashion Week. We had taken a stand at Olympia, not realising that it was entirely for women's clothing. Undeterred, we gave it our best shot. About halfway through the show the Prime Minister, Maggie Thatcher, put in an appearance. I had by then become quite matey with the girl in the organiser's office who made all the announcements and somehow managed to persuade her to put out a message over the public address system: 'Would the Prime Minister and her entourage kindly make their way to stand number 48, Raffateer Limited . . . the boxer shorts that exude masculinity in the bedroom.' Apart from anything else, it also got us a mention on Radio 4's *Woman's Hour*.

Johnny immediately entered into the spirit of or company, while wryly observing that Toyboy 'had fifteen good minutes in him between his first and second drink'. Big trouble, however, was lurking just round the corner.

Out of the blue, an old schoolmate of Johnny's appeared, pleading for help. He claimed some gangsters were hassling and threatening him unless he came up with a source for obtaining large amounts of cocaine. At first Johnny said it wasn't his world and he was sorry but he couldn't help. However, after a little more persuasion, Johnny's desire to help a friend in need, combined with his insatiable curiosity got the better of him. He introduced the hoodlums to some contacts he had been told about and a deal was set up. Unfortunately, the hoodlums turned out to be cops: the whole story that had been presented to Johnny turned out to have been an elaborately staged police sting.

Johnny was arrested and charged as a perpetrator at a motorway services on the M1. On hearing of his arrest, Aunt Boo went into campaign mode and immediately wrote a letter to the Home Secretary expressing outrage.

(Although I have always viewed Johnny as the victim of 'police entrapment' in all this, Johnny does not. When I met up with him recently he very generously told me that I could write what I liked provided he was never portrayed as anything other than an offender getting his just desserts.)

Despite being promised a mere £100 from the purported multi-thousand pound deal, Johnny, at the age of just twenty-one, was suddenly looking at many years behind bars and a criminal record as a serious drugs dealer. The worst thing about it was that he was technically guilty and demonstrating a credible defence was always going to be an uphill struggle.

I was really distressed when I heard what had happened and immediately threw myself into doing what I could to challenge what I saw as a huge injustice. I knew, however, that announcing to the judge that the police are liars wouldn't get Johnny far – not much further than when Sam Cooper's cat-burgling brother-in-law Barney said to a judge when he was asked if he had anything to say before sentencing: 'It's all right for you sitting up there in your fucking wig and what not. I bet you've never done a fucking day's work in your life, you silly old cunt.'

As a start, I introduced myself to Johnny's parents and formed an instant bond with his dad Randal. We both enjoyed a keen interest in DIY and all things mechanical, although his DIY efforts, like mine, sometimes produced unfortunate results. I once surprised him at his Rutland cottage to find him defrosting his fridge. Eager to speed up the process, he had directed a fan heater at the interior. The result was that when he returned some fifteen minutes later to see how things were thawing, he found that it wasn't just the ice that had melted. The entire inside of the fridge had sagged like an old lugubrious face. As a consolation prize I took Randal for a spin in my newly acquired BMW M5 at breakneck speed round the perimeter of a new reservoir.

I persuaded Johnny to dismiss the local solicitors he was using, who I felt were too naive with regard to the police's disingenuous activities, and take on slick, London-based criminal solicitors Offenbach and Co. Everyone was very optimistic about Johnny making bail and, in a moment of wild generosity, I officially offered to put up substantial bail. In the event it wasn't needed: he was remanded in Leicester jail, which was a bitter blow. I drove up to Leicester quite a few times and always found Johnny in surprisingly good form under the circumstances. He later wrote of his experiences in prison that it was 'rather like being stuck at a bus stop in a bad part of town'.

An unusual consolation for me was that I had struck up a good friendship with the mother of James M, one of Johnny's co-defendants. I met Renate in the glamorous confines of the visitor's waiting room in HMP Leicester. She was German and had been married to a rich industrialist. I was very amused by her from the moment I heard her stridently taking on the prison authorities in a strong German accent on behalf of her son. Almost the first thing she said to me was, 'I bet they're all saying, "Oh no, it's that nightmare German woman on the rampage again!"' On the strength of that remark I offered her a lift back to London and for several years afterwards she used to invite me round for dinner at her house in Knightsbridge.

Johnny's case reached the Crown Court, by which time the outcome was pretty much a foregone conclusion. He was finally released early in 1990, some two years and several months after his initial arrest.

A few months following his release, after a stint on a local paper, he went along with a friend who was auditioning for a commercial video. Never one to hold back Johnny insisted on having a go. He turned out to be a natural and his fortunes started to change. Johnny has been a household name now for well over twenty years, presenting the hugely popular *The Big Breakfast* for four years, followed by seven years hosting the Capital Radio show, *Capital Breakfast*.

I wrote him a series of letters while he was incarcerated in the hope that they would entertain him and keep his spirits up. In retrospect they reveal something about me at the time – my feelings of futility about my existence – and the various antics of local characters whom Johnny knew such as the Hobbs, Aunt Boo and my then on-off partner, the irrepressible Bazil.

31 December 1988

Dear Jon,

Thanks very much for your letter. What you said is very much appreciated. If it's any consolation I think you're coping in a nightmare situation with balls, humour and dignity. You have certainly earned my respect (for what that's worth).

Finch and Cooper send you their best. Finch currently has a large overemotional bird in tow what drinks a lot and then gets excited. I think he finds hourly promises of undying love claustrophobic. I drove them to Heathrow to catch a plane for a holiday on some tropical island, the bird was blotto and Finch looked more like a man about to start a life sentence than a pre-nuptial beano. Cooper has fallen in love again for the first time. Only this time it's 'the time' he tells me. I am a go-between for lovey dovey messages.

Lucky Lupin

On Christmas Eve I caught a virulent flu and was unable to leave bed let alone talk. Bazil, little charmer that he is, not only failed to bring me so much as a cup of tea or give me a Christmas card but fucked off to what he described as a more fun Christmas elsewhere. Luckily ex-girlfriend Veronica took pity on me and brought round several tangerines, a maroon waistcoat with brass buttons and a small abstract she'd painted. Christmas was as grim as ever. I managed to immerse myself in a heavy treacle of self-pity and spent several days reflecting, as one does at such times, on the general fuck up one has made of one's life and why yet again Christmas is spent alone vaguely looking out of a window. I suppose the fact that one isn't jumping out of the window must be taken as a plus point.

Aunt Boo is on your case and sends you lots of love. She's convinced the authorities acted too hastily by locking you up (I don't think for once she's too far off the mark) and is threatening now to write to the prime minister. She refers to you as 'my darling Johnny'.

I think John Hobbs has the answer to Christmas. He bought Roy Orbison's greatest hits which he then played at some volume in his custom-built convertible Mercedes whilst he spent the entire day motoring round the home counties. Sebastian H.-P.'s winter break has been strangely quiet after last year's writ-winning performance.

I gather Toyboy put on a fairly interesting display of malevolence at number 12 The Little Boltons after consuming half a litre of vodka. As a result, his allowance is being terminated his father no doubt content that his son will be able to survive comfortably on the substantial income he informed them he got from running London's underworld.

Letters to Johnny (J. R. Vaughan, JA4307)

I will definitely come and see you next week if you could let your mother know when it's okay.

Be lucky and see you soon,

Chas

17 January 1989

Dear Jon,

Thanks for your excellent letter. Sorry not to have written before. I have problems with both lethargy and self-motivation. Somehow living in London makes it almost impossible for me to concentrate long enough to either read a decent book or to write anything of the remotest interest to anyone. Instead I find myself transfixed by mindless dribble on the television such as 'Going for Gold' which I always seemed to end up watching whilst I have my first two Solpadeine of the day and three Marlboro Lights.

The event of last week was poor Minos's funeral, who was tragically murdered at Lockerbie. It took place in a vast and ornate Greek Orthodox church in Bayswater. As you could possibly imagine the entire street was jammed with Mercedes-Benz sedans, all with fully uniformed chauffeurs and curtains. I gather all the big ship-owners were there. A lot of the woman looked not unlike Mrs Robinson in 'The Graduate', sort of tragically expensive. The entire event could have been part of a 1960's film, a decade to which most of the women's clothing seemed to belong. At the end of the two hour service rather than sing 'Abide with Me' we all filed past and in some cases even kissed the coffin before shaking hands with the family.

On Monday I bought a microwave oven, yesterday I gave my

217

first ever attempt at a dinner party, today I have spent in bed with unpleasant food poisoning. I don't think these three events are entirely disconnected.

Everybody I see sends you their best wishes from the Hobbs Bros to that fat fucker Stephen King.

I have decided that I might as well drop out largely because I don't think I've ever really dropped in and I can't think of anything else to do. My plan is to buy a farm in Bordeaux this summer and write a short book in the form of a hundred-page letter to Charlie Shearer. By the time I've finished it I shall probably be able to give it to him personally. I'm not feeling great today which is why this letter is fairly dull. I hope that life with you is bearable and that you're managing to keep your spirits up despite the flak you're probably getting from some of your family. My dad who spent most of the last war in German POW camps said that none of it was quite as bad as the first term at his preparatory school.

I plan to see you this Friday but will check first with your mother to see if that's okay.

Look after yourself and be lucky,

Chas

1 March 1989

Dear Jon,

Sorry I haven't written before. No excuse bar lethargy and lack of application. Thanks for your excellent letter and postscript from James M. I shall be seeing Toyboy when I get back from Devon next week. By that time I will have read the prosecution papers which James's mother is kindly going to show me. Apart from other things, I shall point out to him that despite his strange assertion that you worked for him and that you were a habitual drug abuser, that I had already written to Mr Kiltly [solicitor] as your employer on behalf of Raffateer saying that you were extremely hard working, reliable and that should you get bail we would happily re-employ you. With two such conflicting reports from your so called employers the only solution I can see is that both rat boy and myself appear in court as witnesses. It will be interesting to see how the kindergarten gangster gets on confirming his untruths and disloyalties to you, James and the rest of the court, under oath and face to face.

My holiday. I was rather expecting Morocco to be fun and sun which is probably why I only packed a pair of shorts and a Tshirt. I was therefore no less than a little surprised to find it was about 10 degrees colder than Margate is at this time of year. Frankly hanging around some murky pit masquerading as a swimming pool in sub-zero temperatures for two weeks was so depressing both Nick K and myself decided to head for the nearest warm sounding destination pronto. This happened to be the Sahara Desert. We motored for three days down dried river beds and goat tracks which didn't exactly enhance the condition of our hired Renault 4 which wasn't far short of being an MOT failure when we took delivery of it. On reaching the desert we bought the appropriate gear, rented a couple of virtually moribund camels and hobbled off into a sand storm.

Not much to report from London. I helped John Hobbs now affectionately known as 'The Dada' (Joe Orton's *Loot*) to buy a house in Notting Hill Gate for a shade under three quarters of a million nicker. The plan was to move his entire family in there. This rather ambitious project has not been a success and Hobbs has fled to Dallas to recover from the bloodletting. The house is now known as 'South Fork'. On the flight over he somehow managed to win £7,000 playing backgammon with Fletcher. I work virtually full time with them now. Last week I bought a hideously ornate mirror for rather more than I paid for my flat. Hobbs paid £162,000 for a desk estimated by the auctioneers at £800 which got us a fair bit of amusing publicity. I wrote the press release and mentioned that the desk had been made by cabinetmaker George Bullock so you can possibly imagine the result in the *Sun*, i.e. 'A load of old bullocks'.

I am sorry this letter is a little disjointed but I have to leave for my office in Devon in about three minutes. I have been tartly informed that I haven't put in an appearance there for at least a month and a half.

I will come and see you next week. Hope that life isn't too unbearable.

Be lucky,

Chas

20 November 1989

Dear Jon,

I'm not going to comment on the mind-boggling legal charade that you have been subjected to because whatever I had to say would be inadequate. Suffice to say that dishonest policemen and tunnel-visioned, self-opinionated old cunts masquerading as umpires of fair play and justice are all too common. You have had a raw deal and have every right to feel both bitter and angry because I certainly do. What makes your position so frustrating is that there is so little anyone can do about it. I have spoken at length with Graham Huston [JV's solicitor at Offenbach and Co.] who says the whole case has left a very unpleasant taste in his mouth. He reckons you could be free within nine months which probably, right now, seems to you like nine fucking centuries. That said considering how badly wrong it's all gone the result isn't as bad as it could be, a pretty imbecilic remark in itself, but I can't think of anything much more constructive to say.

Partly as a result of your experiences I am applying to take a three-year law degree at Ealing Poly starting next September. I don't like bullying of any sort particularly by the so-called authorities and by becoming a barrister myself (admittedly rather late in life and if I live that long) I will be able to put my life to some sort of use. Life on the outside isn't exactly a party at present but I won't bore you with my problems.

Last week Josh, Cooper's young nephew was stopped by the Old Bill in Fulham and was taken back to the station to be searched for drugs. He acted very flash because he knew he was innocent. When they eventually released him they kicked him very hard. He turned round outside the station and mouthed wankers at them. Two seconds later two of them got him by each arm whilst another one punched him repeatedly in the face. As this policeman drew back his arm for another blow Josh nutted him and he fell unconscious. Another Old Bill then appeared and between them they rammed Josh's head into three walls and dragged him to a cell semi-conscious. At this point the other Old Bill who was laid out recovered consciousness and appeared like some deranged animal and attacked him again. Josh, who is a big lad, managed to nut him again and they withdrew. Poor old Cooper was rung at three in the morning by a very traumatized Josh. He said, 'I want you to take down the numbers of these police who have beaten me up', at this point he heard somebody shouting in the background to get Josh off the phone to stop him giving out the numbers. The phone then went dead. he drove straight over where he said that the police were very nervous and were if anything being over co-operative. I recommended your solicitor, GH, who arranged a barrister and the next morning Josh was released on bail. The police have now, can you believe, after beating him half to death, the vindictiveness to charge him with maliciously wounding a police officer. Since they have cooled down they want to reduce the charge but Josh's barrister won't let them. He has a medical report of Josh's state and says he wants it to be heard in front of a jury.

Still enough of all that bollxcks.

I hear you have a job in the kitchen. Does that mean you are a cook? I pity any poor sod that ends up with your Hungarian goulash. This letter is more a series of ramblings than anything else, not up to the usual standard I'm sorry to say. I'm probably not depressed enough. You'll be pleased to hear that at the last minute I couldn't bear to part with the M5, so losing my licence now is only a matter of time.

My strange friend the Australian chancellor [Paul Keating] is over here. I said to him on Friday that I was thinking of taking a law degree. 'A law degree mate,' he said (imagine strong Aussie accent), 'that's for mugs. I went into politics aged fourteen without any qualifications bar enthusiasm and I've been running the country's economy for eight years, in fact I've been running the whole fucking country for the past three.' 'What was your reason? What drove you on?' I asked. Then followed a party political broadcast on behalf of the Australian Labour Party with sentences like 'I've given the poor and underprivileged a better

222

deal than they've ever had' etc. etc. and so on, so I responded, 'Why do think that I want a law degree Paul? I want to be a champion of the underdog.' 'Oh,' he said. 'I just thought that you were into some sort of self-betterment shit. If it's a cause you've got going then go for it. You'll piss it, matey.'

On Thursday I'm off to stay with that legendary marriage breaker Seb Lust-Patten. It's now after midnight so I'd better get some kip. Everybody sends you their best, etc. and nobody is unmoved by your predicament. I only wish there was more I could do or say. My dad is eighty on Wednesday, I feel it today.

Be lucky,

Chas

18 January 1990

Dear Jon,

Something fairly strange happened this morning. I was just getting into my bath when I realized as my foot went in that I was still fully clothed. I then panicked and fell in. Maybe I'm really losing the plot? Whatever the plot is. As usual about a million apologies for not writing before. I just find it incredibly hard to actually sit down and use mental application, in fact you are just about the only person I have written to in the last decade or so. Running off at the mouth down the phone I find a whole lot easier.

Christmas was at least marginally less depressing than last year. I was meant to be staying with my godfather in Brighton who decided at the last minute that he'd rather get utterly blitzed and miss out on Christmas altogether. Christmas eve was spent calming Veronica who seemed to be going through some sort of emotional crisis, who isn't for that matter? My ageing parents drove up to Cumberland to stay with a distant cousin who chose the festive season as a good time to leave his wife which made the atmosphere cheerful. On Christmas Day my dad fell ill and demanded to be driven home. My mother having complied with his request then managed to write her car off en route. I then had to drive down and rescue them from Cheltenham Hospital where my dad had refused to be admitted despite cracked ribs and other injuries muttering that this ranked as the worst Christmas he'd ever had including five years as a German POW. I gather after the accident he leaned out of the smoldering remains of my mother's VW Scirocco and shouted at the other driver 'Fuck you, you've killed me you cunt.' I then spent several days trying to defuse a stalemate at my parents' home in that my dad lay in bed refusing to move feigning dead whilst my dear mother got blotto in the kitchen. Having used all the persuasive powers in my possession to sort that one out I then headed off to see in the New Year with Hannah Rothschild.

Arriving a little late I was surprised to literally pass the Prime Minister on the drive (three miles of it) who had just been lunching there. Maggie had, I gather, been on cracking form and at the end of lunch when a toast was proposed in honour of ten years as PM she turned to Arnold Weinstock (head of GEC) and said, 'You might at least smile Arnold,' to which he replied (imagine strong Jewish accent), 'Give me some cause, Margaret, give me some cause and then I'll smile.' As the clock struck midnight and the 1980s ended I grabbed Jacob Rothschild by the hand thinking to myself, 'Everything you touch turns to gold so I might as well be the first one in for the next decade.'

Business is diabolical and I'm feeling very skint. Bazil has swanned off to Bali for a few weeks leaving me with a monumental phone bill. Hobbs is attempting to come off Valium (again!) and has bought a very small and savage dog. Finch thinks he has caught BSE (mad cow disease). Cooper's love life finally caught up with him when his current girlfriend and Mrs C came to blows. Toobad is tottering on the verge of bankruptcy (his flat at 217 is now up for sale).

I ran into Simon Tapper and we both agreed that if possible we would come and visit you together later in the year (hopefully you'll be a free man before then). I really like Simon he reminds me of a Jack Russell plenty of spirit and guts.

I spoke to Randal [Johnny's dad] earlier who said that Lincoln is not much fun. I wish there was something I could do to extricate you from this totally unjust situation. I only hope that life is at least bearable, at least now there is an end in sight.

As always everyone sends you their best, etc.

Be lucky,

Chas

29 March 1990

Dear Jon,

About a million apologies for not having written to you before. Many thanks for your letter. I'm glad that at least you've been moved to a marginally better place than Lincoln. Your experiences during this saga have been little short of a living nightmare. Your appeal being the final farce. I won't bang on with my views on how callously and unfairly you've been dealt with but I can say that it has pissed me off so seriously that I am

225

giving up being a spiv and have (you will be amazed to hear) been accepted on a three years full time law degree course starting this autumn.

This is the first time I've ever used this portable word processing machine bought from Nick K for huge amounts of lolly. I don't care for it all that much but nor do I for most bits of modern technology. Frankly I think I was born into the wrong era, on the other hand where would I be without Solpadeine? (As my dad might say, an example perhaps of Newton's Law on Compensation?) Life has not been short of incidents lately. A couple of weeks ago Finch rang me at about midnight to say that the police had just called him to say that his new bookshop in Bond Street was on fire. As you know nothing cheers me up more than the opportunity to drive at extremely high speed with what I consider to be total justification. Finch spent the entire trip to the West End chewing Valium and burbling on about bankruptcy.

I tried to console him 'I promise you there's nothing to worry about, pet, all you'll find is that the old dosser in the upstairs flat has upset his chip pan. When we get there you'll feel very silly about all this fuss you're making.' When we got there to find Bond Street totally blocked by no less than three ambulances, seven fire tenders and numerous TV news crews someone else felt fairly silly. Finch, actually, has dealt with this disaster with both humour and spirit and I'm now on the payroll as some sort of ageing trouble-shooter cum loss adjuster.

Toobad has finally gone skint having somehow managed to spunk the best part of half a million nicker (of his wife's dough) in the last eighteen months. I sold his flat to Bazil's friend Mark Cohen and have rented the basement out to Boris (drummer with The Cure), currently doing a runner from his wife. I once managed a band he was in, poor sod. Anyway the result is rather a bizarre household here. Serial-shagger Cooper has also gone bust and has been forced not only to go back to work but also to his long-suffering wife. In fact virtually everybody is doing badly financially at present even Grant-Sturgis is down to his last million he reckons and I've recently been forced to flog my favourite painting [*The Muse* by Eileen Agar] to raise a few quid for the inland revenue boys. As yet have still just managed to cling on to the M5. On the other hand the brothers are both on good form and prospering.

It would be good to see you sometime, perhaps I could drive up with Simon Tapper?

My aunt Pam died the other day from emphysema (which was sad) and because my uncle was a general and ex-commander in chief of this and that she had a very large and formal funeral which was made slightly less formal by the behaviour of her two sisters namely Aunt Boo (who rings the Prime Minister about you regularly) and my dear mother. Aunt Boo and her family resembled a shifty gang of Romanian refugees making a midnight break for the border. My mother whilst at least dressed conventionally had had her noggin in the Martini bucket since dawn. It hadn't helped that the previous evening there had been a classic alcohol-fuelled Mortimer family showdown in 'Cuntbury'. During the service the plan was that I did the first reading and my mother the second one. When it came to my mother's turn she had some trouble making it to the lectern and when she got there somehow managed to face the wrong way. After what seemed like a lifetime she realized her mistake and tried to manoeuvre round it. This was not executed successfully as my mother was under the impression that the lectern was fixed to the floor. It wasn't. The result was she fell over taking the lectern, the Bible and everything else with her. All this in front of around 400 astonished (understatement) mourners. The whole thing was so surreal that I was absolutely paralysed to the spot thinking 'this just cannot be happening'. Finally, a sergeant in the Parachute Regiment came to the rescue and in a very kindly fashion put both my mother and the lectern back on their feet. But this wasn't the end. Having regained some composure and at least now facing the congregation my mother then launched into a very sombre Bible tract as if she was auditioning for a leading role in a weird mixture of *Hamlet* and *West Side Story*. Otherwise she did very well. Later I saw my father offering £100 for anyone other than my mother to drive him home.

It's now about two in the morning and I'm flying to Scotland at daybreak so I'd better get some kip. Once again, I'm sorry this letter took so long in coming. I'll try to write more regularly.

Nick K went skiing last week with one of the directors of his firm, Wandering Moonbeam. Sadly, the director skied flat out over a small ravine, collided with a boulder and died.

As always everyone sends you their best and all are equally appalled by the way you've been treated.

Finch has just had a son called Jack. I'm a godfather if I live as long as the Christening.

Be lucky,

Chas

Letters to Johnny (J. R. Vaughan, JA4307)

Summer 1990

Dear Jon,

Because it's in the attic my bedroom recently has been more like the punishment hut in the film 'The Bridge over the River Kwai'. In last year's heat-wave I came out in a rash which my doctor told me was normally only found in tropical jungles. To escape experiencing a similar fate this year I'm off to Zambia this afternoon with Nick K. Last Friday, which I am told was the hottest day recorded since 1911, an old friend of mine shot himself in full view of his wife and two children. He was affectionately known as 'Pebble specs', for fairly obvious reasons. I liked him a lot as he was invariably rude to everyone in a rather stylish way which I, for one, found highly entertaining. The last time I saw him it was at a party. 'Oh Christ,' he exclaimed on seeing me 'it's the fucking resurrection. Good God, Charlie, I thought you'd died years ago!'

The Hobbs are on spirited form although business according to John is 'fucking diabolical' so to keep ourselves amused we are suing difficult customers. I have recently been given a shareholding in Nick K's computer company, as yet (our mutual friend) his brother Toyboy, whom I haven't acknowledged for over two years, is unaware of my new status. I believe he is the only other shareholder which should prove interesting. I am also now a salaried partner in Finch's rare book firm. So I am not as bored and depressed as usual. That said I am still fairly skint and sadly had to very reluctantly flog the M5. I recently wrote an account of my final trip when I drove it to Amsterdam with Nick K for Easter, a journey made not without incident. On the strength of it there's a small chance I am to be part time motoring correspondent for *Tatler Magazine*.

I start school at Ealing in September. Do I need to buy a satchel? Bazil and his friend Mark Cohen have now moved into Toobad's old flat on the ground floor. Bazil now lives in far greater style than I do.

More importantly, how are things with you? I spoke to your ma the other day who persuaded me to buy you some rather strange and expensive underwear from Harvey Nichols (what's wrong with Raffateer Boxers may I ask?). She said that your first crack at parole comes up soon. If you want any books, computer manuals or anything let me know. After Nick K's tuition I've become rather a computer buff which should impress your dad. I've just persuaded poor old Finch to spend about twenty thousand nicker on PCs and software which depresses him a lot since he is incapable of even turning it on. He is also convinced that all his confidential information will by stolen by infiltrators. I suggested that possibly they wouldn't be that interested. Since getting married most of his wife's family have either died or been committed to secure hospitals and his Australian nanny is always getting pissed and then gets shagged by local Irish labourers. He sends his best and is now a confirmed Solpadeine man. I have bought an old Mercedes sedan which resembles an Athens mini cab, the interior is bile green and dead nasty but at least it has air conditioning.

A couple of months ago I was given some filthy pills [AZT] by the Aids Clinic which made me feel perpetually seasick morning, noon and night. After a memorably appalling month I ceremoniously binned them and resumed my daily (hourly sometimes) ration of Solpadeine etc. and feel much better as a result. Some bossy lady doctor at the hospital told me that I was totally irresponsible. I responded, 'Don't worry, love, it might never happen.' This annoyed her considerably, which was, of course, the intention.

I now have about fifteen minutes left to pack and get to the airport.

I'll next be in touch from central Africa if World War Three hasn't broken out by then.

Be lucky,

Chas

20 November 1990

Dear Jon,

As usual I'm sorry for not having written for so long. Many thanks for your letter and message on the ansaphone. I'm up to my eyeballs in old shit and work and it's largely your fault! If you hadn't ended up inside I would never have gone to law school. I started almost three months ago and is harder work than I could ever have imagined in my wildest dreams. This particular school takes people that have the sort of qualifications (or lack of) that wouldn't get you a job in a car wash and after three years turns out the same percentage of first degrees as Oxford and Cambridge. I am now discovering that this doesn't happen by magic. The age of students ranges from around sixty down to sixteen. When we have a roll call it sounds like entries for the Miss World Competition. I've made two friends 'Black Kevin from Reading' and an ex-sergeant from the Flying Squad. To date I've only been sent home once. I was looking out of a window during rather a dreary class on contract law when the old bag of a lecturer suddenly exclaims, 'You are clearly not with us, Mr Mortimer. What exactly out there is so fascinating?' So I

231

responded, 'I'm sorry, Miss, but I think that your broomstick is being clamped. If you get your skates on you might just catch them.' Although I'm older than most of the staff I find that being back at school brings out the dormant delinquent in me.

I spoke with Ed Butcher this morning who told me that you are out for a weekend on 3 Dec and that with any luck this nightmare saga ends on 31 Jan. The last time I wrote to you in August I was, I think, just off to Zambia with Nick K. As it happens it turned out to be a deeply unpleasant experience. For starters I thought it might be fairly warm so I failed to even pack a jersey. During the first week the temperatures were about one degree above freezing. I was under the impression that our work for the Zambian government (can you believe?) would take maybe a day or so and the remaining time could be spent lurking around having a good time. How wrong was I? I was obliged to drag myself out of bed every single morning at 6.45 a.m. to be collected by a government car, which would have failed an MOT in the Republic of Ireland ten years ago, and work through till seven in the evening. We would then be returned to a bleak concrete building that masqueraded as a hotel; apparently we were lucky as it was considered to be the best in Lusaka. We then had an hour for dinner which made an evening meal at Colditz look like haute cuisine before spending the remainder of the evening writing dreary reports. There was a national outbreak of cholera and when we visited the general hospital, with a view to computerizing it, the mortuary had instead of the maximum of 40 bodies in it nearer 400. The first one I saw was being eaten by a dog outside in the roadway. Due to the Gulf crisis there was no petrol for love or money so even if we had had the time to go anywhere we couldn't. The only way out of

Letters to Johnny (J. R. Vaughan, JA4307)

Zambia in the end was, at vast expense to Nick's company, to take the only seats available which were first class to Paris where we spent several days attempting to recuperate. Nick at the very last minute put on quite an unusual performance of eccentric behaviour on the runaway. In any other continent I am sure we would not have been allowed to board the plane. Once safely under way I took full advantage of the free alcohol on offer and ended up singing my interpretation of 'My Way' to the pilot. On the subject of Frank Sinatra I have just read his biography by Kitty Kelley. It doesn't exactly make him out to be the most endearing of characters.

Raffateer has finally been wound up and I now have sufficient samples stored in my attic to last me several lifetimes.

Yesterday I drove Aunt Boo to the country for the day, an interesting experience, which surprisingly I rather enjoyed. I cannot keep up with her various political alliances, however she still asks fondly after you. Very little else of interest to report.

The Hobbs are on good form and we hope to serve our writ on Jake Rothschild next week which should cheese him off a bit. Finch claims to be very depressed. He has just made me a director of his company, enough to make anyone feel depressed. I last heard that fat Sam Cooper was flogging water filters outside tube stations. I think the fashion industry is in the doldrums. Bazil tells me he's buying a convertible Maserati.

I must crack on with the absurd amount of homework I've been set for tomorrow. Give me a call when you are out for the weekend if you can.

Be lucky,

Chas

Johnny was released a month or so after this letter. Both of us being ardent Elvis fans, we promised ourselves a trip to Graceland. Sadly, to date we have never got round to it and the way things are going for me healthwise, we'd better get our skates on if it's ever going to happen.

9

Collecting Stuff

In recent years Tim and I have adopted three criteria for acquiring art, loosely based on our personal interpretation of the Waverley Criteria: 1. We have to be absolutely shit-faced when we agree to buy it; 2. We both have to love it; and 3. It has to be of museum quality. (As opposed to: 1. Is it so closely connected with our history and national life that its departure would be a misfortune? 2. Is it of outstanding aesthetic importance? 3. Is it of outstanding significance for the study of some particular branch of art, learning or history?)

I realised some time ago that I don't come from wealth but from the fag-end of wealth. This wasn't the end of the world since I've spent most of my life attempting to reinvent myself as a yob. As it turned out it didn't require much effort to effect the transition. I have never been happier than holding forth with congenial company over a full English breakfast in a transport café. I was, however, to discover that in one specific area of life something buried deep in my DNA was about to dictate otherwise.

My great-uncle was Thomas Geoffrey Blackwell, of food company Crosse & Blackwell fame. He was a huge patron of the arts and by the time he died in 1943 he owned any number of Impressionist paintings by such artists as Monet, Manet, Sisley and Sargent. I had an early relationship with a Blackwell-owned Monet, as one hung in the dining room at my school in the 1960s. Affectionately known as 'the old bird on the motorbike', it depicted the rear view of an elderly peasant lady carrying a bundle of firewood making her weary way through a small village. Sometimes my friends and I would flick scrambled eggs, made from almost inedible powdered tuff left over from the war, at her posterior.

Thomas Blackwell had also amassed one of the finest collections of eighteenth-century English furniture by such cabinet-makers as Chippendale, John Cobb and William Vile. My godfather John Blackwell loved to tell the story of how, when a boy, he was in the bath with his father following a day's foxhunting. The butler knocked on the door and said he had a message that Mr Percival Griffiths, another great collector of furniture, had just broken his neck on the hunting field and died. My great-uncle was out of the bath in a flash and on the phone to Griffiths's agent, R. W. Symonds, in an attempt to acquire all his best pieces. Sadly, most of the Blackwell collection has since been flogged off by the various impecunious relatives.

I used to visit my godfather fairly regularly at his penthouse suite of flats in Brighton. He frequently told my father that I would be his heir, so he probably ended up having more visits from me than would have been the case otherwise. In old age he was something of an acquired taste. When I first met Tim

I took him down to meet John. Dispensing with any form of introduction, he opened the conversation with: 'Are you rich?' Tim replied in the negative. 'Well, more fool you,' gushed my godfather. 'I'm very rich.'

John had inherited a sizeable chunk of his father's world-class collection of paintings and furniture, which he would survey as he buzzed around in a modified electric golf cart in his penthouse fiefdom in Brighton the bulk of which, I had been told many times, would one day be coming my way, but then tragedy struck. An old friend of the Blackwell family who was also a director of Christie's auction house came to stay and persuaded John to put virtually everything into a one-owner sale. I felt this was a bad move, not least because it was driven more by a desire to irritate the rest of the family than anything else. Financially it was a catastrophe. Seeing as all the pieces were of national importance, they had been exempted death duties in 1943 and had he chosen to leave the entire collection under the same status to an institution, he (or his heirs) would have avoided the 80 per cent tax on the sale and the collection would have remained intact. Even though I was a director of Carlton Hobbs Ltd with billionaire clients all over the world, prior to the Christie's sale John derived a perverse pleasure from not asking my company's advice on anything. Now the sale was over that changed.

The only lot not to sell at Christie's was a huge eighteen-century barometer that my godfather was convinced was worth a million pounds. Clearly it wasn't, but nevertheless he insisted that I collect it from Christie's and sell it on his behalf through Carlton Hobbs. I took it all on the chin and cheerfully collected the barometer, had it all buffed up at my expense and put it up for sale in our showroom in Belgravia hoping to score a few brownie points.

What I hadn't bargained for though was the daily phone call from Brighton. On one occasion, I accidently pressed the redial button and found myself calling my godfather back which was a big mistake. The ensuing conversation got progressively muddled as he couldn't get his head round the fact that it was me. In the end slightly exasperated I implored him: 'It's me, Charlie Mortimer . . . Roger's son . . .' 'Yes, yes, I'm fully aware who Charlie Mortimer is,' replied my godfather angrily. 'I've just spoken to him on the telephone. The five thousand dollar question is who the bloody hell are you?'

After four months, an Irish businessman made what I thought was a very decent offer for the wretched barometer. His representative Sebastian and I headed down, barometer in tow, to lunch at John's flat in Brighton, where the offer would be formally made. To describe the goings on in my godfather's penthouse as eccentric would be something of an understatement. His butler had recently died and so his elderly and rather alcoholic boyfriend Keith, who had an incontinent Labrador, had taken over the role. In almost every area Keith's qualifications as a butler were somewhat questionable; he had just been severely reprimanded having been caught peeing in the kitchen sink over all the dirty dishes. Unattractive, possibly unhygienic, but not exactly the end of the world. When Keith greeted us as we exited the lift, he was wearing beige polyester trousers and it was fairly obvious that he'd had a slight accident down one leg. The fact that he was not wearing shoes or socks was of little account. He assured us that there was an excellent lunch waiting, together with a splendid claret which he had personally chosen from John's collection of vintage wines, stored in the cellar of a terraced house nearby purchased for that specific purpose. Keith was shaking so badly from the DTs that he was unable to transport the extremely dry slices of pork luncheon meat from the trolley to our plates so I was obliged to take over serving duties. Over lunch John held Sebastian riveted by a series of stories, all well known to me, such as the time when, together with another headmaster of a local preparatory school, he had visited a gay sauna in Amsterdam and someone had touched his bottom. John, unwisely in my opinion, declined Sebastian's offer and insisted that he wanted at least half a million pounds for the barometer. But at least the cursed instrument was now out of my hands, or so I thought.

Keith now took it upon himself to hang it in a suitably prominent position. Unfortunately, a four-inch nail in plaster board was a somewhat unsatisfactory means of support for an extremely fragile antique that weighed the same as a small sack of spuds. I gather that when, inevitably, the wretched barometer fell from the wall and hit the parquet floor, it smashed into a thousand pieces. My godfather, for reasons known only to himself, was convinced that I had surreptitiously driven down to Brighton in the dead of night, scaled the outside of his block of flats, sneaked in through a window and then thrown the barometer on the floor and jumped on it. No argument from anyone could move him from this conclusion. The lawyers were summoned and I was removed from his will. 'The Lord giveth, and the Lord taketh away.' The whole unhappy saga was so crazy that I actually found it quite funny. Thank God, I thought rather pragmatically for me, if I've inherited nothing else from my family, at least I've inherited a sense of humour.

———•———

Moving on from the baked-bean and Branston-pickle side of the family to my dear mother's mob the Denison-Penders. By comparison, the Denison-Pender art collection was also pretty impressive boasting many famous artists including Turner, Gainsborough, Reynolds and Canaletto to name but a few, but taken as a whole was not a patch on the staggering Blackwell stuff. My great-grandfather, who in portraits looked like quite a self-important gentleman, published in 1894 a sizeable leather-bound tome, embossed in gold lettering and rather modestly inscribed, 'Catalogue of pictures, drawings, and sculptures forming the collection of Sir John Pender'. The frontispiece, of course, was a portrait of the great man himself. My father always considered the Denison-Penders to be complete philistines and enjoyed winding my mother up by telling her so frequently.

By descent, as they like to say in auction catalogues, my mother owned a large oil painting by David Roberts of the interior of St Jacques, Antwerp, acquired by John Pender the year it was executed in 1849, which she gave to me a few years before she passed away. My father used to describe it as 'ghastly' and 'unspeakably gloomy'. After she died, Tim and I took the unusual decision to spend several thousand pounds having it cleaned and restored and by doing so, quite accidentally, reversed the recent family habit of selling. Thus, almost by default, we subconsciously detonated a desire – to acquire art of one sort or another.

Our first major purchase came from Sotheby's. Tim, who is rather an accomplished artist in his own right, specialising in homoerotic three-dimensional art, loved the work of the two iconic gay French artists Pierre et Gilles. To glean some advice on art, we had lunch with the controversial art critic Brian Sewell. I don't think it unfair to say that Brian was not a big fan of modern art. Charles Saatchi generously wrote about him, 'I have missed being shredded by you so much. It was a real treat to get the cane from the headmaster once more in your review of our little Brit show'. Tim enthusiastically recalled that we had once met Pierre et Gilles in Berlin, and I chimed in, 'And do you know what, Brian, to my utter astonishment they seemed to think that I was moderately attractive.' Brian, sharp as a stiletto, instantly responded in his unmistakable nasal twang, 'And do you know what, Charlie, that is what we call being polite.'

After discussing the pros and cons of buying a Pierre and Gilles with Tim, I rang their dealers, Gallerie de Noirmont, in Paris and enquired how much a reasonable work might cost. 'About eighty thousand euros, monsieur.' 'Fuck me slowly' was what I thought, but 'let me give it some thought and I'll get back to you' is what I actually said. I told Tim that at these prices we'd probably missed the boat as far as Pierre et Gilles were concerned. However, Tim spotted that by chance one was coming up for auction in Sotheby's, wrongly catalogued in a photography sale, with a modest reserve. We pitched up rather excitedly to view the high-camp interpretation, *St Michel, Archangel*. We decided to bid rather more to have a chance of getting it. After a four hour-wait, I managed to constrain myself until it was just about to be withdrawn unsold (there were no other bidders) and made just one bid. To our complete disbelief it was ours. At first we thought perhaps we'd made a right fuck-up and bought a copy or part of a limited series so kept re-reading the description in the catalogue. When we took delivery of the piece, I couldn't resist opening the back of the frame. To my horror I found that this multi-thousand pound 'work of art' was just a painted photograph. I immediately rang my new friend at the Noirmont gallery.

'Jérôme,' I exclaimed, 'it's just a painted photograph. That can't be right, can it?'

Cool as *un concombre* he responded, 'But what did you expect? All Pierre et Gilles are painted photographs. I thought you would have known that before you bought it.'

He also told me that this was a classic work from 'The Saint' series, which by bad luck they had missed. 'You are very lucky to have acquired such an important piece for such a price.' Champers all round.

Now keenly interested in all things Pierre et Gilles, Tim and I kept an eagle eye open for what was either available or coming up for sale. One afternoon I called Tim at work in the local Jobcentre to go through one of Jérôme's catalogues. I had already decided that these works were not what we were looking for, especially the 'crying-boy-dressed-as-a-sailor-clutching-a-crucifix-whilst-being-burnt-at-a-stake-with-in-the-background-a-galleon' piece, which was way out of our price range and off the Richter scale in the camp stakes.

'Oh, there's this incredibly camp painting of a boy being burnt in front of a galleon. I don't personally much rate it and in any event it's eye wateringly expensive,' I said casually.

There was quite a long pause before the reply: 'But that one is by far my most favourite. I just absolutely adore it.'

'Oh, Christ,' I thought with grumpy resignation, 'it just would be your bloody favourite, wouldn't it.'

Two days later we were being given lunch at the Hotel Bristol in Paris by the two Jérômes. After all the years of working at John Hobbs it was a treat to be the client.

'Interestingly,' I said as a conversation opener, 'a really good friend of mine hanged himself in this very hotel a few years back.'

The Jérômes looked completely horrified and suggested that we lunch elsewhere.

'Oh, no,' I replied, 'I'm sorry, I was just as the English say, making small talk.'

After lunch, I made a cheeky offer which I knew would be too low. Absolutely futile really: had we left Paris without having first acquired the painting it would have been me being burnt at the stake. I'm happy to say that *The Burning Sailor Boy* still holds pride of place above the sofa in our living room.

Emboldened by our relative successes to date we decided to look at other artists. Tim had shown a keen interest in a transvestite potter, who had been awarded The Turner Prize in 2003, called Grayson Perry. From a distance many of his pots looked rather charming but on closer inspection depicted rather unsavoury scenes – bizarre mixture of Cath Kidston and Hogarth. In 2009, we were due a final pay-out from a pension plan that had, thanks to the collapse of Lehman Brothers the previous year, been the width of a cigarette paper from bankruptcy itself. As a result we had sworn never again to commit our life savings to the vagaries of the financial markets and the charlatans who manipulate them. We decided to invest this small windfall in contemporary art. It was just good luck that the receipt of funds coincided with a major exhibition of Perry's work at the Victora Miro gallery in London. Seeing as the entire show had virtually sold out, we asked Elke Seebauer, the delightful director of sales, if there were any other pieces on offer. In the basement we passed a pair of pots about five foot in height. 'Blimey, Elke, these are huge. They can't be by Grayson can they?' They were in fact classic Grayson: in that from a distance they gave the appearance of two wonderfully proportioned chinoiserie vases, whereas on closer inspection they were smothered from top to bottom with depictions of swirling used condoms and penises clearly designed to shock, contrasting with smiling photo transfers of the artist portrayed as 'a bunch of pale blue and burgundy carnations'. The vases had the rather innocent title of *Entrance to the Forest* and had, we were told, been inspired by John Singer Sargent's painting *The Daughters of Edward Darley Boit*, in which two huge Chinese vases stand like the guardians to adulthood and sexuality. I wasn't surprised to find that they were far beyond our budget.

Over a 'two for the price of one' lunch of sausages and mash, Tim and I debated the vases using only the logic of the art collecting simpletons that we were. The fact that they were the largest pots Grayson had ever made or was ever likely to make was a plus. The minus was their price and the fact that we would need to hire a crane to get them into our modest flat. We decided we had to at least try to buy them and would make an offer substantially lower than the asking price. In a high state of excitement we rushed back to the gallery, found a surprised Elke and made our offer. That evening Elke called to say our offer had been accepted. Elation, however, was extremely short lived when running through the figures I discovered she assumed that our offer was 'plus VAT' whereas in fact it was inclusive of. I said there was no way we could pay an extra fifteen per cent on top. Fortunately not entirely sober by then we readily agreed a generous compromise. Under the terms of our deal we didn't take possession of the pots for six months, and in the intervening period it dawned on us that we really hadn't got a clue as what to do with them, so I wrote to Grayson:

Dear Grayson,

I apologise for writing to you out of the blue.

In brief, about a month ago, my partner Tim and myself went to Victoria Miro to view an exhibition of your art. It was not our intention to buy anything major but in a moment of extreme enthusiasm we ended up purchasing your wonderful diptych 'Entrance to the Forest' of which we take possession in February.

As it happens we live in quite a small flat and, although we would love to have the vases here, they would virtually touch the ceiling, and it might require some skill to manoeuvre round them to actually get anywhere.

However, it has since occurred to us that a better alternative might be to lend these spectacular pieces (free of charge) to a museum or gallery, on say a five-year loan, so that everyone could enjoy them. To that end, we were wondering if this idea held any appeal for you and if you could advise us as we have no experience whatsoever in this area.

Best wishes etc.

We received no response. Perhaps, understandably, he just dismissed us as a couple of crackpots (excuse the pun). As time ticked by we became somewhat desperate. It seemed a shame just to stick the vases in storage somewhere, so we asked the gallery to get in touch with the museum that had previously expressed interest, to see whether they fancied having them on a long-term loan. Fortunately they did and a year later Tim and I found ourselves having dinner courtesy of Manchester Art Gallery. I sat next to Grayson and Tim next to a very beautiful red-haired lady, whose husband Tom Bloxham was a hugely successful Manchester businessman. Tim had struck gold.

Jo Bloxham's opening remark in a strong Scouse accent was along the lines of 'I guess you're one of those floppy-haired posh knobs from West London?'

'No darling . . . actually I work in a job centre,' said Tim.

'You don't smoke as well do you?'

'Yes I do, heavily.'

'Magic! . . . outside now.'

Jo is a highly successful business woman in her own right and one of the world's leading curators of avante-garde jewellery; she can also tell a great, usually self-deprecating, story as rivetingly and amusingly as John Hobbs (which coming from me is a great accolade).

In retrospect it wasn't a great idea to seat a fairly egocentric alpha-male artist, dressed in the style of Christine Hamilton, next to an equally egocentric old poof who, after a bottle or two of whatever is available, also likes to hold court. We did not end the evening exactly best of mates. However, five years on, the two vases still hold pride of place on either side of the grand central stairway in an imposing Georgian mansion, home to Manchester Art Gallery's Gallery of Costume. Since that evening, we have acquired more of Grayson's art, including a sizeable tapestry depicting his take on a scene from Hogarth's *A Rake's Progress* rather aptly named *The Upper Class at Bay*, which is also on loan to Manchester Art Gallery. (On a personal note, Tim and I now chat away merrily with Grayson and his other half Philippa whenever we bump into him. She kindly sent me her book *How to Stay Sane*.)

The following year, we managed to wangle a VIP pass to Frieze London in Regent's Park. Sensing vast quantities of complimentary champagne and other goodies, which sadly never materialised, we stormed off there. Frieze was not really our cup of tea, and we spent much of our time there sniggering at absurd objects presented as art. As we were about to leave, we stumbled across a highly amusing five-foot photograph of two Saluki dogs lying on a shag pile carpet in a fashionable minimalist interior, intensely watching heterosexual porn on their owner's television. Little did we know it at the time that this was the beginning of our next art adventure.

The photo was being sold by David Zwirner gallery from New York and the photographer was Philip-Lorca diCorcia. We hadn't heard of either of them. We were told by charming Angela Choon at David Zwirner that PL (as he's called) was a very famous photographer and this particular photo had been released especially for Frieze in a limited edition of eight, over half of which had already been sold. Employing our usual highly sophisticated logic, we reckoned that if more than half of the editions had already sold, and Frieze had barely started, it must be worth a punt. Moreover, we both loved dogs, and Tim porn, gay or straight.

Three months later we were thrilled to receive an invitation, 'David Zwirner invites you to a private dinner honouring Philip-Lorca diCorcia', to be held at his home in New York. What made this more exciting was that, prior to 2010, I could not travel to the USA, due to my HIV/Aids status, without first going through a laborious palaver known as a 'waiver of inadmissibility to travel to the US'. This procedure was surely designed as a barrier as it took months and was by no means certain to succeed. Had I travelled without the waiver and been caught at customs (quite a strong possibility given that I travel with enough medication to open a medium-sized pharmacy), the penalties would have been severe. These included being arrested, held without representation and deported in a cage to RAF Northolt. This would be our first trip together to New York and we leapt at the chance.

Tim and I had the time of our lives. It was as if we had won a competition in *Hello* with first prize a trip of impossible glamour to New York for four days. We had no idea what a big deal Philip-Lorca diCorcia was in contemporary photography and certainly no idea of the importance (in the tiny world of high art) of David Zwirner. We felt like the Beverley Hillbillies, though after a few glasses of bubbly, we entered into the spirit of things, and by the end of the evening I had to be physically restrained by Tim from joining in the speeches by delivering one of my own.

PL, disarmingly off-the-wall in his maroon Sgt. Bilko style safari suit, was more interested in discussing where the next drink was coming from than the pigmentation of his recent works. At supper we sat with his immediate family and friends who were delightfully eccentric and dysfunctional with the result that we felt entirely at home.

The following evening we were due to meet my old friend Lex Fenwick (who was a big cheese in Bloomberg) and his young Japanese girlfriend, now his wife, Ikue. Lex had booked a table at The Waverley Inn, at the time we hadn't a clue that The Waverley Inn was so exclusive it didn't have a phone line and makes The Ivy look trashy. Apparently to book a table you are advised, 'to get your people to call their people'. Lex took us to a few clubs, where I finally fell asleep with my head on the bar. An unkind person posted a photo of this with the heading: 'In the city that never sleeps!'

We also found time to meet up with old friends Hugo Guinness and Chris Brooks, go up the Empire State Building, walk through Central Park in the snow and go to the Metropolitan Museum of Art and the Guggenheim. To describe the weather as nippy would be, frankly, an understatement.

Over the next couple of years we bought three more of PL's photos always dealing with the lovely Angela. However the most memorable PL moment for us was when he agreed to have a retrospective exhibition at the Hepworth Wakefield gallery. Prior to the opening, there was a celebration dinner to which Tim and I were, rashly in my opinion, invited. PL had been there for several days, and by the time we pitched up he was looking to let his hair down a little. Earlier in the week, there had been some fairly controversial moments when the 'Dogs watching porn' photo was removed on the grounds of offending public decency. PL is happily from that school of Americans who, like Hunter. S. Thompson, assume, on their first encounter with a meagre pub measure of spirits, that it's a free sample. By the early hours Tim and I enjoyed the surreal experience of ending up with PL in the 'Sky Lounge' at the hotel in Leeds where we were all staying.

I have, through a haze of vodka cocktails, only the vaguest of recollections of the final hour or so. Nevertheless I do clearly remember Tim at one point describing the mechanics of 'fisting' in some considerable detail, with PL earnestly responding, 'Hey little buddy even for me that's just too much damn information'. By any standards it was a unique and thoroughly entertaining evening and for Tim and I to spend time getting tanked up and talking enthusiastic old bollocks with PL was frankly, without wishing to sound like some star struck teenage girl, beyond our wildest dreams.

The icing on the cake came not long after. We had arranged to meet Elke for lunch on a Saturday at the Victoria Miro gallery. A couple of days earlier she texted to say that she had to go to Germany for the weekend so could we make Thursday instead. We turned up to find the final touches being applied to an exhibition of new works by an artist we had never heard of called Idris Khan. As we came into the downstairs gallery we were confronted by seven large and very dark paintings. Elke was clearly very enthusiastic and explained that although oil on aluminum they were not paintings but words and sentences stamped over and over again thousands of times. 'Blimey,' I observed, 'what does he do? Live in a nut house?' I had no idea the artist was standing about one foot behind me. More amused than offended we ended up joining him in a local pub for lunch. It turned out that Idris had already recently shown some of his work at the Whitworth in Manchester. We began to think about buying one of the huge works in his exhibition 'Beyond the Black' with the purpose of lending it to Manchester on a long-term loan. After outlining our plan, we made a ridiculously low offer that was politely turned down. After a couple of drinks at home that evening Tim and I more or less simultaneously agreed that if we missed this opportunity we would regret it. Fortunately I managed to get hold of Elke on her mobile as the show began, rapidly agreed a deal and got her to ask Idris which one of the seven works he would most like to go to Manchester. We emailed Maria Balshaw (director of the Whitworth and Manchester Art Gallery and hotly tipped for great things, as if her achievements to date weren't already pretty jaw-dropping), who agreed enthusiastically to display the work. We had met Maria a few years back, when Tim introduced himself along the lines of, 'Hello darling, what's your star sign?' We had absolutely no idea of her standing in the art world and our friendship has since blossomed.

Over the following year we were lucky enough to get our hands on another couple of significant pieces by Idris destined for Manchester. However the real coup was achieved by following our three buying criteria to the letter.

By now Idris and his wonderful wife Annie, who is also a highly accomplished artist in her own right, had become close friends of ours. They are a lot of fun to hang out with. One night Idris invited us along to the launch of an exclusive art journal *E.R.O.S.* for which he had produced an oil painting inspired by Malevich's *Black Square*. To accompany the launch Idris had produced five new works, entitled *Death of Painting (1 to 5)*. Of these he was keeping one and another had been allocated elsewhere. The highlight of the evening was a conversation about the paintings between Idris and the editor of *E.R.O.S.* Fond as I am of Idris these intellectual chats between artists and writers are not really my cup of tea. I remember once going up to the Manchester International Festival, when Tim received a text from our hosts suggesting we meet them at a gallery to hear two artists discussing conceptual art in some detail. Tim texted back: 'The philistine that is my husband says he would rather hang himself.'

To get in the mood Tim and I had availed ourselves of the free bar, so by the time Idris began his talk we were both fully aware of having had a drink or five. After a few minutes I whispered to Tim, 'I'm going to liven things up a bit' and with that crept off to find Elke and Idris's agent Fabian. I launched into a garbled theory of why I thought these five works should stay together as one body of work. Fabian, as I suspected, thought it was a great idea but out of the question as only three were now available. When Idris finished his thirty-minute chat I said, 'Idris, with the best will in the world I didn't really understand the majority of what you were talking about. That said it's an absolute no brainer that these paintings must stay together as one work. They should be on public view preferably at the Whitworth together with a written narrative from you as to what inspired you to create something so special and so personal.'

The following morning, I had little recollection of any of this until I received a text from Elke: 'So wonderful to see you last night! Fabian and I had to guide Idris out of the room, mumbling Charlie's right this body of work should stay together . . . I am not joking, he is very inspired.' Now sober, I was slightly appalled to be confronted with a fast-moving situation that I had started just hours previously as some light-hearted hijinks. However, on the positive side Idris's oil paintings were astonishing as a group and presented an opportunity not to be missed; on the negative side we hadn't been exactly planning to fund anything on this scale and had no idea how we were going to. Tim and I decided to email Maria in Hong Kong. 'Charlie and I think this is an unprecedented opportunity not just to acquire a major work from Idris but a small show that stands on its own merit. We now just need your stamp of approval to proceed.' We decided that if Maria was up for it then even if we had to beg, steal or borrow we would get the cash together one way or another. Considering Maria was the other side of the world and extremely busy, we were over the moon to get an enthusiastic email back within hours. 'I think this could work brilliantly for us at the Whitworth and I'd be very pleased to work with Idris and Miro to make it happen. So an enthusiastic, resounding yes all the way from Hong Kong.' I was in a café with Tim enjoying a bacon sandwich when Maria's email came through. It is almost unheard of for me to abandon a half-eaten butty, but overcome with excitement I rushed outside to call Fabian and cement the deal. I can think of few transactions where everyone involved, not least future visitors to the Whitworth, are winners. But this really was such a one.

In the end the purchase was funded entirely by Tim and my share in the sale of the very last parcel of land left by Thomas Geoffrey Blackwell, the great connoisseur and collector himself.

I'd like to think the old boy would have heartily approved.

Tim and I genuinely get more kicks out of Manchester than any other city we have ever visited. It's lucky we don't live there as neither of us have ever woken up there without a hangover of gargantuan proportions. We have also made some really excellent new friends up there. The parties are in a whole new league of lunacy compared to those down south. We once ended up at a beano in the Manchester Art Gallery thrown by artist Raqib Shaw. Raqib is famous for both his prodigious talent, his works – which sell for millions and resemble massive Fabergé eggs flattened by a steam-roller (in a good way) – and for his legendary lifestyle which takes excess and generosity out into the stratosphere. An evening once spent as guests of Raqib's at his 30,000 sq. ft. private paradise in Peckham made a dinner with Dalí seem pedestrian. Raqib, originally from Kashmir, lives in a style more in keeping with a nineteenth-century maharajah. Tim and I lead the lives of Trappist monks by comparison.

I spotted Tim from the other side of the room and sauntered over to find him deep in conversation with Raqib's gallerist Jay Jopling, the charismatic owner of White Cube.

'Oh this is my other half, Charlie,' enthused Tim.

They then proceeded to talk about me in the third person.

'How long have you been together?' Jay asked Tim.

'Pushing on for eighteen years.'

'Christ, what did he do . . . steal you out of a perambulator? Anyway, what does he do?'

'Nothing much.'

At this point I drew myself up. 'Well, since you ask, old fruit, I've just written a book.'

Jay gave Tim a knowing nudge. 'What privately published I suppose? Does it have a name?'

'Yeah, actually it's called *Dear Lupin*.'

'Christ,' said Jay incredulously, 'you're fucking Lupin?'

(Virtually the entire party ended up in a gay bar in Canal Street. I gather locals usually drop the 'C' and the 'S'.)

Like our friends Idris and Annie Khan, Tim and I are passionate about art being for all and not just for the fortunate few. When we can afford it we love to acquire and lend pieces of contemporary art that are current, significant and appealing to museums, particularly those outside London, free of charge – Manchester Art Gallery and the Whitworth in particular.

A couple of years ago our good friend Geordie, famous for his explosive missives, sent us a classic 'when you're not busy reinventing yourselves as patrons of the arts perhaps you might have the decency to respond to my bloody email!' It's somewhat ironic, given my rackety lifestyle, that the philistine otherwise known as Lupin, in his twilight years, has somehow managed to end up as a sort of junior patron of the arts. My father and John Hobbs would be more than just a little astonished.

10

From Nut Pressure to
No Pleasure

If I confide in someone that I feel depressed and their response is, 'What on earth have you got to be depressed about?', it's pretty clear that they haven't got a clue about mental stuff. If you then try enlightening them, more often than not, you might as well waste the next ten minutes of your life barking at the moon.

Being diagnosed and living with HIV/Aids has for me been a walk in the park in comparison to nut pressure. There is no magic pill, and when depression hits, it's like waking up in some joyless vacuum with the challenge of confronting the day ahead about as inviting as the prospect of running a thirty-mile marathon wearing a fat suit. Nothing leaves you more vulnerable and less prepared for the daily rough and tumble of existence than depression; nothing is more effective at ruthlessly grinding you down until the prospect of leaving the planet has considerably more appeal than remaining on it. Given the choice between winning the Euromillions lottery and being guaranteed a depression-free future to me is a no brainer.

One of my closest friends took his own life, having suffered from appalling mental health problems for several decades. Nobody could have done more for him over the years than his two sisters. They were clearly devastated and obviously thought they could or should have done more. The truth is that nobody could have done more than they did. Mental illness is no different than physical illness in many respects: you can't try to save someone from terminal cancer and then blame yourself for not managing to do so.

In many ways it's a lose-lose situation, and somewhere deep inside you just know at times that there isn't going to be a happy ending. Tragically this was to be the case with our friend Geordie. He was only fifty-two when he died.

My father once compared me to a rather suave friend of mine, 'In respect of manners and sophistication he is Lord Chesterfield and Charlie some uncouth moujik from the Siberian Steppes.' I could say the same about Geordie and myself: we were not obvious friend material.

But despite our differences ver the years, our flat became a sanctuary of last resort for Geordie when things were too much for him. He and I would talk about our respective mental health issues (or 'nut pressure') and other personal issues with the casual ease golfers might discuss their game in the clubhouse. These conversations formed the cornerstone of our friendship and were quite outside the remit of his outwardly much more conventional existence. Despite disabling mental health, Geordie got on with his life and held down an excellent job in the city for many years. He always brought a lot to the table: he was as loyal and as trustworthy a friend as the day is long, enriched the lives of all those who knew him and as a result was much loved by many in return. Given the maelstrom that frequently played out in his head, presenting himself to the world as he did took some doing. He never once played the victim card and knowing at times what he was going through I would actually hail his stoicism as truly heroic; not a term often associated with mental health. If someone dies from cancer or some other ghastly disease, a death announcement might read, 'long illness bravely borne'. So why not so with mental illness?

The other day I was talking to a good friend Anya who, lucky lady, has never had a day's depression in her life but her ninety-year-old dad suffers from it periodically. She had mentioned to her father that I had told her that ending up in a wheelchair would be preferable to a future of clinical depression. She had expected her father, an extremely astute and intelligent man, to ridicule such a statement but much to her surprise he simply replied, 'Despite the fact that I've never met him I could not agree with your friend Charlie more.'

Having suffered from a variety of mental illnesses from my mid-teens onwards, I realize that there are no easy fixes and, frequently, just no fixes at all. The brain is a complex living sponge and current treatments are not, despite claims otherwise, all that sophisticated. It's not that different from giving the television (or PC) a really good thump to get a better picture. Sadly, neither doctors nor psychiatrists are possessed of mystical powers. I remember my young godson once observing, 'Uncle Charlie, did you know that we only use about ten percent of our brains?' To which I replied, 'I am not so concerned about that Sam, it's the disturbing messages coming from the other ninety percent that seems to be the problem.'

My younger sister Lumpy and my mother have also been closely shadowed by depression. Paradoxically, it often surfaces when things are, on the face of it, going rather well. I remember when Lumpy was 'in one', as we would say, I called to tell her that she was due an unexpected and quite substantial sum of money. From her reaction I might have just told her that her beloved border terrier, Marley, had just been run over. 'I can't handle this . . . not now . . . I mean what am I meant to do with it?' she said with some alarm.

An example of just how nonsensical depression can be if rules of ordinary life are applied. Following the same topsy-turvy pattern, Lumpy received some really challenging news in that she required an urgent and highly-specialised operation on her spine. Result? She was on cracking form all winter without so much as ten seconds gloom, despite everything that had been thrown at her.

If I call up Lumpy, bless her, I can tell within two seconds what state of mind she's in. It's pretty obvious if she answers along the lines of 'HIYA! How are you, hoo-hoo-hoo-hoo-HOO!' that she's floating around at the top end of high somewhere. On the other hand, if she picks up the phone and merely responds in a manner that gives monosyllabic a whole new meaning, then clearly she's seriously browned off.

Lumpy is on mood-levelling medication for life, as am I and, indeed, as was our mother. It is unfortunately not a cure but certainly makes life at times more endurable.

Lucky Lupin

One thing that Lumpy has certainly mastered is the ability to say no. Getting Lumpy to do anything she doesn't want to do is like dragging a deep freeze around on a rope. I, on the other hand, have a habit of becoming wildly enthusiastic, particularly after a couple of drinks, and once ended up inviting a gaggle of comparative strangers to come on a bicycling holiday in the foothills of the Atlas Mountains. As I haven't been on a bicycle for over thirty years and have no intention of ever doing so again it seemed a strange choice of vacation.

When Tim and I do go on holiday we insist on a room with a view, preferably with a balcony, which we seldom leave. I always travel with two identical hamper-sized boxes of medication together with a letter from my consultant Mark Nelson: 'This gentleman attends my clinic for a chronic condition, and needs to carry his medication with him at all times.' One box goes in the hold and the other as hand luggage to lessen the chances of the catastrophe of finding myself stuck, pill-less, in the middle of nowhere. (We are not now great travellers and on one particular holiday someone commented that, from the tortured expressions on our faces, we looked as if we were en route to be guillotined.)

I have always found sleep a welcome respite from the storm, whereas waking up is little less than an exquisite form of torture. A very old friend of mine, Patrick, clearly feels much the same. He has been diagnosed as suffering from classic and chronic bipolar and once told me in a very slow and languid tone not unlike Morrissey, 'I wake up in the morning, I pull back the curtains, look out of the window and think to myself, "Oh my goodness me, not another day."' My mother's often repeated mantra, when she was old and on a downer, was

'Stop the bloody world, I bloody want, to bloody well, get bloody off.' Both of these really used to strike a chord.

After my dad died, Tim and I would go down to my mother's for the weekend. I used to leave Tim and my mother to consume vast quantities of cheap white wine, while I got on with practical stuff. After doing a few tasks round the place I would walk in to find my mother, wig slightly askew, clutching her beloved Chihuahua Danny and happily announcing, as she held out a hand with two fingers crossed, 'Of course, Tim and I are absolutely d'accord!'

To my mother, having congenial company was absolutely essential to keep her from feeling utterly abandoned One evening she tried to engage with me rather than Tim after supper. I was otherwise engrossed in some newspaper story. When I refused to respond she launched into a very articulate appraisal of how she felt.

'You don't bloody know what it's bloody well like to be in this bloody house all bloody week with no bloody person to bloody well talk to!'

It was said with such feeling that it made my blood run cold and still does. My mother needed to be needed and contact was vital. (I always rang her twice a day wherever I was in the world.) Just after my dad died, I tried to persuade her to buy an ansaphone. By far her biggest objection to getting one was 'But just imagine how desolate I'd feel if I came home and found that no one had rung me.'

On Bank Holiday Monday in May 1998, Tim, my mother and I all went out for a pub lunch by the River Thames. It was a happy occasion, devoid of any family drama. When we returned to my mother's house she went upstairs for a nap. At about

5 p.m. Tim announced that he would like to go back to London earlier rather than later so I went upstairs to wake my mother.

I was shocked to find her lying on the floor, clutching a rose. She was obviously having difficulty breathing. My immediate thought when I couldn't get any response from her was that she had suffered a stroke so I shouted for Tim and telephoned our local GP, Dr Yates. Astonishingly, given the fact it was a holiday, he was round within minutes.

As he walked into my mother's bedroom, he took one look at her clutching the rose and announced, 'Drama queen to the last.' Dr Yates and my mother had been having a bit of a love-hate thing going on since my dad had died.

Within seconds he unblocked her airways, which did not make him very popular with my mother when she found out what had happened. It turned out that she was desperately trying to kill herself. 'The man's a pocket bloody Hercules,' she complained.

I subsequently found a hastily scribbled note:

SORRY . . . I do love you all three BUT I can't cope anymore.

NN

Please look after Danny [her Chihuahua].

Once it had been established exactly what she had taken (about forty Distalgesic tablets and a bottle of whisky) Dr Yates told me (very pleasantly) to kiss her goodbye as there was no way she could possibly survive for long. However after twenty-four hours in intensive care, survive she did, her first words to a nurse being 'Have I missed Ascot?' (She would live to see quite a few more Ascots.)

When the default position is deepest gloom, which it was

with my mother at the time, quite suddenly the thought of ending it all comes as a tremendous release. With depression comes indecision and so any decision, however drastic, can be a huge relief. I think that for my mother, the thought of us going back to London and leaving her alone again all week was too bleak a prospect for her to face up to right then.

———•———

Sometimes behaviour brought on my mental health issues, such OCD, can have unexpected consequences.

Several years ago, I developed from nowhere a seemingly unshakeable compulsion to collect red rubber bands left on the pavements by postmen; ultimately any rubber band proved irresistible. Tim, always tolerant of my latest foible, nonetheless warned me on a daily basis that in the long term it wasn't going to do my back any favours. In addition, my good friend and co-director Will had, bizarre as it may be, an unnatural phobia of rubber. A walk down a London street with Will was on occasion fairly challenging for both of us. If in a frivolous mood (fairly unusual), I'd chase him waving a couple of rubber bands. Not very sophisticated behaviour from a senior citizen, I grant you. However, there was a price to pay for all this nonsense, and it was just around the corner.

After a lifetime of hunting accidents, my mother had for many years suffered from back pain. For as long as I can remember she swore by a purported expert in these matters based in Oxford. For myself I had long held suspicions that in reality his only qualification was the white doctors' coat he wore like an actor on TV advertising remedies for influenza. It turned out I was spot on. When I finally persuaded my mother to see a specialist in London it took him less than five minutes to diagnose that she needed a hip replacement. The resulting trip to the hip-replacement surgeon was not without incident. Sarah, who was also the Queen Mother's surgeon, was a well-known transsexual who was both highly professional and extremely charming. My mother listened intently to everything that was said. Prior to us leaving, Sarah asked my mother if she was happy to proceed with the operation as planned.

'Oh very happy,' enthused my mother, adding in a loud whisper as we left, 'just as long as I don't wake up with a bloody penis.'

One Sunday, I was strolling casually back from one of our regular jollies with friends Caroline, David and her two sons Alex and Fergus (who, poor boy, is my godson). Without warning, walking became extremely difficult and I was overcome by an agonising pain in my leg and back that increased hour by hour. I could take no more and Tim called an ambulance. It took two very lovely ambulance-women, several shots of pure morphine and some Entonox gas to prize me from our bedroom. I vaguely remember remarking that it was ironic that I would normally be using both gas and morphine to entice people into our bedroom not the other way round.

A&E was a kind of bedlam all of its own making. I had previously ended up there with a life-threatening variant of pneumonia. On that occasion I was so ill and full of morphine that I barely noticed that I had been effectively dumped in the middle of a Hogarth cartoon. The fact that two drunk people were trying to strangle each other in a nearby curtained cubicle was, I found, more amusing than threatening. Two days later, feeling rather better, I was surprised by a professor doing his ward round with a gaggle of enthusiastic medical students. He breezed towards me in a rather flamboyant manner verging on the camp. 'Here we are presented with a white male in late middle age and poor condition' was his opening line. 'Speak for yourself, dear' was mine.

This time round, I spent the entire night drugged up to the eyeballs on a hospital trolley with about as much give in its mattress as a scaffolding plank. In the morning, the doctor in charge said to Tim, 'Well there's nothing more we can do here. Take him home and get an appointment with a back specialist.' Tim, unlike me, is usually one to avoid any form of drama, yet this time he went ballistic. Going home without a drip full of class A painkillers and a private ambulance wasn't really an option so, in anger, Tim commandeered a wheelchair.

(Tim tells me his more laid-back attitude to creating a scene, compared to my very much more proactive approach, is purely because he's Libra and I'm Aries. A classic example of this in action is when we travel together on the London underground. As a train pulls in to our platform and I can see one or two seats available, I crouch ready to throw myself like a decrepit fly half into a rugby scrum. As the doors open, I pounce. Tim on the other hand, and much to my frustration, dithers politely on the platform in case there still may be someone deep in the bowels of the train who wants to get off. When Tim does finally deign to board the train, I am given a severe reprimand 'Someone is going to hit you for behaving like that one day.' The fact is, though, I have a seat and Tim doesn't.)

As luck would have it I had an appointment that very morning with my HIV/Aids consultant Mark Nelson in the adjacent block, the Kobler Clinic. I first came across Mark back in 1992, when he looked like a mischievous schoolboy out of the *Beano* comic. Much loved by his patients, not always so by the administration, he was and is one of the finest Aids brains in the world; he is the 'Columbo' of the medical world. Entirely thanks to Mark's intervention I ended up in the brand new NHS Ron Johnson Ward which made a Four Seasons hotel look positively down market.

By the following morning I had, thank God, recovered some composure. As I reclined in my electric bed watching daytime TV having eaten a full English breakfast washed down with a hefty does of 'Oramorph', I could have gladly kissed both Mark Nelson and Mr Johnson.

When I left the hospital a few days later it was strongly suggested that I saw a back specialist as an MRI scan had shown all sorts of depressing stuff. Before I got round to it, two days later while walking through the nightmare that is Fulham Broadway, my legs just stopped working midstride. I flew through the air with all the control of someone mid-epileptic fit and braced myself for rather a hard landing on my face. Fortunately, I fell into the arms of a very substantial tattooed gentleman who appeared from nowhere. Tim in his wonderfully whimsical way reckoned it was a special guardian angel that he'd organised to look after me via an order to the universe. Wherever the truth lies, in heaven or here on earth, I am to this day truly grateful. The following day, Tim dragged me off to see the expert he had selected. After a quick physical once-over, followed by an MRI scan, Dr H, clearly not a man to waste words, delivered his verdict: 'If I could I would operate today but it being Friday now I can fit you in first thing on Monday.'

'Well, the thing is Doctor, I'm going to a dinner party next Thursday with the Brudenell-Bruces and then it's Christmas. Shall we say sometime early in the New Year?'

His reply was delivered with just a hint of menace. 'That all depends, doesn't it Mr Mortimer [he might just as well as called me 'mate'] on whether or not you want to spend your Christmas flicking through wheelchair brochures?'

Point well made.

'See you Monday,' I said.

Thus, it was at some unearthly hour we pitched up at a clinic that looked more like a VIP waiting room to the after-life. I was wheeled away, looking like I was en route to be executed by lethal injection. Not that far from the truth. I remember an affable man with rather hairy arms injecting me with a gadget that looked almost horticultural in size and nature. Ten seconds later, I was sparko. Tim had been told that the operation would take no longer than an hour and a half. Tim now merrily skipped off down the road to Selfridges.

Having not heard a squeak out of the hospital for a full 300 minutes, Tim started to panic. When he eventually tracked me down, he found me busily vomiting into a bucket. To this day we have never had anything approaching a satisfactory answer as to why it took over three and a half hours for me to regain any form of consciousness despite the best endeavours of the anaesthetist. I could swear there were burn marks on my chest and a slight whiff of charred skin surrounding my person.

The hospital, beyond giving advice on how to get in and out of bed, offered no assistance on any other practicalities, such as walking with 'drop foot' on the left hand side and 'seriously numb foot' on the right. The only positive I could think of was that, in the event that I was crucified, I wouldn't feel the nail going through my right foot. Tim tracked down some plastic gismo that I strapped to my left leg, thus eliminating most of the problems there. For the uninitiated 'drop foot' is where you lose all muscle strength in the foot. Every time your foot hits the pavement, it sounds like a wet fish being slapped down on a Formica worktop. It doesn't make walking with your other half a particularly relaxing experience, more so if they keep coming out with really unfunny jokes comparing my recent disability to Michael Flatley and *Lord of the Dance*.

The thing about back trouble is that almost everyone has something to proffer in the form of advice, most of which can be dispensed with pronto. Pilates, in my opinion, falls into this category. About a month on, I was persuaded to see a physiotherapist. I have never really gelled with physios, and this little session was to prove no exception. The lady was on the mildly irritating side of pleasant, and I endured an hour's worth of improving posture and a variety of, for me at any rate, impossibly complex exercises. Given that I have no attention span, combined with both dyslexia and dyspraxia, these were an absolute nonstarter. As I left I was instructed to make an appointment to come back in a week, having mastered a whole series of mini manoeuvres I had been shown. 'Madam,' I said in a rather patronising tone. 'If you honestly think for one minute that I am going to attempt even one of these exercises at home you must need your head examined.'

Lounging on my bed about a week after I got home, I suddenly realized that my sex drive had just gone. And when I say gone, I mean G. O. N. E. – just as effectively had Sky disconnected my sports channel. With rare optimism I presumed it would come back with time – how wrong was I. There were, however, some positives. At sixty-two, it was hardly the end of the world; and certainly when I was younger the idea of older people shagging was rather unappetising and frankly still is. I remember once suggesting to my dad, when he was about the same age as I am now, that he got himself a young girlfriend.

'Don't be so ridiculous, sonny boy,' he retorted. 'It would be like trying to stuff a marshmallow into a kiddie's money box.'

Eminent thinkers such as Socrates and other less eminent thinkers such as John Hobbs observed that losing their libido was akin 'to being unshackled from a lunatic'. Certainly, I found myself with considerably more time on my hands, happily labouring under the illusion that this was just a temporary setback.

Did this have any effect on Tim and me as a couple? Well, no it didn't. Tim, who is twenty years younger, and I had been together for seventeen years and, as with many gay relationships, the initial sexual explosion diminished with time. In our case, mutual devotion wasn't demonstrated by sex but by affection, tolerance and intimacy (with a few other bits and bobs thrown for good measure). Tim enjoyed joking with close confidantes such as my younger sister that he 'was actually rather relieved'. As I could barely move unaided, even had I had the sex drive of Casanova on crystal meth any serious action would for the time being have been in my dreams.

Come April something vaguely resembling normal service was resumed. Cheap champers was quaffed once again on a nightly basis, the plastic leg brace was binned, the other leg is permanently but not inconveniently numb. As for my libido, it's now just a dim and distant memory, a bit like my youth.

11

Lucky Lupin

John Hobbs loved telling anyone who would listen, 'If you had known Charlie before he met Tim, he was the moodiest, most miserable fucker you could ever imagine.' The fact is that meeting Tim back in 1996 was an absolute game changer for me. We practise a mutual survival pact on a daily basis and not an hour goes by that I don't thank my lucky stars for him.

We have been together now for twenty years and should anything happen to him I plan on leaving the planet pronto. There is no way I would last a minute on my own. Although much of my life reads – and sometimes feels – like a romp through one catastrophe after another, I have few complaints. I consider myself very lucky at least to have had a life and I only have myself to blame for my health and other problems, which are entirely a consequence of my somewhat disorderly conduct.

Having to live with the diagnosis of a terminal illness was actually a turning point for me. There is a rather bizarre

Texan saying for transforming a negative into a positive: 'I've seen the elephant'. Well, I believe I have seen the elephant. And yet, I would rather not have to have gone through the torture of mental illness and depression. Clinical depression is akin to being personally abused by God, and I can think of nothing positive to come out of it bar empathy to others in a similar position (even that isn't guaranteed). That said, I consider it a triumph that should I die tomorrow I would now leave life happy to have lived. A conclusion inconceivable for me thirty years ago, when on some nights I used to practise, with relative success, something that I called my 'death camp' therapy. In the early 1980s, when driving aid trucks to Poland, I visited quite a few of the extermination camps. My dad had interrogated some of the senior Nazis during the Nuremberg trials, and I remember, as a teenager, finding a book of his called *The Incomparable Crime: Mass Extermination in the Twentieth Century*, which was full of many deeply disturbing factual accounts of the Holocaust. I was both fascinated and horrified in equal measure. As a result I produced, aged fourteen, the only piece of work at Eton for which I ever got highly commended in the form of a poem called 'War Guilt'. I still remember the line, 'Butt meet woman's jaw frail as a leaf, she gets up bleeding and vomits her teeth.'

For all my reading, I wasn't prepared for the sites I visited. Who on earth could be?

So when I was particularly depressed I would read accounts of life in these extermination camps and felt beyond grateful for my life as it was. My much-repeated mantra: 'Man up, and stop feeling so fucking sorry for yourself.'

I have always felt that suicide was 'on the cards' if required, some days just having it as an option got me through but fortunately for the past fifty years it's never been more than a comfort blanket of sorts. I once read an article in *The Times* about a man in his early fifties called Jeffrey Spector, who had a cancerous tumour on his spine and on any morning could have woken up paralyzed from the neck down. While still in control, and with the support of his wife and family, he had chosen to end his life at Dignitas in Switzerland. I blogged into the debate online: 'I can't remember signing any sort of contract agreeing to a life of slavery on this planet. Thus, I'll leave it as and when I feel like it. Jeffrey Spector made an informed and pragmatic decision while still in a position to do so, and I admire him for having the balls.' To my surprise I received more support than not for my views, which shows the way things are changing.

I have only really had one epiphany about dying. In 1975, I was desperately ill in Basingstoke Hospital with chronic liver failure. Because I was considered to be highly infectious I was 'barrier nursed' in a room of my own. By chance one evening, as my condition deteriorated, I overheard snippets of a conversation between two consultants outside my room: the gist of which suggested that my chances of survival were at best fifty-fifty. Later that evening, unable to sleep, I lay there thinking that whatever my circumstances in life – rich, poor, hugely popular or not, or even if I were married with children – everything that formed part of my life was completely irrelevant. I was facing death alone, and I may as well get used to it. It was a sobering thought, but not an unpleasant one – in fact, from that moment on, I found the thought of death, if not exactly comforting, then reassuring. Those with religious and other beliefs may have a different take, however this is how it was for me and I have never forgotten it.

It is now just over thirty years since I was diagnosed with a killer virus and given a life expectancy of just a few years, and over forty years since that moment of clarity in Basingstoke. Compared to mental illness, having HIV/Aids for me has been pretty much a breeze, although many others have not been so lucky. I have concentrated on the life that I can lead, and not to get stressed out about the one I can't. In the early years I was perhaps doing about 80 to 85 per cent of the things other people of my age could do but recently this has narrowed dramatically. The immune system ages somewhat faster for people with HIV/ Aids than it does for healthy individuals. I reckon I am now about ten to fifteen years older health-wise than my contemporaries, which makes me virtually an octogenarian.

Narrow as my life is, it's much better than I could ever have dreamt of. I've found one of the really great things about being on this planet is that if, for some reason, you suddenly can't smell the roses, then there is plenty of other terrific stuff in the garden to get a kick out of. Tim and I have taken to walking down to the Thames at Putney every afternoon to watch the changing seasons and the tides coming in and out. All very different from chain-sawing a makeshift doorway through Robin Grant-Sturgis's drawing-room wall during a dinner party.

I have been very lucky in having had excellent doctors; however at times trying simultaneously to balance the benefits versus the side effects of specialist drugs have at best been 'trial and error' or more accurately 'hit or miss'. It is nigh on impossible, sometimes, to try and isolate why one is feeling a particular way and whether it's chemical, psychological or a mixture of both. I recently emailed long-suffering Mark Nelson regarding a proposed change in my medication, 'Nothing terrifies me more than depression and mental illness generally. Given the choice, I would rather get up twelve times a night for a pee (the current side effects) than be depressed. In fact, I would I think on balance rather be beheaded by Daesh than feel depressed again right now'.

Recently, it so happened that I sat next to the avant-garde jewellery artist Bernhard Schobinger at an informal dinner in an Italian café off Brick Lane. Bernhard is several years older than me, has a strong Swiss accent and, much as I like and admire him, is quite hard work to sit next to for an hour and a half. So biting the bullet, I inquired: 'Bernhard, are you one of those people who when they go to sleep at night is frightened that they might never wake up? Or are you, like me, one of those who is frightened knowing that they will wake up?'

His eyes suddenly alight with interest, Bernhard turned to me and replied, 'In England you have an expression . . . it is how you say, "small talk" . . . this,' he said, pausing for maximum impact '. . . this is not small talk.'

Appendix

Post-op
Dr Mortimer's Observations

In the mid-nineties, as well as working with John Hobbs, I became the junior partner in an antiquarian book company, Simon Finch Rare Books Ltd., based just off Bond Street. Simon had become fixated with launching an upmarket literary magazine. In 2002, he was introduced to the young and ebullient Dan Crowe, recently literary editor of *Another Magazine*, they hit it off and so *Zembla* magazine – 'Fun with Words' – was born. The acclaimed art director Vince Frost was signed up to design the layout with the brief that *Zembla* should be both interesting and funky visually. The whole project was bankrolled by Simon. Because I was the financial director of Simon Finch Rare Books by default I became the finance director of *Zembla*. This would have been challenging at the best of times but given my lack of experience in publishing, even more so. A consolation prize was, however, negotiating with Dan that I should write a column (ex gratia) for *Zembla* to be called 'Dr Mortimer's Observations'. I knew that I would never again have such an opportunity, as the likelihood of any other publication giving me my own column was remote to say the least. As it happened Dan was nothing if not astute and he worked out pretty quickly that it was a cute move to give the magazine's finance director his wish. If the worst came to the worst he could always have the column rewritten and plead editorial necessity. Thus a protocol was established that should Dan need any additional funding for some pressing project or if a large bill required paying urgently, I would receive a casual softening-up call, usually along the lines of 'Hiya, Chas, a good friend of mine who just happens to be editor of *Vanity Fair/Rolling Stone/GQ* just happened to read your column the other day and they think it's: a work of enormous literary merit/so humorous that they have now stuck it on the fridge door/just world-class satire on every front.

Being a sucker for the odd compliment for a while I did of believe him (which I now see, with the benefit of hindsight, was insane). I think it was the day that he mentioned the distinct possibility of a Nobel Prize for Literature that the penny dropped.

Notwithstanding Dan's disingenuous habit of hiding unpleasant *Zembla* invoices behind the filing cabinet when he had gone seriously over budget, I hugely enjoyed working with him. Despite the fact I thought Simon needed his head examining by a really good man for taking on *Zembla* in the first place I must give him credit for having had the chutzpah and vision to do so.

Somewhat astonishingly during its brief two year existence, *Zembla* attracted contributions from all sorts of heavyweight literary figures (most of whom I had never heard) from Paul Auster to Harold Pinter and Hanif Kureishi.

Zembla (2003 to 2005): the only magazine, according to Johnny Vaughan, that had more awards than it did readers.

For anyone needing a sedative, here are my columns:

September 2003

As I was moving into a new flat my neighbour Natalia knocked on the door to introduce herself, 'Would you like to come round on Thursday to meet some really nice people?'

'I'll tell you what, pet,' I responded, 'if we're going to be living next door to one another I'd like to get one thing straight and that is I never want to meet some really nice people.' In my limited experience really nice people are, more often than not, not very nice people pretending. A good friend of mine tends to acquire houses all over the world, sometimes at an alarming rate. He's decent enough to suggest that I can use them with the added incentive that they are situated in areas inhabited by 'very interesting people'. Uncharitably I translate that as 'not very interesting who clearly think otherwise'. The result of this social cynicism is that I spend a lot of time at home with the blinds down and the air-con up.

I remember my father once depicting a character on the racecourse thus: 'with his distinctly individual clothes and inevitable cigar he was an easily recognisable figure as he no doubt intended to be . . .' which leads me onto to self-contrived individuals who take great pride in both presenting and describing themselves as eccentric. For what it's worth, I find persons who have gone to great lengths to stand out from the crowd with both considered premeditation and intent rather fraudulent (understatement). They are as a Picasso print sold in Woolworths is to an original.

There is nothing I love more than the genuine article – clearly one stop short of East Ham (Barking), totally original and 100 per cent sincere that they are as normal as 'the man on the Clapham omnibus'. My Aunt Boo, who missed genius by a whisker, was a tireless campaigner for unusual causes, when she wasn't holding forth from her collapsible mahogany steps at Speakers' Corner she was standing as an independent parliamentary candidate for a variety of previously unheard of parties. 'Keep Dorking White' in 1958 and 'Women against the Common Market' both ring a bell. The fact that she always lost her deposit was no great surprise; the fact that over a hundred people were always mad enough to vote for her was.

Not a million miles away are those of us, myself included, with mental problems of one sort or another. Often fun to hang out with, but things can get out of hand fairly rapidly. Several years ago whilst a patient in the Priory, Roehampton, I became quite matey with an ex-serviceman dressed as Spiderman. I guess the fact that he had a minder and was under section should have alerted me more. However, from what I remember, we seemed to enjoy pretty regular conversations from time to time about this and that. One day he asked me to his room for a cup of tea and a digestive biscuit. After about twenty minutes of conversation he mentioned he had recently visited California, which in itself was fine . . . 'and whilst I was there,' he went on to say, 'I created another planet.' And then with very deliberate articulation and just a hint of menace, 'Now don't you think that makes me just a little bit special?'

Very recently I acquired a haemorrhoid. This was a first for me so I was unaware of its normal margins of operation. After two days of acute discomfort I went to Boots the chemist. 'Do you have any strong haemorrhoid cream?' I asked the pleasant lady. Her response, pointing vaguely to the middle of the shop somewhere, 'All our haemorrhoid creams are over there, sir.' My response was also to point: 'Madam, what I need won't be found over there but over here with you on your side of the counter, in the heavy-duty section.' What I noticed from this brief exchange was that acute pain had forced me to overcome any normal sense of shame or embarrassment and that simultaneously the mood of the queue at prescriptions had brightened perceptibly as it became aware of my plight. The following evening Dean, my flatmate of ten years who has more tattoos per square inch than the Sistine Chapel has illustrations on its ceiling, returned to our flat with his girlfriend looking and acting morose. I took him aside. 'You think you've got problems. I've got a haemorrhoid the size of . . .' Within a nanosecond his entire demeanour had changed; I might have just intravenously injected him with a Carry On film. For the rest of the evening, whenever I hobbled past his room, I heard cackles of laughter.

Talking on the telephone this morning to my mother I endured, as I do from time to time, a fair bit of stick about what she considers to be my unhelpful attitude to any proposed social commitment. 'But mother,' I responded, 'the fact is that life itself is completely meaningless anyway. All we are, are pointless self-important things meandering around on some tiny spinning ball in the middle of a massive and endless nowhere.' 'Now don't you get scientific with me boy,' she retorted, and hung up.

Winter 2003/2004

For many years it has been my ethos to leave hotel rooms in a better state than when I found them. For this specific purpose I usually carry with me a small toolkit when travelling so that I can spend hours amusing myself by re-attaching the loose soap dish or overhauling the mechanical plug in the bidet. On the subject of hotels, I think it would be much more original if rock stars and footballers staying in five-star hotels, rather than launching the television set off the balcony, instead gave it a damn good going-over with a can of Pledge and a duster before shampooing and vacuuming the entire suite. Imagine, in retrospect, the headline 'Hotel manager in total shock as wild man of rock leaves presidential suite spotless', and goes on to enthuse that 'not only can you see your face now in the faux mahogany veneer, but Keith Moon has even managed to get rid of those unsightly stains left by Sheik-a-leg and his extensive harem. Wow!'

Bearing all this in mind I recently booked into a quasi-luxury hotel in Northumberland for my older sister's wedding. The first evening, the extremely grumpy barman asked for my room number in exchange for an armful of intoxicating drinks. 'Strangely,' I responded, 'there doesn't seem to be a number on the door just a brass plaque with "Hadrian" written on it.'

'Ooohh,' he replied with an unexpected deference more in keeping with those addressing minor royalty, 'you're in the

Hadrian Suite are you?' This was news to me but appeared to be the case and for the remainder of the evening my other half Tim and I made the most of our elevated status as the occupants of what I gather was the only suite in town.

Unfortunately, the following morning events took a slight downturn. I ran a bath in the slightly (understatement) impractical shag-pile carpeted bathroom and then wandered off for a short while. Returning what seemed like a mere two minutes later, I discovered to my horror that I had run enough water to fill about three baths – two of which, it seemed, had disappeared through the floor into the room below. Not quite grasping the magnitude of the unfolding catastrophe, I attempted to right matters by ripping up the carpet and mopping the floor with an immaculate set of white bath towels, which became very dirty very quickly without having much impact on the deluge. The occupants of the room below appeared in disarray, sprinkled with builders' debris and not surprisingly dangerously disgruntled. My partner's yoga session now a washout, I wasn't popular in that quarter either. By now an army of domestics had appeared and I retreated alone to the dining room for a 'full English', where I choked on a white-hot pork sausage and knocked a vat of scalding black coffee all over the pastel carpet. A short time later I went in search of the manager to explain, apologise, and grovel for permission to stay another night. As I passed a small group of hotel employees I heard them whisper, 'He's the one who trashed The Hadrian Suite.'

Negotiations with the management team started off okay – that is until I began. I was sweating both heavily and obviously by now, as I endeavoured to explain my ethos and how as a result of it I personally felt extremely traumatised. 'Pray continue, Mr Mortimer,' invited the senior day manager. So I did, and as I painstakingly described my practice of carrying a small toolkit, etc. ('I can fetch and show it to you if you like') I saw all colour drain from his face as he and his team rapidly reached a certain, very permanent and wholly unsatisfactory conclusion about me, my ethos, my toolkit and my mental state.

By sheer coincidence shortly afterwards we went to another wedding – my second only in more than a decade. We stayed at a moderately chi-chi hotel on the outskirts of Bury in Suffolk. Other guests included a significant number of down-at-heel aristocracy from central Europe. An ageing countess mistook me for the hall porter and as a consequence instructed me to carry about a hundred massive suitcases from one end of the hotel to the other. Had her general demeanour suggested that a decent tip might have been on offer I would have obliged. Tim fared little better when the concierge displayed total incredulity that he was going to 'That wedding . . . as a guest . . . you're kidding me!'

After the service I somehow got stuck in the disabled toilet in the vestry with an ancient rock star (Bill Wyman) whom I knew a little.

That evening, at a sit-down dinner, I was placed next to Lady F whom I hadn't seen since I set fire to my bed while staying at her home in 1983. She is one of my firm favourites being of the 'no-nonsense' school of thought. Having once eaten an entire catering can of cold Heinz baked beans, I accompanied her to the cinema in the Fulham Road. After about forty minutes Lady F announced, I thought quite loudly,

'Charlie, unless you stop doing what I think you are doing either you or I are going to have to leave this cinema in the very near future.'

A couple of years later I went to the same cinema with rather a wild friend of mine, now very sadly deceased, called Lars, who lived on the island of Lamu. As we walked in the film had already started and two young men were pulling the lifeless body of a beautiful young lady from a swimming pool. 'Oh God, what shall we do now . . .' one said to the other. 'Fuck her while she's still warm!' shouted Lars. We were escorted out by the manager shortly afterwards.

Continuing the theme. My younger sister Lumpy took my mother to the same cinema to see the comedy *A Fish Called Wanda*. During the film, after the third small dog had been squashed by falling crates, my mother marched off to complain to the manager (my mother owned Chihuahuas). At the end of the performance Lumpy went off to find my mother and was a little surprised to find her propping up the bar with the Indian manager expounding to him the extensive benefits of foxhunting. 'Oh, do meet Amar, he really is the most delightful man . . . we've had a wonderful chat. Of course, he completely understands . . .'

I once went to watch a very dull film in Exeter with larger than life Nigel Knight-Bruce. 'I need a large drink . . .' said someone in the film. 'So do I,' agreed Nigel, loudly, and we left.

The final cinematic incident that comes to mind was when my companion JB set fire to the hair of the person sitting in front of him because he couldn't see the screen . . . that did the trick.

Moving on ... my neighbour Natalia has a passion for redistributing junk. Several months ago, Tim and I had a major clean-out from our flat and, as has always been the understanding, we deposited with her several bin-liners full of stuff. Natalia, in her turn, passed quite a lot of this on to her delightful mother in Shropshire, who in turn donated it to her local Conservative Party fundraising bazaar. Amongst this particular consignment were some videos put there by accident. Thus it was that the local association vice-chairman of the Tory party (Lieut-Col. something or other) ended up watching *Gary Gets a Fat One*.

Last weekend, I visited my mother, currently looked after by a keen young carer from South Africa, who feels quite strongly that my mother should grasp this late opportunity to repent and embrace Jesus. 'My dear girl,' I overhead as I passed her room, 'I don't need Jesus. I just need a strong drink!'

Spring 2004

In a perfect world I would like to have been a motoring correspondent, 'Mort the Sport, connoisseur of fine motoring'. That sort of thing. Several years ago I had a bash at doing a column for *Tatler Magazine* and managed to wangle a brand new BMW M5 for a few days. To put it through its paces a good friend, Steve W, and I decided to drive to Amsterdam for Easter. To spices things up a bit Steve videoed me complete with commentary as we hurtled along at between 130 and 150 mph. After about an hour of this we decided to pull into some motorway services for a cup of tea and a jam doughnut and simultaneously found ourselves surrounded by police vehicles of every description.

'I'm most frightfully sorry, officer, I had no idea that there was a speed limit over here . . .' seemed to be making a moderately favourable impression, despite the fact that apparently a specially modified Porsche had been dispatched from Rotterdam to intercept us. Unfortunately, gaining in confidence by this point, I clearly made a hideous misjudgement by following quite unnecessarily with '. . . and in any case officer, even if there is a speed limit, with your country's current attitude towards child pornography and hard drugs, I didn't think speeding would be taken too seriously.' What relationship there was fell off a cliff and Steve and I found ourselves behind bars for the rest of the day, sans video recorder. Eventual persuasion that the car wasn't actually mine followed by a trip to a nearby cashpoint to extract and hand over some £400 (no paperwork, no receipt) got us back on our way. Later on we discovered that there wasn't a single room to be had in Amsterdam that night and we had to drive all the way to Cologne, which as resorts for Easter go, is not exactly a barrel of laughs. The eventual piece I submitted to *Tatler* was declined. No definitive reason given.

Just for the record, Steve and I decided to have another go at Amsterdam the following year but this time flew there to celebrate New Year. On this occasion it was the return trip that caused all the drama. It all started when Steve asked me if I wouldn't mind packing a few of his 'things' in my suitcase. 'If some things mean any of that hideous collection of perverted porn currently adoring your bedspread then the answer, old bean, is no.' End of subject till arrivals at Heathrow Airport. 'Anything to declare sir?' asked the kindly customs man. 'No nothing, officer.' 'All the same, sir, would you like to open your bag?' he said to Steve. As my companion released the catches his suitcase literally exploded with pornographic paraphernalia. The nice officer suggested that it might be better if they went to some room behind the scenes.

As it happened I was actually studying for a law degree at Ealing Polytechnic at the time, so when the officer returned a while later and asked me if I was indeed Mr W's solicitor, I thought 'Fantastic, my first case.' I therefore replied in the affirmative before being led backstage into a small room now bulging at the seams with massive flexible dildos, chicks-with-dicks videos and such like. In the middle of all this merchandise sat my friend, now stripped down to his underwear, which to my surprise seemed to consist quite simply of black and red lace ladies' knickers and a matching bra. To be fair, the customs man made it clear that as far as he was concerned, although he was very sympathetic to Steve's predilections, approximately 98 per cent of what he had in his possession fell into the category of obscene material and was therefore categorised as an illegal import. For my part I explained that my companion's fiancée was waiting for him in the arrivals foyer and would be 'most distressed to see her future husband under these most harrowing of circumstances'. A deal was therefore struck – the porn was confiscated – a £100 fine was levied – and we were on our way. I felt well pleased with my first official legal performance, which was just as well since it was also my last as I failed all my first-year exams shortly afterwards.

Another arrival which ended up in a concealed backroom accompanied by, on this occasion, a not-so-pleasant immigration officer was when disembarking from the Hamburg to

Harwich ferry when I was asked for my passport. 'I'm very sorry, officer, I seem to have eaten it, or at least most of it,' I replied, at the same time producing a few tooth-marked shreds of unconsumed dark blue cardboard. In retrospect a more prudent course of action would be to have simply said, 'I'm very sorry, officer, but I appear to have mislaid it', rather than launch into a lengthy and detailed scenario revolving around the ship's discotheque, the Beatles song 'Nowhere Man', the collapse of the British pound and a schnapps-drinking competition.

On the subject of run-ins with officials, pleasant or otherwise, I was recently reminded of an incident I will come to shortly by a series of adverts that appear from time to time in the *Spectator* magazine entitled 'My first Krug.' The gist of them is, more or less, along the following lines: '. . . after papa had parked the Facel Vega in the owners' car park at Royal Ascot he produced from a massive Fortnum and Mason picnic hamper, concealed in the boot, an ice-cold bottle of vintage Krug and four champagne flutes . . . it is a memory that I shall always treasure . . .' (You get the picture.) Well this got me thinking about my first Krug. The occasion was the launch party of my extremely short-lived Kensington-based estate agents Tips, Butler and Co. At the advertising agent who were kindly hosting the evening I came across two bottles of Krug in a fridge and, having never drunk Krug before, was unaware that it was not usually consumed direct from the bottle like Lucozade. Before long – in the words of Mr Kipling – I felt 'exceedingly' inebriated, albeit in rather an expensive sort of way.

Not long afterwards I was driving, or rather attempting to drive, my then business partner and old friend Colin Pool home. Unfortunately, whilst seeing double I drove the wrong side of a lamppost in full view of a police car. I was promptly pulled over. I am told that when the amenable officer approached the car he took one look at me helplessly and hopelessly fumbling for a door handle and decided from that moment on only to converse with Colin rather than me. This altercation eventually resulted in me blowing up some sort of a bag, such as existed then in the early days of breathalysers. The policemen then went off to examine whether or not the crystals had turned colour. I am told he looked alarmed as he examined and re-examined his findings in front of each headlight of his patrol car. Eventually, addressing Colin, he announced, 'Well, I don't understand this at all but I'm obliged to give your friend the benefit of the doubt.' The only condition was that Colin drove.

Due to go foxhunting with my uncle General Sir Kenneth Darling in Oxfordshire the following morning I insisted that Colin took me halfway across London to collect my suitcase before heading to the country. This supreme effort on Colin's part turned out to be largely pointless as I discovered the next morning I had failed to put anything in it. In addition to arriving at the Guinness's Farm at midnight curled up in the foot-well of my Fiat, the following morning, on my way to the meet, I brought up a full English breakfast virtually intact within seconds of swallowing it, which was nice for my young ward Anita. If things weren't bad enough I then fell off my horse and onto my head at the first fence. 'You really are the bally limit!' boomed Sir Kenneth.

During the last war my mother, inter alia, worked for the aircraft firm Westland as a draughtswoman, the result was that she fancied herself as a bit of an engineer. So when my then brother-in-law, now sadly deceased, Paul Torday [then MD of a substantial engineering company and subsequently a highly successful author of such books as *Salmon Fishing in the Yemen*], came to stay after a very late and boozy night my mother eagerly made off to bed with a copy of his company's latest colour brochure. The following morning, we were all rather the worse for wear. Not so my mother, who despite having drunk as much as all of us put together appeared as bright as a button. It was rumoured that she once had a hangover in about 1948. 'I must say, Paul,' she enthused, 'I was most awfully intrigued by your simply enormous crankshaft.'

Summer 2004

On the subject of stress – several years ago I ran into Leonie Gibbs, the young wife of a very good friend of mine, Joe Gibbs. She was in a bit of a state having just reversed into a parked car. I told her not to worry but instead to simply adopt my new philosophy in life, namely a totally stress-free existence. 'Nothing bothers me,' I enthused. 'In fact, I'll call Joe this evening and tell him all about it.' A minute later I was opening the door of my own car when a largish truck laden with scaffolding whizzed past purposely scaring the life out of me by missing both my door and myself by millimetres. Without a sensible pause for thought I gave the truck a couple of fingers whilst shouting something appropriate. To my surprise the lorry stopped and all three scaffolders jumped out to confront me. 'Wanna do that again?' one of them said with menace. Unwisely, rather than beat a hasty retreat, I took him at his word and responded along the lines of 'Not especially, old bean, but by kind invitation only too happy to oblige.'

I don't actually remember how much of this little speech I got out before I was knocked totally sparko. The next thing I remember was regaining something that vaguely resembled consciousness with Leonie, who had witnessed the entire incident, attempting to pick me up from the road. 'These bastards aren't going to get away with this,' I assured her before I apparently jumped into my car and chased off down the road after the scaffolders. Unfortunately for me I caught up with them.

My next memory was about half an hour later lying on the Gibbs's kitchen floor with a wet towel wrapped round my head. It seems that after the second altercation I had somehow, in total blackout, got back in my car and driven to Leonie's house, arriving on her doorstep pouring blood and rambling something along the lines of 'Please tell me who I am and how I got here?'

Emerging from the blackout was a little like, I imagine, being beamed up by Scotty. Quite simply one was transported from one reality to another with absolutely no interim whatsoever.

In medical parlance I guess I was suffering concussion because now back in some sort of control I thanked Leonie and shot off to Queensgate, still with a wet towel wrapped round my head and a heavily bloodstained shirt. It was there that I had an appointment with record tycoon Chris Blackwell whom I had recently discovered was a distant cousin. There I met up with Nick K whose band (Blame It All on Lex) I was then managing. Between us we were hoping, together with our demo cassette tape, to make a favourable impression. Unfortunately, Mr Blackwell was less than impressed (understatement) with both my rhetoric and disorderly appearance with the result that Nick and I were shown the door pronto.

As it turned out there was an unexpected upside to all this as I was inexplicably launched into a really excellent mood for all of a month, a bit like some crude form of stone age ECT. The downside was a certain lack of credibility chez Gibbs and a hairline fracture of the jaw. 'If you aren't careful, Charlie, I'll have to wire it up,' said Michael my doctor whilst perusing the X-rays. 'How would I eat then?' I not unreasonably inquired. 'Through a straw,' he responded cheerfully. 'And communicate?' I continued. 'By signs chiefly interspersed with the odd grunt,' he replied, clearly warming to his theme. 'With the greatest of respect, Michael, it was communicating largely by signs that got me into this predicament in the first place,' I concluded.

On roughly the same sort of theme, in the 1960s whilst at school flicking through the *Oxford Dictionary* I came across the word 'spiv', explained in the blurb as 'one who survives without regular employment'. 'That suits me just fine,' I thought and to this day have never sought to depict myself as anything else although these days I tend to embellish it if someone asks me what I do by describing myself as 'a middle-aged, middle-class spiv.' [My father once wrote to my tutor Michael Kidson: 'I agree with everything you said in Charles's report except for the comparison to a chimney jackdaw; I thought that was unfair on the bird. As you say he is a sort of inverted Lord Rosebery.']

By the time I hit thirty not that much had changed and I received a letter from my dad stating in his own inimitable style, 'Now you've reached middle age why not accept that in life's race you're an also ran but never shown, but don't worry about it, sonny, by the time you get to forty you won't much care anyway.' For the record, I reckon he was about ten years out, forty now being middle-aged and fifty marking some sort of benign acceptance of the way things are and likely to remain. To be fair to my dad he went on to say that it was a status that he had personally reconciled himself to years previously.

Around the same time (1982) my younger sister Lumpy sent my father a saucy Valentine card and signed it 'Mrs McQueen'. My mother (née Denison-Pender) was convinced that it had actually come from the popular hostess of the local pub, the Carnarvon Arms. As a result, my father was given a fearful bollocking, followed he said by 'many hostile comments on my alleged drinking and amorous habits, combined with severe reminders that no member of the Denison-Pender family ever received Valentines from barmaids'.

Summer 2004

Some random thoughts and scenarios which will, with any luck, fall into a vague semblance of logical order . . .

Some years ago whilst staying in Bangkok to organise the manufacturing of underwear for our fledgling company Raffateer (slogan: *You're never alone in a pair of Raffateer boxer shorts*) Ltd with my then business partner Johnny K (nicknamed Toyboy) we came across a nightclub which advertised its star attraction of the night outside on a blackboard. 'She shove egg up her cunt' left little to the imagination; to this day I can't think of a more economic or descriptive ad. Later on that evening in another club one of the prettiest girls I have ever seen parked herself on Toyboy's lap. Whilst stroking his hair she asked the nineteen-year-old Westminster-educated Toyboy, who had a bit of a reputation as a ladies' man around Chelsea, 'Kiss me darling.' 'Kiss you?' exclaimed Toyboy. 'I can't possibly kiss you . . . I don't even know you.'

Whilst on the subject of Thailand; the previous year a friend, Julian Keeling, and I rented a couple of trial bikes near the Golden Triangle, with adventure in mind. Within hours we ended up with rather more adventure than we'd bargained for when an elderly lady literally threw herself in front of Julian's machine with a view to sustaining some minor injuries and then suing for a few quid. Unfortunately for all concerned, her in particular, she well underestimated Julian's speed and all I saw (no disrespect intended) was what I thought was a sack of dirty laundry flying through the air followed by a bareheaded Julian and his motorbike somersaulting down about the only stretch of asphalt in Northern Thailand. I cannot speak for the other parties but although actually uninjured myself I was clearly going to be severely disillusioned if I really thought that, having surveyed the carnage, digging around in my sponge bag for a tube of Germolene was going to achieve anything. There were no hospitals in the vicinity and the victims were in a poor state.

The injured lady was removed by a small army of relatives, the bikes by the police and we were placed under arrest. After some negotiations somehow I got Julian to a hotel in Chiang

Rai where he bled so profusely I was obliged to buy the mattress off the proprietors in order to keep the peace. Despite the awfulness of our situation we developed a kind of gallows humour which kept us unnaturally amused. I spent the next couple of days, despite savage diarrhoea, applying bandages, tracking down antibiotics and painkillers, and making large numbers of absurd phone calls back to a gullible hotel reception, pretending to be various world leaders (such as Paul Keating, the then Prime Minister of Australia) enquiring after Julian's state of health. At night, in order for me to get some sleep, desperate measures were sometimes required. 'If you don't stop all that groaning and moaning, old fruit, I shall be obliged to spit my Aids-infected sputum into your open wounds.' That usually did the trick.

Several days later, I wheeled Julian, together with our new-found interpreter Mr Boonsong, into a Nissen hut masquerading as an intensive care unit for a pre-arranged rendezvous with about two dozen policemen and concerned relatives at the old lady's deathbed. The only person who seemed remotely interested in the wellbeing of the poor lady was our taxi driver who from time to time lifted a blanket, prodded her with a stick, and then sighed and gloomily shook his head. Since Julian looked like an accident victim in *Carry on Matron* I took control of the proceedings.

It was pointed out to me that despite the fact that I was riding a separate motorcycle and was a good twenty yards behind all the action I was, under Thai law, equally culpable. The police wasted no time in demanding the equivalent of £5,000 or 'you prison very long time mister'. In return I offered £20 which was not well received. Six hours later I was up to about £100 when a policeman stuck a machinegun in my throat. At this point I said to Mr Boonsong, 'Can you inform these gentlemen that if we are sent to prison we will immediately go on hunger strike, thus provoking a major international incident?' Mr Boonsong translated and to my surprise the entire room erupted into howls of laughter – bar of course Julian and myself. Drawing myself up a little. I responded, 'Mr Boonsong, frankly I would have thought that laughter was most inappropriate at this juncture.' To which he said in conclusion, still sniggering, 'They say in Thai prison no food anyway so hunger strike no problem.' This spiked my guns somewhat and eventually we agreed on £400 which was split 50 per cent to the old lady's nearest and dearest and 50 per cent to the police 'benevolent fund'. I regret that I am unable to confirm whether or not the lady survived.

For no obvious reason, this reminds me of a story I once heard. I was at the time an inmate in a drug/alcohol treatment centre near Weston-super-Mare. During one of our frequent group therapy sessions we were supposed to be giving personal examples of 'Powerlessness' (i.e. the inability to predict once you had had your first drink or drug of that particular day when you were, if ever, going to stop) and 'Damage' (i.e. emotional damage, in particular, mainly to your partner, family and friends caused by your unpredictable behaviour whilst on the rampage). Andy, from Birmingham, recently released from prison, on being asked for his example of P and D launched in a strong Brummie accent into one of the maddest stories I've ever heard. It involved vast quantities of drugs in sacks (for sale), stolen hi-fis, TVs and other electrical goods being piled high in the back of his Tranny (Ford Transit van) which was then pursued at breakneck speed (apparently) for hours over endless humpback bridges by half the West Midlands serious crime squad whilst he and his mates dropped LSD and smoked spliff in the front of the van. 'Very interesting, Andrew,' commented the counsellor. 'Now where exactly do you see the damage in all of this?' Andy thought for a minute before replying with great seriousness, 'It didn't half fuck up the suspension on my Tranny.'

Moving onto the other night – whilst motoring back from the country I turned on the radio, heard a few bars of some hideous song and promptly turned it off again. My other half Tim immediately started laughing. 'What's up?' I inquired. He responded that I was the only gay man that he had ever met who having turned on the radio and heard 'Dancing Queen' by Abba could possibly turn it off again.

I guess the fact that we are so different makes us a constant source of amusement to each other and in part explains why we get on so well. He spends large amounts of time watching Kylie Minogue and reality TV shows (often involving makeovers or plastic surgery), reading very expensive and obscure Italian fashion mags and applying moisturiser. He can spend literally hours working out the right combination involving simply three different coloured T-shirts, two pairs of jeans and a pair of trainers. For myself, I now realise that my seduction techniques before meeting him, which usually involved a fry-up, a viewing of *Sweeney 2* (the movie) and then a close inspection of my matt black metal and rubber pump-action twelve-bore Beretta shotgun with collapsible stock was laughable in its inappropriateness. But there you go. You live and learn. Luckily we have two TV sets so he can watch Britney Spears live from Miami whilst I am tragically glued to repeats of *Taggart* and *Hi-de-Hi!*

On the subject of 1970s classics, towards the end of that decade my mother, worried not for the first time about my general wellbeing, telephoned John Hobbs for a tête-à-tête. Their markedly different take on the subsequent conversation was as follows: My mother, commenting on John's distinctive accent, 'I really do applaud people who have had huge success and yet still keep their roots.' John: 'I spoke to Charlie's mum for forty-five fucking minutes and I didn't understand one fucking word she said.'

Autumn 2004

In the hope that I could spare myself the effort of writing a column for this anniversary edition of *Zembla* I came up with the idea of persuading our esteemed editor (Mr Daniel Waterfall Crowe) to interview me. I had assumed that Crowe was a trained journalist of some sort. My plan was that I should do sweet FA apart from answer a string of predictable questions, Crowe would do all the work, and presto problem solved. We rendezvoused last week at a moderately chi-chi hotel in Notting Hill. Crowe was dressed in a loud and unusual way. I think it involved shorts. He had prepared a few questions, few being the operative word, and seemed to think it was possible to conduct an interview without a pen, notepad or tape recorder. However, our Crowe may be many things and slippery just happens to be one of them. So that said, it didn't take (even) Dr M long to work out that all he wanted to do was to scoff a gargantuan breakfast at our long-suffering publisher's expense, talk crap for twenty minutes (always a pleasure with Crowe) and then fob me off with a crumpled sheet of paper on which there were half a dozen inane questions such as 'Do you like Christmas? Tell me about your underwear?', together with a suggestion that I go away and interview myself, to return next week with the result. Nice one, Crowe.

So using the above-mentioned questionnaire and accompanying blurb here we have the Crowe DIY interview:

Crowe: Now Dr M just relax. Tell me about your father.

Dr M: Not until you tell me about yours, which is usually good for a laugh. (Crowe's family takes the description 'dysfunctional' to unheard of levels.)

Crowe: Who is Dr Mortimer?

Dr M: Some sad old sucker who writes a column for no dough who also happens to be financial director of this magazine. So I suggest you watch yourself if you want a wage packet at the end of the current month.

Crowe: What makes him so twisted?

Dr M: Dealing with you on a daily basis might have something to do with it.

Crowe: Does he ever have a happy, sunny day?

Dr M: Not with you around he doesn't.

Crowe: Do you like Christmas?

Dr M: Give me a break. What sort of question is that? For the record the last family Christmas we had was more like *Straw Dogs*. (A film before your time I guess but ring Johnny Vaughan and he'll tell you all about it.)

Crowe: Tell me about your underwear? (Clearly an obsession for Crowe.)

Dr M: I don't wear any. What's yours like?

Crowe: Clean and ironed. Who is someone you admire?

Dr M: Your wife.

Crowe: What is the point of it all?

Dr M: Do you mean this interview or have you got something more significant in mind?

Crowe: Are we all equal?

Dr M: You're having a laugh now.

Crowe: You have endured a life-threatening illness for almost twenty years now. Has this allowed you to cultivate attitudes towards people that you may not have had otherwise?

Dr M: Carry on like this, matey, and I could easily end up biting you.

Crowe: Who is the kindest person you have ever met?

Dr M: Me – for putting up with all your old bollocks for the past fourteen months.

Crowe: Do you rely on your friends?

Dr M: Yes – they're called Solpadeine and Valium.

Crowe: Who is your favourite author?

Dr M: The guy who edits *MIMS Monthly Index of Medical Specialties.*

Crowe: Do you have a motto?

Dr M: Yes – don't suffer fools gladly, so I'm off now.

Crowe: Are you going to pay for breakfast?

Dr M: Do I have a choice?

EDITOR'S NOTE: Mr Mortimer did end up paying for breakfast and indeed my wages for this month. Contrary to the above exchange, he is in fact a very kind man with a penchant for wild flowers.

Winter 2004

On 1 September I received a rather smug and self-congratulatory letter addressed to Mr C. Mortimer from our London Mayor, Ken Livingstone. The gist of it was to take an opportunity (i.e. the third anniversary) to thank each couple who had supported his same-sex London Partnership Register. He went on to say that, to date, some 800 couples had registered (at a cost of some eighty-five quid a throw) and that, as a result, we had in some way contributed (apparently) to the development of this historic piece of legislation. It droned on encouraging all registered couples to lobby the government to restore the Civil Partnership Act and said that cuddly old Ken looked forward to the day when gay people in this country were recognised as equal before the law. All very commendable. However, it is probably a good start to at least pay lip-service to what you preach and, despite the fact that Tim (the other half) were, in fact, only the fourteenth couple to register back in September 2001, dear old Ken saw fit to send a letter addressed in every respect to the Mortimer half only, with no mention whatsoever being made to my partner.

Nice one, Ken. No chance, I suppose, of us getting our eighty-five nicker back is there?

As it happens the actual registration process itself was rather more entertaining than anticipated. On the day in question three of us pitched up at the allotted hour and were asked to wait for a short time before the registrars appeared. Tim and I had brought along as witness our quasi-adopted son Dean who lived with us. Dean was straight and had the air of a young and much better looking Sid James. He was very much the ladies' man. Unfortunately, he thought this was an ideal moment to ask Tim's opinion on whether or not he had recently caught 'crabs' as he considered Tim to be something of an expert in the area of sexual health. I did not participate at all in this medical evaluation which culminated in a rather personal inspection being conducted. Dean was not known as 'Conga' for nothing and predictably it was at this precise moment that the two lady registrars made their appearance. There was some initial consternation (understatement) made worse when they realised that the couple actually getting hitched (for want of a better expression) was in fact Tim and myself. Any attempt at explanation along the lines of 'he's our adopted son . . . well sort of' or 'it's all right he's straight and has a girlfriend' were guaranteed to make matters much worse so we kept schtum, signed the forms, handed over our cheque and legged it.

On the way home we stopped at a chemist's in Pimlico. Tim had advised Dean he didn't think there was a problem but to be on the safe side he should apply some Quellada lotion for a couple of days. Tim offered to go into the rather crowded chemist's to purchase a bottle. When it came to his turn in the queue he almost whispered his request to a bubbly sales girl. She bounced off to some store room before shouting out to the entire shop, 'Is it crabs or scabies you've got there?' For Tim, mortified didn't cover it.

On the subject of gay marriage, etc. I was astonished to find myself truly grief-stricken by the ban on hunting and in no way compensated by the Civil Partnership Bill passing into law in the same twenty-four hours. The fact is that it's simply a bonus for Tim and I to have various tax concessions and for our domestic arrangements to be officially validated. For hunting folk their whole way of life has been decimated by a mean and spiteful bill driven through a questionable process by a bunch of hypocrites as some bizarre trade-off for backing the invasion of Iraq. At least Hitler (who also banned hunting) was a vegetarian. I have actually been foxhunting on several occasions (admittedly all over twenty-five years ago) and I have to say that nothing on this planet would ever induce me to go again. I vaguely remember someone seriously suggesting that my horse and I jump over (stone cold sober) some massive five-bar gate – and this before noon. The moment I hesitated (and frankly who in their right mind wouldn't) an elderly lady, riding side-saddle, barged past shouting, 'Get out of my bloody way, you bloody little man!'

The next time I took to the hunting field I found that half a dozen whisky macs made the experience almost endurable although being stuck on a huge horse and absolutely desperate to have a pee was also memorable. Now we're on the subject, I guess the fact that much of Siegfried Sassoon's *Memoirs of a Fox-hunting Man* was inspired by his close friendship with my great-uncle Master of Foxhounds Norman (Loder) combined with the fact that various members of my family were either MFHs or killed in the field has brought out in me this surprisingly strong view that the tradition should survive at any cost – provided of course that I am not obliged to participate personally. I now look forward to participating in some really serious civil disobedience. Ultimately (and God knows where I got this from) it is not those who break an unjust law who are the criminals but those who made it.

Lucky Lupin

Lex iniusta non est lex.

Moving on. In January 1986, after several unexplained illnesses, I was diagnosed with HIV (or HTLV 3 as it was then). My friendly doctor gave me a max of two to three years to live. His nurse Rosie started crying. I remember thinking, 'That's very nice of you, pet.' No such niceties, however, from the magazine distributed annually by my old preparatory school which simply reported my death in the section headed 'Old Boys News'. The tragedy of it for me was that only one person noticed and called my sister to console her. For myself, I kept meaning to put them straight but thought I'll probably snuff it soon anyway so why bother. That said I was rather surprised when I saw an emergency dentist around that time. I had serious toothache (what toothache isn't serious for that matter?) and he told me the only solution was to pull a tooth. That done I thanked him and suggested I made another appointment to plan for some sort of replacement. 'Don't bother,' he replied. 'There's no point really, is there?' I have to say even with my 'let me have it straight, doc' attitude, it did rather take the wind out of my sails.

Three years ago I went to my godfather's wake held at my old prep school in Broadstairs where he had once been a master. Worth mentioning in passing, he had liked boys so much he'd actually bought a school of his own. Today he would be subject to satellite tagging, put on a list and not allowed within a million miles of a school of any description. In his defence he was actually totally harmless, just rather unusual (understatement). Anyway, while at this wake I was introduced to the editor of the school magazine and pointed out to him that he had erroneously killed me off in the

304

mid-1980s. He seemed genuinely mortified. I was more amused than put out. The result is that I now feature regularly in 'Old Boys News' as some sort of big shot in the London art and antiques market next to such success stories as Henry Wyndham (Chairman of Sotheby's). This, I guess, is compensation of sorts.

This is actually leading somewhere and that is that I will be intrigued to see how 'Old Boys News' deals with my contemporary Simon Mann. Simon is currently languishing in some dreadful gaol in Zimbabwe for purportedly doing something that, as far as I can see, showed remarkable initiative. I remember Simon quite well because at school he always had the best 'war mags'. Reputedly, aged ten or less, he carried out a practice parachute jump from the rear of his mother's Morris Minor as she was barrelling down a country lane at speed. She was unaware of his little plan and thus there was some consternation when on arriving back home she found he was not in the car.

The other day I was asked by a firm compiling a report on behalf of our bank what sort of qualifications I had for being financial director of a medium-sized company. I replied that I left school with one more O-level than Nicholas Soames (of whom I am a big fan) and one less than Mark Thatcher, whom I believe has three.

Whilst in the vicinity of big shots . . . in the 1960s my dad and I sometimes caught the train from Camberley to Waterloo. From time to time a stout self-important individual called Colonel Oakshott would board en route at Bagshot station. He was known, not without affection, as Oakshott, the Big Shot from Bagshot.

Dan Crowe, our esteemed editor, has made me aware that the *Spectator* magazine has recently had a dig at *Zembla* along the lines that one of our contributors, Manolo Blahnik, a mere maker of footwear, cannot possibly have anything valid to say about literature. Despite many tries, I have never found the *Spectator* is really my cup of tea, unlike *Exchange and Mart*. At Eton Jerry Soames kindly rechristened me *Exchange and Mort*. I did, however, always enjoy Jeffrey Bernard's candid observations in his truly excellent column 'Low Life' in the *Spectator*. [The fact that his favorite book was my dad's tome, *The History of the Derby Stakes*, endeared him to me even more.]

Not long ago my mother's boiler packed up. As a result, the manufacturers required her to fax them an order for the requisite new part, which the local plumber 'Terry' was intending to fit. That evening, my mother informed me triumphantly that she had indeed sent them a fax. I replied that that was interesting as she didn't have a fax machine. On further interrogation she told me that she had rung the fax number and when it had 'squawked' at her she had shouted her message down the phone and then replaced the receiver.

Summer 2005

I've found quite a good way of dealing with stress is to send emails to the BBC's 'have your say on some suggested topic' website. To date not one of my communications has ever been published; unsurprising really, since I guess (and perhaps they guess) my sole intention is to offend someone and thus feel better. Recently religion has featured quite strongly, what with the death of the Pope. However, I was astonished to read the other day that whatever authority deals with this sort of thing had received more than 800 complaints over an advert for Mr Kipling's mince pies which had (Heaven forbid) mocked the birth of Christ. The question the BBC asked was along the lines of 'Do you find the mocking of religions wrong?' Since the BBC moderator declined to print my response here goes: 'I actually find most religions pretty damn offensive. In particular, their attitude towards gay people. With regard to mocking the birth of Jesus let's lighten up here; it's not exactly the end of the world and anyway Mr Kipling does bake exceedingly good cakes (or mince pies in this case).'

Since we're on the subject, I wasn't exactly wild about the late Pope John Paul II despite the fact he sent me a nice blessed hanky (subsequently lost by Parsons Green launderette) and a wooden platter as compensation when I was unable to attend an audience with him in the early 1980s. No, I'm not joking, although I agree it all seems rather unlikely. The invitation to the Vatican was in connection with my work and support for Solidarność. Together with the elderly but extremely sprightly Mollie, Marchioness of Salisbury, we used to take medical and other supplies in an articulated truck all round Poland usually ending up in Krakow where John Paul had been Cardinal. I had along the way acquired an HGV1 licence, which meant that I did all the driving. The Marchioness was great company and a real sport. On one occasion we came across a narrow bridge with a ten-ton weight limit. The gross weight of our rig was nearer thirty. To one side was a sign pointing out a detour, which was around 60 km long and avoided crossing the bridge. I glanced at her and in return she gave a barely perceptible nod. I pushed the accelerator to the floor and we literally flew over the bridge at about 60 mph without a word being said.

Returning briefly again to the main theme, on John Paul's watch the world was rightly taken to task on poverty whilst at the same time the Vatican was (and is), by its frankly criminal teachings on its use, or rather non-use, of condoms for Aids prevention, causing millions of unnecessary deaths and subsequently much more misery and poverty. It wasn't that long ago that the Catholic Church tried to halt evolution in its tracks, for around 200 years, by threatening to string up anyone who supported the recently discovered premise that the earth went round the sun and not vice versa. The Vatican's nonchalant attitude to mass paedophilia within its own ranks, its dismissal of same sex partnerships as evil (the very first edict from Benedict XVI to the Spanish government was against its proposals for gay marriages), its refusal even to consider women priests, along with the Aids issue, are in my view deeply hypocritical and unsatisfactory from an organisation that burbles about faith and love. Fortunately, I am agnostic, i.e. 'haven't got a clue and suspect no one else has either'.

In conclusion to this minor religious rant. Shortly after my dad died, my mother was persuaded by a well-meaning relative to attend a born-again Christians group. At the end of the meeting, the chairwoman invited any 'newcomers' to stand up and introduce themselves and perhaps say a few words. After taking a decent-sized swig from the old hip flask, and clutching her adored Chihuahua Danny, my mother made it to her feet.

Dr Mortimer's Observations

'Hello, I'm Cynthia,' she started, 'and I've been most awfully intrigued by everything that everyone has said, but I have to say that my life's experiences and in particular the recent illness and death of my late husband has made me believe that God is in fact the most frightful shit.'

Acknowledgments

To my publisher the late and delightful Nick Robinson for taking the risk.

To my endlessly patient and long-suffering editor Andreas Campomar, agent Maggie Hanbury and her assistant Harriet Poland. Not forgetting, of course, the astonishing array of colourful characters that have punctuated my existence and made life just that little bit more entertaining.